Q&A on Japanese Taxation for Multinational Corporations

Q&A on Japanese Taxation for Multinational Corporations

Yukiyasu Nakata

Wolters Kluwer

Published by:
Kluwer Law International B.V.
PO Box 316
2400 AH Alphen aan den Rijn
The Netherlands
E-mail: lrs-sales@wolterskluwer.com
Website: www.wolterskluwer.com/en/solutions/kluwerlawinternational

Sold and distributed by:
Wolters Kluwer Legal & Regulatory U.S.
7201 McKinney Circle
Frederick, MD 21704
United States of America
E-mail: customer.service@wolterskluwer.com

ISBN 978-94-035-4310-9

e-Book: ISBN 978-94-035-4311-6
web-PDF: ISBN 978-94-035-4312-3

About the Author

Yukiyasu Nakata is a Certified Public Tax Accountant (Japan) and Certified Public Accountant (Japan). He commenced his career at Arthur Andersen Japan as an auditor for 4 years, where he was involved in auditing multinational corporations engaged in international transactions.

Subsequently, Yukiyasu was with PwC Tax Japan for 16 years, providing international tax advisory services. During this time, he prepared Japanese tax returns for multinational corporations and provided advice on international tax matters. He also provided tax consulting relating to corporate reorganisations and indirect tax consulting, including Japanese consumption tax and European value added tax (VAT).

During his career at PwC Tax Japan, Yukiyasu was seconded to PwC's Dusseldorf office for three and a half years. His focus while on assignment was primarily supporting Japanese multinational corporations on German domestic taxation issues, intra-European reorganisations, and European VAT.

In September 2017, Yukiyasu opened his own tax firm. Since that time, the majority of his time has been spent on consulting services in relation to international taxation, including taxation of multinational corporations in Japan, and taxation for Japanese corporations expanding their business overseas.

Table of Contents

List of Abbreviations

CFC	Controlled Foreign Corporation
CTA	Corporation Tax Act
CTAEO	Corporation Tax Act Enforcement Order
CTAER	Corporation Tax Act Enforcement Regulation
Consumption Tax	National Consumption Tax and Local Consumption Tax
Corporate Tax	Corporation Tax, Local Corporation Tax and Local Tax
Dividends	Dividends of Surplus, Dividends of Profit, Distribution of Surplus, or Interest from Funds
Enterprise	Individuals Carrying on Business and Corporations
GST	Goods & Services Tax
ITA	Income Tax Act
ITAEO	Income Tax Act Enforcement Order
ITAER	Income Tax Act Enforcement Regulation
JCT	Japanese Consumption Tax
JCTA	Consumption Tax Act
JCTAEO	Consumption Tax Act Enforcement Order
JCTAER	Consumption Tax Act Enforcement Regulation
Local Tax	Corporate Inhabitant Tax, Corporate Enterprise Tax, and Special Corporate Enterprise Tax
LTA	Local Tax Act
LTAEO	Local Tax Act Enforcement Order
LTAER	Local Tax Act Enforcement Regulation
NTA	National Tax Agency

PE	Permanent Establishment
STMA	Special Taxation Measures Act
STMAEO	Special Taxation Measures Act Enforcement Order
STMAER	Special Taxation Measures Act Enforcement Regulation
Transfer of Assets	Transfer or Lease of Goods Located in Japan and Supply of Services
Transfer of Taxable Assets	Transfer of Assets Other Than Those That Are Non-taxable
VAT	Value Added Tax
Withholding Tax	Income Tax, Including Special Income Tax for Reconstruction, Deducted at Source

This book is based on legislation effective as of 1 January 2022.

Preface

This book provides an overview of various tax issues that may be faced by tax professionals managing multinational corporations operating in or doing business with Japan.

This book has been compiled in a Q&A format, organised around actual tax issues that I have consulted on during my twenty + years as an international tax specialist. As a result, many of the questions in this book are those that tax professionals managing multinational corporations may face in practice.

As each question is based on a specific factual situation, it is unlikely that many of the answers will be directly applicable in practice. However, I hope that you will be able to apply them to your own situations, referring to them as basic knowledge and underlying concepts of Japanese taxation, to support your Japan tax strategy.

Yukiyasu Nakata
May 2022

CHAPTER 1

General Taxation in Japan

Q1 Overview of Taxes in Japan

Please provide an overview of the main Japanese tax items for foreign companies operating in Japan.

A:

A number of taxes are levied on companies operating in Japan. Japanese taxes vary according to the nature, size and/or type of business being operated in Japan. However, the following are the major taxes imposed on companies in Japan.

Discussion:

1. Corporation Tax

Corporation tax is a national tax and is levied on the taxable income of a corporation. As a general rule, corporation tax returns must be submitted to the competent national tax office for the corporation, and the relevant tax must be paid within two months from the end of the corporation's fiscal year. However, it is possible to extend the filing due date for the corporate tax return by submitting an 'Application for Extension of the Filing Due Date', giving appropriate reasons for such application to the competent national tax office by the end of the first fiscal year in which the taxpayer would like to extend the filing due date. A one-month extension can generally be granted upon the filing of such an application. The reason why such applications are commonly made and granted is because a corporation tax return must be prepared based on the corporation's finalised financial statements. However, the articles of association of most Japanese corporations stipulate that the annual general shareholders' meeting must be held within three months after the fiscal year end. For most corporations, the financial statements are therefore not finalised until the annual general meeting.

On the other hand, even if the filing due date for the tax return is extended, the payment due date cannot be extended. Interest will be charged for the period from the day after the statutory payment due date to the actual payment date. This interest is called 'interest tax' for the period from the day after the original payment due date to the extended tax return filing due date, and 'delinquent tax' for any payment made after the extended tax return filing due date. Interest tax is deductible in the fiscal year in which it is paid, whereas delinquent tax is not.

In order to minimise the amount of interest tax due, it is common practice for corporations to calculate and make payment of the estimated amount of corporation tax before the statutory payment due date (generally called the 'estimated tax payment').

The corporation tax rate is 23.2% for fiscal years beginning on or after 1 April 2018. For small- and medium-sized corporations, a reduced tax rate of 15% applies on income up to JPY 8 million. However, excluded corporations, which are small- and medium-sized corporations whose average taxable income for the previous three fiscal years exceeds JPY 1.5 billion, will be taxed at the rate of 19% (refer to Q27).

2. Local Corporation Tax

Local corporation tax is a national tax and is calculated based on the corporation tax amount. The local corporation tax return is combined with the corporation tax return, and the due dates for filing and payment are the same as for corporation tax. Interest will be charged for the period from the day after the statutory payment due date to the actual payment date.

The local corporation tax rate is 10.3 % (4.4% for fiscal years beginning before 1 October 2019) of the corporation tax amount.

3. Corporate Inhabitant Tax

Corporate inhabitant tax is a local tax and is levied by both prefectures and municipalities. The corporation must submit corporate inhabitant tax returns and make tax payments to each separate prefecture and municipality in which they are located.

Corporate inhabitant tax comprises a corporation tax portion and per capita portion. The corporation tax portion is calculated based on the corporation tax amount. The per capita tax is based on the combination of the capital for tax purposes and the number of employees. Therefore, even when a corporation has no taxable income, it is still possible for that corporation to have a corporate inhabitant tax liability (i.e., arising from the per capita tax portion).

For corporations that have offices in more than one prefecture or municipality, the corporation tax portion is calculated by dividing the corporation tax amount among those prefectures and municipalities, generally based on the number of employees. The per capita tax portion is levied on each office location.

The filing due date for corporate inhabitant tax returns is two months after the end of the fiscal year, as for corporation tax returns. However, if the due date of corporation tax return filing is extended, the filing due date of the corporate inhabitant tax return can also be extended, by filing a 'Notification of Disposition for Extension of the Filing Due Date of Corporate Tax Return' to the competent local inhabitant tax office by the end of the first fiscal year in which the taxpayer would like to extend the filing due date. As in the case of corporation tax, even in the case that the filing due date for the tax return is extended, the payment due date cannot be extended. Similarly, interest tax will be charged on late payment of corporate inhabitant tax for the period from the day after the statutory payment due date to the actual payment date. On the other hand, unlike corporation tax, there is no distinction in the name of the interest tax according to the original tax payment due date. However, as in the case of corporation tax, interest tax up to the extended filing due date of the tax return can be deducted in the fiscal year in which it is paid.

It is also common practice to make estimated payments of corporate inhabitant tax in the same way as for corporation tax.

The standard tax rate for corporate inhabitant tax is stipulated in the Local Tax Act (LTA), but each prefecture or municipality can determine the actual tax rate they wish to use up to a maximum rate. Therefore, in order to calculate the actual corporate inhabitant tax amount, it is necessary to multiply the corporation tax portion by the relevant rates after it has been allocated to each prefecture or municipality where the corporation's offices are located. The standard tax rate for prefectural corporate inhabitant tax is 1% (with a maximum rate of 2%), and the standard tax rate for municipal corporate inhabitant tax is 6% (with a maximum rate of 8.4%).

4. Corporate Enterprise Tax

Corporate enterprise tax is a local tax and is levied by prefectures. The corporate enterprise tax return is combined with the prefectural corporate inhabitant tax return, and the due dates for filing both tax returns and for both tax payments are the same.

The tax calculation method for corporate enterprise tax differs depending on whether a corporation's registered capital amount is JPY 100 million or less or more than JPY 100 million.

(1) Where the registered capital amount is JPY 100 million or less (income-based taxation)

The corporate enterprise tax is levied on taxable income for most industries (income-based taxation). The tax base for corporate enterprise tax is taxable income, which is essentially the same as taxable income for corporation tax purposes. However, as corporate enterprise tax is levied on taxable income related to domestic business only, there are some differences from taxable income for corporation tax purposes. Examples of taxable income for corporation tax purposes but which are excluded from taxable income for corporate enterprise tax are as follows:

- income attributable to permanent establishments (PEs) outside Japan; and
- foreign taxes which are added to taxable income when claiming foreign tax credits.

The tax rate for corporate enterprise tax is as follows:

- 3.5% (with a maximum rate of 4.2%) for taxable income up to JPY 4 million per year;
- 5.3% (with a maximum rate of 6.36%) for taxable income between JPY 4 million and JPY 8 million per year; and
- 7.0% (with a maximum rate of 8.4%) for income over JPY 8 million per year.

However, the tax rate for corporations with registered capital of JPY 10 million or more and which have a physical presence in three or more prefectures at fiscal year end is fixed at 7.0% (with a maximum rate of 8.4%).

(2) When the registered capital amount is over JPY 100 million (factor-based taxation)

Corporations with a capital of more than JPY 100 million are subject to factor-based taxation, under which corporate enterprise tax is calculated based on three factors: an income factor, a value-added factor, and a capital factor.

(i) Income factor

Under the income factor, taxable income is the same as for corporations with registered capital of JPY 100 million or less, i.e., the same as for income-based taxation. However, the tax rate for the income factor under factor-based taxation is as follows:

- 0.4% (with a maximum rate of 0.68%) for income up to JPY 4 million per year;
- 0.7% (with a maximum rate of 1.19%) for income between JPY 4 million and JPY 8 million per year; and
- 1.0% (with a maximum rate of 1.7%) for income over JPY 8 million per year.

However, the tax rate for corporations that have a physical presence in three or more prefectures at fiscal year end is fixed at 1.0% (with a maximum rate of 1.7%).

(ii) Value-added factor

The tax base for the value-added factor is the total of salaries, net interest, net rent and taxable income for the year, minus a credit for employment stability.

(a) Salaries

Salaries for the purposes of the value-added factor are the total of:

- any remuneration paid to directors and employees, which are deductible for corporation tax purposes and which are classified as salary or retirement income in the hands of the recipient for individual income tax purposes;
- contributions to defined benefit corporate pension schemes (i.e., a Japanese 401K); and
- 75% of any amount paid to a dispatch (temporary staffing) corporation as compensation for the provision of temporary staff under a dispatch contract prescribed in the 'Act for Securing the Proper Operation of Dispatch Arrangements and Improved Working Conditions for Dispatched Workers'.

(b) Net interest

Net interest for the value-added factor is interest expenses less interest income.

Interest expense includes interest on debt that is deductible for corporation tax purposes.

Interest income includes interest received, which is added to taxable income for corporation tax purposes.

(c) Net rent

Net rent for the value-added factor is rent expense less rent income, where rent relates to land or buildings, whose rental period is one month or more.

The total of (a) to (c) is generally called the 'revenue distribution amount'.

(d) Taxable income

Taxable income for the value-added factor is the same as taxable income for income-factor purposes. However, any tax loss carry forward cannot be deducted from taxable income.

(e) Credit for employment stability

If the amount of salaries (defined in (a) above) exceeds 70% of the revenue distribution amount, a credit for employment stability is applied. The amount of the credit is calculated as:

credit for employment stability = salaries – revenue distribution amount * 70%

The tax rate for the value-added factor is 1.2% (with a maximum rate of 1.44%).

(iii) Capital factor

The tax base for the capital factor is the capital amount for corporate enterprise tax purposes, which is the same as the capital amount for corporation tax purposes (i.e., registered capital + capital surplus for tax purposes) at the end of the fiscal year. The standard tax rate for the capital factor is 0.5% (with a maximum rate of 0.6%).

5. Special Corporate Enterprise Tax

The special corporate enterprise tax was created by separating out a part of income-based taxation or income factor under factor-based taxation (*see* 2(i) above), however is applicable to all corporations regardless of their registered capital.

Although the special corporate enterprise tax is a national tax, the tax return is combined with the corporate enterprise tax return, and payment should also be made to the prefectural government, as for corporate enterprise tax.

If the corporation is subject to factor-based taxation for enterprise tax, the tax base for special corporation enterprise tax is the tax amount for income factor. If the corporation is not subject to factor-based taxation, but instead is subject to income-based taxation for enterprise tax purposes, the tax base for special corporation enterprise tax is the enterprise tax amount.

The tax rate for special corporate enterprise tax is:

- 37% for corporations not subject to factor-based taxation;
- 260% for corporations subject to factor-based taxation.

The above corporate inhabitant tax, corporate enterprise tax, and special enterprise tax are often collectively referred to as local tax.

In addition, corporation tax, local corporation tax and local tax are often collectively referred to as corporate tax.

6. Consumption Tax

Japanese consumption tax (often referred to as JCT) is a tax on the sale of goods and the provision of services. It is similar to value added tax (VAT) or goods and services tax (GST) in other countries.

Consumption tax consists of national and local components, which are included in a single consumption tax return, submitted to the competent national tax office. Both national and local consumption taxes are paid to that national tax office.

Consumption tax is an indirect tax, and enterprises are required to collect the tax from customers when they sell their goods or services. The consumption tax paid to the national tax office is the difference between the consumption tax received by an enterprise from the customers ('output consumption tax') and the consumption tax paid to other enterprises at the time of the purchase of goods and services ('input consumption tax'). If input consumption tax is greater than output consumption tax, the difference should be refunded to the corporation upon the submission of the consumption tax return.

In principle, the taxable period for consumption tax purposes is the fiscal year of the corporation, but it is possible to apply for a shortened taxable period.

The filing due date for a consumption tax return is two months from the end of the taxable period, but if the filing due date for the corporation tax return has been extended, it is also possible to apply for the same one-month extension for the consumption tax return.

The standard national consumption tax rate is 7.8%, and the local consumption tax rate is 2.2%, which produces a combined rate of 10%. A reduced rate applies to food and drink purchased for consumption off the premises of the retailer, and certain newspapers, with a national consumption tax rate of 6.24% and a local consumption tax rate of 1.76%, which produces a combined rate of 8%.

7. Withholding tax

Income tax and the special reconstruction income tax should be deducted from certain kinds of income payments. These deductions are generally collectively referred to as withholding tax.

Multinational corporations in Japan would typically be required to deduct withholding tax on the following payments:

(1) When the beneficiary is a Japanese resident:

- salaries and directors' remuneration;
- severance payments; and
- certain fees:
  - fees for manuscripts, translation, interpretation, and royalties for intellectual property;
  - professional fees, such as those paid to lawyers, certified public accountants, certified public tax accountants, judicial scriveners, and labour and social security attorneys.

(2) When the beneficiary is a Japanese corporation:
- dividends.

(3) When the beneficiary is non-resident or foreign corporation:
Domestic source income including:
- dividends;
- salaries (excluding remuneration paid to directors of Japanese companies) for work performed in Japan;
- in relation to domestic operations:
  - interest on loans;
  - royalties or fees relating to:
  - intellectual property;
  - consideration for the transfer of intellectual property; and
  - usage fees for machinery or equipment.

Withholding tax rates vary according to the type of income or beneficiary, but are generally 10%, 15% or 20% for income tax, and 2.1% for the special reconstruction income tax.

As a general rule, withholding tax should be paid by the 10th of the month following the month in which the relevant taxable income is actually paid. However, the withholding tax agent (i.e., all corporations and certain self-employed persons) with ten or less directors and employees can adopt a half-year withholding tax payment for salaries and certain fees upon special application to the tax authorities.

The withholding tax agent is required to prepare and submit annual summary reports for all withholding tax for each calendar year by 31 January of the following year.

- Salaries

The payor of salaries and directors' remuneration must prepare two copies of an 'Employment Income Withholding Record' (*kyuyo syotoku no gensen choshu hyo*) on a calendar year basis, showing the annual salary or director's remuneration paid to an individual, and the withholding tax amount. One copy should then be submitted to the competent national tax office by January 31 of the following year. The other copy should be given to the relevant employee or director.

In the following cases, however, the Employment Income Withholding Record does not need to be submitted to the competent national tax office:

- Directors' remuneration: the director whose annual remuneration is JPY 1.5 million or less.
- Salaries to employees: the employee for JPY 5 million or less.

Note that the same information must also be submitted to each local tax office as a 'Salary Payment Report' (*kyuyo shiharai hokokusyo*) where the directors and employees are domiciled, regardless of the amount.

- Severance payments to employees or directors.

The payor of severance payments to employees or directors who retire during the course of a year must prepare two copies of a 'Retirement Income Withholding Record' (*taisyoku syotoku no gensen choshu hyo*) and should submit these to the competent national tax office within one month from the date of retirement. However, the Retirement Income Withholding Record can be submitted to the competent national tax office by 31 January of the year after the year of retirement, together with the annual Employment Income Withholding Records.

- Payments other than salaries or severance payment.

The withholding tax agent must prepare a 'Report of Payment' and submit it to the competent national tax office by January 31 of the following year. There are several types of 'Reports of Payment', such as fees, real property, or payments to a non-resident. The Report of Payment states the payments made, the tax amounts withheld, and the individual or corporate number of the payor and of the recipient of each payment.

There is no obligation to provide the Report of Payment to the recipients of payments listed therein. However, it is common practice for withholding tax agents to provide a copy of the Report of Payment to recipients.

- Annual Withholding Tax Summary (*hotei chosho gokei hyo*).

In addition to the above Employment Income Withholding Record, Retirement Income Withholding Record, and Report of Payment, an Annual Withholding Tax Summary must be prepared and submitted to the competent national tax office by 31 January each year. The Annual Withholding Tax Summary is prepared as the total of all withholding taxable income and all withholding tax amounts for the calendar year, regardless of the submission of the other reports.

8. Business Premises Tax

Business premises tax is a municipal tax levied on business premises in cities with a population of 300,000 or more.

The business premises tax consists of an asset factor and an employee factor.

(1) Asset factor

The asset factor is calculated based on the floor area of the premises, which is exempt from taxation if the floor area is 1,000 sqm or less. However, if the floor area is more than 800 sqm, a business premises tax return must still be submitted, even if the corporation is exempt.

(2) Employee factor

The employee factor is levied on the gross salaries and remuneration of a corporation. Where the number of employees and directors is a hundred or less, the employee factor is not applicable. However, where the number of employees and directors is more than eighty, a business premises tax return must still be submitted, even if the corporation is exempt.

The deadline for filing and paying business premises tax is within two months from fiscal year end, with no extensions.

The tax rate for the asset factor is JPY 600 per square metre. The tax rate for the employee factor is 0.25% of gross salaries and remuneration.

9. Fixed Asset Tax

Fixed asset tax is a municipal tax levied on the owners of fixed assets. The fixed asset tax is levied by the municipality based on the assessed value of the fixed assets. Fixed assets for the purposes of the tax include both real estate (i.e., land and buildings) and depreciable fixed assets (e.g., machinery, equipment).

Real estate value is assessed by the municipality and reassessed every three years.

Corporations with depreciable fixed assets are required to submit a depreciable asset return to the competent municipal tax offices where depreciable assets are located as of 1 January each year. The due date for submitting a depreciable fixed asset return is 31 January.

Each municipality calculates fixed asset tax based on the assessed amount of real estate and the depreciable fixed asset return submitted by a corporation, and sends a notice of the fixed asset tax payment in May each year. The fixed asset tax must be paid in principle in four annual instalments.

The fixed asset tax rate is 1.4%, but depreciable assets with a total assessed value of less than JPY 1.5 million are exempt.

You may also be required to pay stamp duty upon the execution of certain documents, and registration tax upon the registration of a corporation or real estate. Depending on the type of business in which you operate, alcohol tax, gasoline tax and/or international tourist tax may also be imposed.

An example of the tax calendar for a corporation with a fiscal year ending on 31 December is shown in the following chart:

Tax calendar for a corporation:

1. which has a 31 December fiscal year end

2. which is located in Tokyo

3. which has obtained approval for a one-month extension for filing of both corporate and consumption final tax returns

4. which has a monthly interim consumption tax return filing

January	February	March
4 January – Monthly interim consumption tax return (Oct) filing and payment	10 February – Withholding tax return filing and payment (Jan)	10 March – Withholding tax return filing and payment (Feb)
10 January – monthly withholding tax return and payment (Dec)	Fixed assets tax payment (4th)	31 March – Final corporation tax return and local corporation tax return filing and payment
31 January – Annual withholding tax report	28 February – Estimated consumption tax payment	31 March – Final consumption tax return filing and payment
31 January – Depreciable assets return filing	28 February – Estimated corporation tax and local corporation tax payment	31 March – Final corporate enterprise tax, special corporate enterprise tax, and corporate inhabitant tax return filing and payment
31 January – Monthly interim consumption tax return filing (Nov) and payment	28 February – Estimated corporate enterprise tax, special corporate enterprise tax, and corporate inhabitant tax payment	
	28 February – Business premises tax return filing and payment	

April	May	June
10 April – Withholding tax return filing and payment (Mar)	10 May – Withholding tax return filing and payment (Apr)	10 June – Withholding tax return filing and payment (May)
Fixed assets tax payment (1st)	31 May – Monthly interim consumption tax return filing (Jan, Feb & Mar) and payment	30 June – Monthly interim consumption tax return filing (Apr) and payment

July	August	September
10 July – Withholding tax return filing and payment (Jun) 31 July – Monthly interim consumption tax return (May) filing and payment	10 August – Withholding tax return filing and payment (Jul) 31 August – Interim corporation tax return and local corporation tax filing and payment 31 August – Interim enterprise tax, special enterprise tax and corporate inhabitant tax return filing and payment 31 August – Monthly interim consumption tax return (Jun) filing and payment	10 September – Withholding tax return and payment (Aug) 30 September – Monthly interim consumption tax return (July) filing and payment Fixed assets tax payment (2nd)
October	**November**	**December**
10 October – Withholding tax return and payment (Sep) 31 October – Monthly interim consumption tax return (Aug) and payment	10 November – Withholding tax return and payment (Oct) 30 November – Monthly interim consumption tax return (Sep) and payment	10 December – Withholding tax return and payment (Nov) Fixed assets tax payment (3rd) Notification for Ultimate Parent Entity Master File

Q2 Overview of Japanese Tax Audits

We have been contacted by the National Tax Agency (NTA) about the start of a tax audit. Please explain the typical audit process in Japan.

A:

A tax audit is a procedure for the tax authorities, typically the taxpayer's competent tax office, to check the taxpayer's tax returns against the taxpayer's accounting books and other source documents.

Tax audits are usually conducted every three to five years for each category of tax.

Discussion

A tax audit is an investigation by the relevant tax body, which includes prefectural or municipal tax offices, as well as tax offices under the direct jurisdiction of the NTA, to check a taxpayer's tax returns.

Since Japanese tax compliance generally adopts a self-assessment approach (i.e., taxpayers calculate their own tax and submit tax returns reflecting that calculation), there is always the possibility that there may be errors in the returns or in the calculation of the tax payable, or that false tax returns may be submitted by unscrupulous taxpayers.

Tax audits are conducted by the relevant body responsible for each tax category, usually every three to five years. For the main tax categories, the relevant bodies are as follows:

(1) Corporation tax, consumption tax, stamp duty: the competent national tax office or national Regional Taxation Bureau.
(2) Withholding tax: competent national tax office.
(3) Local tax: Tokyo Metropolitan Tax Office, other prefectural or municipal tax offices as appropriate.

In most cases, the competent national tax office may conduct tax audits of several categories of tax at the same time.

Regional Taxation Bureaus are primarily responsible for corporation tax, local corporation tax and consumption tax for large corporations with registered capital of more than JPY 100 million. However, the Regional Taxation Bureaus sometimes designate smaller corporations (i.e., those with registered capital of JPY 100 million or less) to be within their jurisdiction, or conversely, some large corporations to the jurisdiction of a competent tax office.

In the case of foreign-based companies, a Regional Taxation Bureau is likely to be designated as the relevant body.

At the conclusion of a tax audit, if there are items that need to be corrected in a tax return, the taxpayer may either submit an amended tax return or may be subject to an assessment. The key difference between these two results is that submission of an amended tax return is an acknowledgement by the taxpayer of the error and a self-correction. Consequently, taxpayers submitting amended returns cannot pursue competent authority or legal appeals processes.

It may not be common practice to submit amended tax returns at the conclusion of a tax audit in other countries. However, the intention of this process in Japan is to encourage taxpayers to self-correct errors in their tax returns, which will ideally contribute to the submission of correct tax returns in the future. In addition, the submission of amended returns is consistent with the logic of the self-assessment system. Given the above philosophy, although the amount of additional tax will not change, submission of an amended tax return will often result in smoother completion of a tax audit than the issuance of an assessment. However, taxpayers under audit must consider all the consequences of submitting an amended tax return or receiving an assessment before determining the appropriate approach for their particular audit.

If additional tax is payable as a result of a tax audit, taxpayers will also be liable to pay penalty tax and interest tax.

CHAPTER 2
Withholding Tax

Q3 Scope of Domestic Source Income

What is the scope of domestic source income subject to withholding tax in Japan?

A:

Domestic source income is the income, the source of which is Japan. The categories of domestic source income are defined in the Income Tax Act (ITA) and Corporation Tax Act, as set out below. In principle, a Japanese permanent resident or a corporation established in Japan is subject to taxation on all its income, regardless of whether it is earned within or outside of Japan (worldwide income). In contrast, a non-resident or foreign corporation is subject to taxation only on its domestic source income.

Discussion

Domestic source income includes the following categories of income (ITA Article 161, CTA Article 138):

(1) Income attributable to the business of a permanent establishment in Japan, income arising from the use or holding of assets located in Japan, and income arising from the transfer of assets located in Japan.
(2) Certain profits arising from business conducted through a permanent establishment pursuant to a Nini Kmiai (NK) and similar partnership agreement (i.e., 'partnership agreement'), which are distributed in accordance with that partnership agreement.
(3) Consideration for the transfer of land, rights over land, buildings, leasehold improvements and other structures located in Japan.
(4) Consideration for the provision of personal services in Japan by a person whose main business is the provision of personal services. For example, consideration for the provision of services by professional entertainers

such as actors and musicians, professional athletes, lawyers, certified public accountants, other freelance professionals, or persons with specialist knowledge or skills in science, technology, or business management.

(5) Consideration for the lending of real estate or rights over real estate located in Japan.

(6) Interests on Japanese government bonds, local government bonds, or corporate bonds issued by domestic corporations, interest on bonds issued by foreign corporations that relate to business conducted through permanent establishments in Japan, and interest on deposits and savings deposited in domestic business offices.

(7) Dividends made from capital surplus, distribution of profits or distribution of surplus, received from domestic companies.

(8) Interest on loans provided to a person conducting business in Japan for the purpose of using such loans for domestic businesses.

(9) Royalties for industrial property rights, or any other right relating to technology, production methods involving special technology or any other equivalent right or method, copyright or consideration for the transfer thereof, royalties for copyrights or consideration for the transfer thereof, and royalties for machinery and equipment, received from a person performing services in Japan which relate to a business conducted in Japan.

(10) Salaries, bonuses, remuneration for the provision of personal services which are based on work or the provision of services performed in Japan, and public pensions or retirement allowances, which are based on work performed or services provided during the period in which the individual performing the work or providing the services was a resident in Japan.

(11) Advertising prizes for a business conducted in Japan.

(12) Pensions arising from insurance contracts concluded through offices located in Japan.

(13) Complementary benefit payment from term deposits accepted by domestic business offices located in Japan.

(14) Distribution of profits based on silent partnership contracts (*tokumei kumiai* or TKs), with respect to investments in businesses located in Japan.

(15) Other domestic source income.

This includes, for example, insurance payments and compensation payments or compensation for damages in respect of businesses conducted in Japan or assets located in Japan.

(Source: Translation of NTA Tax Answer No. 2878: Scope of domestic source income (2017))

If a tax convention has provisions relating to the taxation of domestic source income that are different from the provisions under domestic law, the provisions of the tax convention should be applied (ITA Article 162, CTA Article 139).

The taxation of domestic source income may be accomplished through the imposition of a withholding tax, through the inclusion of the relevant domestic source income in the taxpayer's tax return, or both. The method of taxation will differ depending on the type of domestic source income, whether there is a permanent establishment, and whether the domestic source income is attributable to a permanent establishment. It is therefore necessary to understand the type of domestic source income that has been earned, and the physical presence of the taxpayer in Japan, in order to pay the appropriate amount of Japanese tax.

Q4 Tax Conventions

What is a tax convention and how does it impact withholding tax payable on domestic source income?

A:

A tax convention is an agreement between two or more countries dealing with various tax matters. It is often referred to as a tax treaty.

Discussion

1. Types of tax convention

There are four main types of Tax Conventions as listed below. However, the terms 'tax convention' and 'tax treaty' are generally used to refer to (1):

(1) A convention between two countries for the elimination of double taxation with respect to taxes on income and to certain other taxes and the prevention of tax evasion and avoidance ('Tax Convention').
(2) An agreement between two countries for the exchange of information relating to tax matters.
(3) A convention on mutual administrative assistance in tax matters.
(4) The Multilateral Convention to Implement Tax Convention Related Measures to Prevent Base Erosion and Profit Shifting ('Multilateral Instrument' or 'MLI').

2. Objectives of Tax Conventions

In general, Tax Conventions are expected to contribute to the promotion of investment and economic exchange between two countries by ensuring the stability of taxation, eliminating double taxation, and addressing tax evasion and avoidance.

Among the above objectives, the elimination of double taxation is generally considered the most important for taxpayers. More recently, however, there has been increasing focus by tax authorities on addressing tax evasion and avoidance.

In order to eliminate or reduce double taxation, Tax Conventions may exempt certain income from taxation in the source jurisdiction or may provide for a maximum tax rate. Tax Conventions also provide for mutual agreement procedures (primarily in relation to transfer pricing), and include provisions for corresponding adjustments.

In order to address the issues of tax evasion and avoidance, recent amendments to many Tax Conventions have eliminated double tax exemptions and restricted access to benefits to certain categories of taxpayer only.

3. Tax Conventions and domestic tax law

In Japan, Tax Conventions are generally considered to take precedence over domestic tax law. If a Tax Convention has provisions on domestic source income that are different from the provisions under domestic law, the provisions of the Tax Convention should be applied.

Since the classification of income often differs between domestic tax law and Japan's Tax Conventions, it is often necessary to confirm which income category under domestic tax law corresponds to which income category under a particular Tax Convention (e.g., the provision of personal services under domestic tax law may be classified as business income under a Tax Convention). Alternatively, domestic tax law determines the source of certain categories of income based on the place of use of an asset or the conduct of a business, while certain Tax Conventions determine the source based on the location of the payor of the income. In these cases, the source of the income should be determined by the Tax Convention.

Tax Conventions also prohibit the tax burden under a Tax Convention from being higher than that imposed by domestic tax law (the 'Preservation Clause'). Therefore, even if a Tax Convention provides for a tax rate higher than the domestic tax rate, taxpayers cannot be taxed at that higher rate.

In addition, Tax Conventions are considered to apply only to residents of the other country covered by the Tax Convention, and do not apply to residents of the home country (the 'Saving Clause'). For example, the Tax Convention between Japan and Australia provides exemptions to Australian residents from taxation in Japan, but does not affect the taxation of residents of Japan in Japan.

4. Japan's Tax Convention network

The Tax Convention network in force in Japan as of 1 January 2022 is as follows:

«82 conventions,etc. applicable to 149 jurisdictions; as of January 1, 2022»

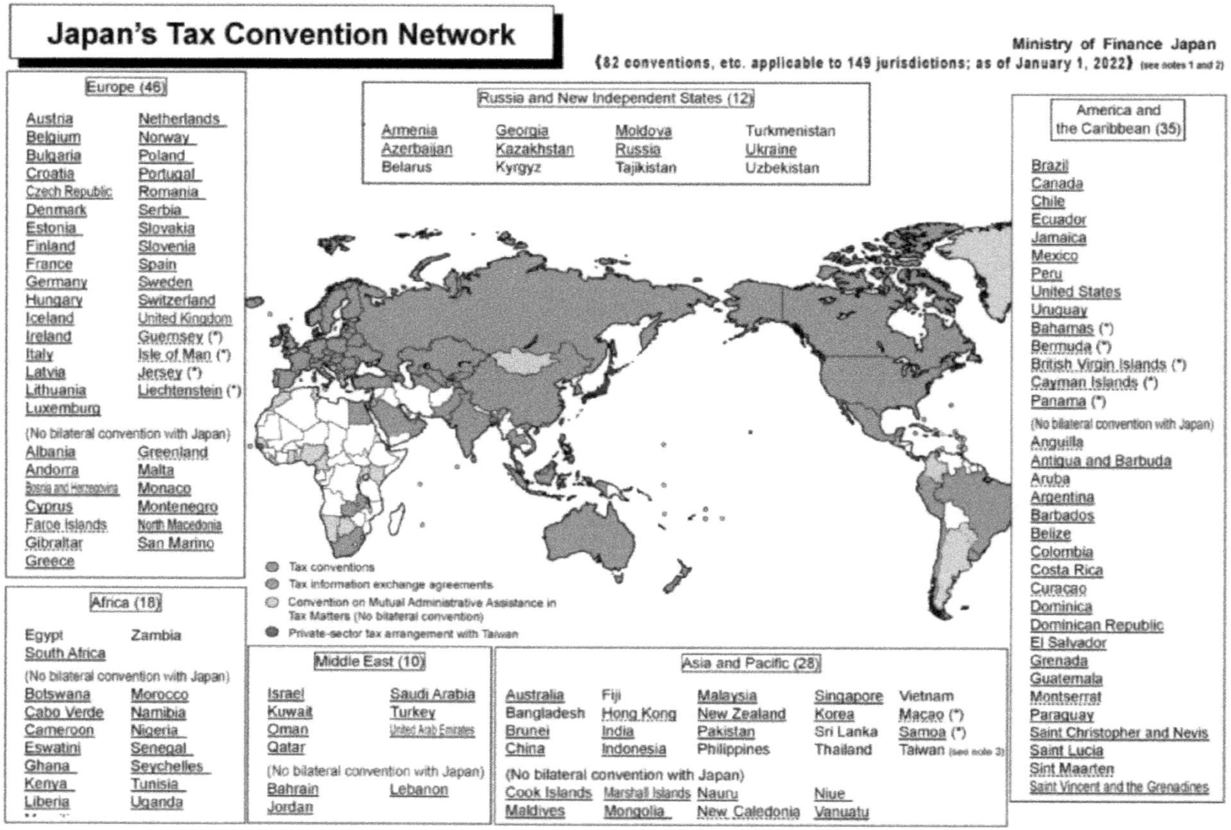

(*Source*: Ministry of Finance website)
(Note 1) Since the Convention on Mutual Administrative Assistance in Tax Matters is a multilateral convention, and the Tax Conventions with the former Soviet Union and with the former Czechoslovakia were succeeded by more than one jurisdiction, the numbers of jurisdictions do not correspond to those of Tax Conventions, etc.
(Note 2) The breakdown of the numbers of conventions, etc., and jurisdictions is as follows:

- Tax convention (a convention principally for the elimination of double taxation and the prevention of tax evasion and avoidance), 69 conventions applicable to 77 jurisdictions.
- information exchange agreement (a convention principally for the exchange of information regarding tax matters), 11 conventions applicable to 11 jurisdictions (these jurisdictions are marked with (*) above).
- Convention on Mutual Administrative Assistance in Tax Matters, entered into force by 117 jurisdictions (not including Japan) (these jurisdictions are underlined above) and applicable to 135 jurisdictions due to the extension of the application of the Convention (jurisdictions to which the Convention is extended are underlined above with dotted lines). Sixty jurisdictions out of 135 do not have a bilateral convention with Japan.
- Private-sector tax arrangement with Taiwan; 1 jurisdiction.

(Note 3) As for Taiwan, a framework equivalent to a tax convention is established in combination of: (1) a private-sector tax arrangement between the Interchange Association (Japan) and the Association of East Asian Relations (Taiwan) and (2) Japanese domestic legislation to implement the provisions of the private-sector tax arrangement in Japan (the two associations are now named Japan-Taiwan Exchange Association (Japan) and Taiwan-Japan Relations Association (Taiwan), respectively).

Q5 Withholding Tax on Unpaid Dividends

We are a Japanese subsidiary of a foreign-based corporation. At our annual general shareholders' meeting, we declared a dividend. However, due to cash flow problems, payment of this dividend may be made more than a year later. When can we pay the withholding tax due on the dividend in this case?

A:

As a general rule, withholding tax should be paid by the 10th of the month following the month in which the dividend is actually paid. However, if payment of a dividend is not made within one year of the date on which it is fixed, payment is deemed to have been made one year after the date on which the dividend is fixed. As a result, withholding tax must be paid by the 10th of the following month of the deemed payment date of the dividend.

Discussion

Dividends from capital surplus, distributions of profit, distribution of surplus, or interest on funds ('Dividends') received from a domestic corporation are classified as domestic source income (ITA Article 161(ix)). A person who pays Dividends to a non-resident or a foreign corporation in Japan is required to withhold income tax at the time of payment and pay it to the competent national tax office by the 10th of the following month in which the payment is made. The withholding tax rate is 20.42% (ITA Article 212(1) and Article 213(1)).

As a general rule, tax should be withheld at the time of the actual payment of Dividends, and paid to the competent national tax office by the 10th of the following month.

In the case of unpaid Dividends to a Japanese resident or a Japanese corporation, if payment of the Dividends is not made within one year of the date when the Dividends are fixed, the Dividends are deemed to have been paid as of the day when one year has passed ('deemed payment date'). Withholding tax is required to be collected by the corporation paying the Dividends by the 10th of the month following the deemed payment date (ITA Article 181(2)).

This provision also applies to unpaid Dividends owed to a non-resident or a foreign corporation (ITA Article 212(4)). Therefore, if actual payment is not made for more than one year after the dividend declaration date, the payment of the Dividends is deemed to have been made on the date on which one year has passed from the shareholders' meeting. Again, withholding tax must be paid by the 10th of the month following the deemed payment date.

If the foreign corporation to which Dividends are to be paid is located in a country with which a Tax Convention has been concluded, the withholding tax rate may be reduced or exempted if the foreign corporation is entitled to benefits under that Tax

Convention, and if appropriate administrative procedures such as submission of an 'Application Form for Income Tax Convention' are followed (*see* Q7). If Dividends are not paid for more than one year after the declaration date, the deadline for submitting the 'Application Form for Income Tax Convention' will be the day before the deemed payment date.

Form of withholding tax payment slip for domestic source income of a non-resident/foreign corporation is given below:

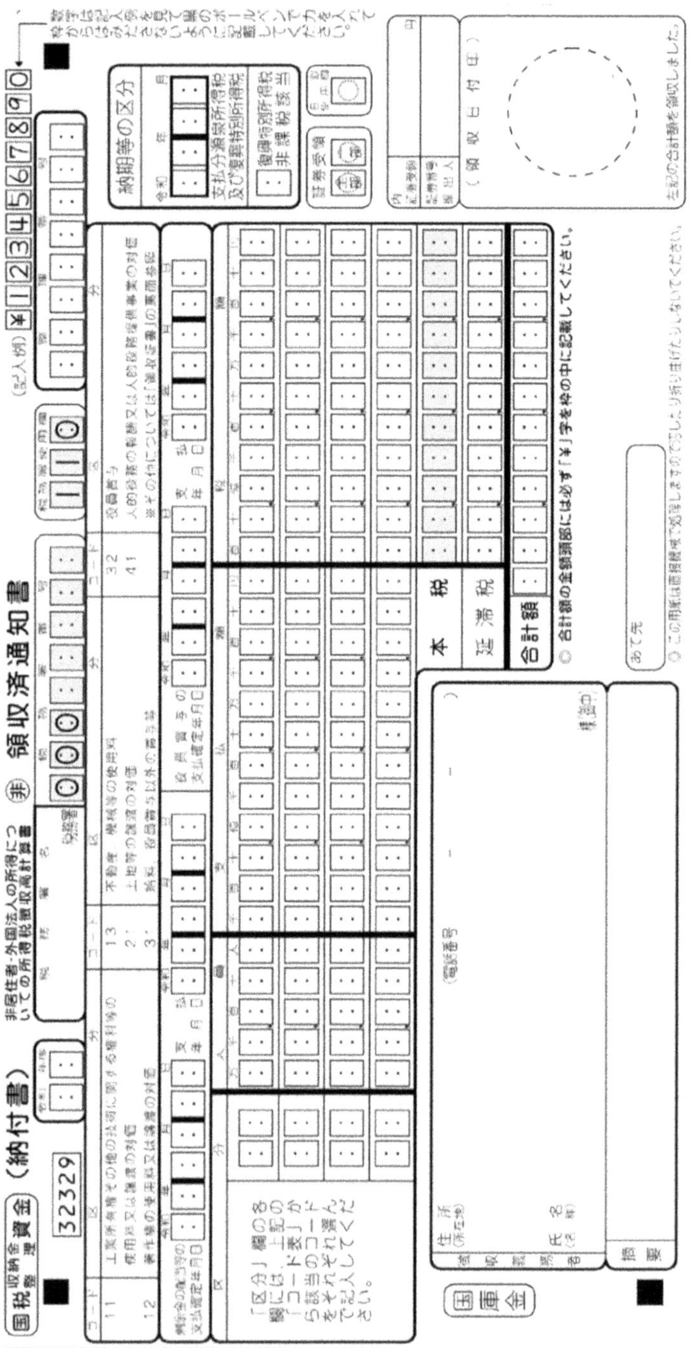
国税 収納金 整理 資金 32329 （納付書） 非居住者・外国法人の所得についての所得税徴収高計算書 非 領収済通知書

（記入例） ¥ 1 2 3 4 5 6 7 8 9 0

コード	区分	コード	区分	コード	区分
11	工業所有権その他の技術に関する権利等の使用料又は譲渡の対価	13	不動産、機械等の使用料	32	役員賞与
12	著作権の使用料又は譲渡の対価	2	土地等の譲渡の対価	41	人的役務の報酬又は人的役務提供事業の対価
		3	特定の社債等の利子		※その他については「源泉徴収のしかた」の裏面参照

「区分」欄の各欄には、上記「コード表」のコードの該当するものをそれぞれ選んで記入してください。

本税 / 延滞税 / 合計額

◎ 合計額の金額頭部には必ず「¥」字を枠の中に記載してください。

納期等の区分 / 支払分源泉所得税及び復興特別所得税 / 非課税 / 証券受領 / 住所 / 氏名 / 摘要 / 国庫金 / あて先 / 領収日付印 / 上記の合計額を領収しました。

Q6 Exemption from Withholding Tax for Japanese Branches of Foreign Corporations

We are a Japanese branch of a foreign corporation that provides management consulting services to corporations in Japan. Do those corporations need to withhold income tax when they pay our consulting service fees?

A:

As a general rule, corporations are required to withhold income tax when they pay for domestic consulting services provided by a non-resident or foreign corporation. However, if the service provider obtains a 'Withholding Tax Exemption Certificate for Foreign Corporations or Non-residents' and provides a copy to its customers, those customers are not required to collect withholding tax.

Discussion

1. General treatment of withholding tax

Where a non-resident or foreign corporation provides personal services in Japan, the consideration for the provision of such personal services is classified as domestic source income (ITA Article 161(vi)). In addition:

> The provision of personal services includes businesses whose principal activity is the provision of services by a person who has expert knowledge or special skills in science, technology, business management, or other fields, by making use of such knowledge or skills (ITAEO Article 282(3)).

In general, management consulting services are treated as such personal services, and, therefore, consideration for management consulting services performed in Japan is classified as domestic source income.

Since you are a foreign corporation, and since your clients are paying domestic source income to you, in principle, your clients need to collect withholding tax regardless of whether or not you have a branch in Japan (ITA Article 212(1)). The withholding tax rate is 20.42% (ITA Article 213(1)(i)).

2. Withholding Tax Exemption Certificate for Foreign Corporations or Non-residents

Foreign corporations with permanent establishments in Japan that satisfy certain requirements may be exempt from withholding tax on certain domestic source income if they obtain a 'Withholding Tax Exemption Certificate for Foreign Corporations or Non-residents' ('Exemption Certificate') from the competent national tax office and present that Exemption Certificate to the payor of the domestic source income (ITA Article 180(1)).

The requirements to obtain an Exemption Certificate are (ITAEO Article 304):

(1) The foreign corporation has submitted a 'Notification of Becoming a Foreign Corporation' to the competent national tax office.

(2) The foreign corporation has legally registered under the Companies Act Article 933(1) or the Civil Code Article 37(1).
(3) The domestic source income to which the withholding tax exemption applies is included in the taxable income for corporation tax purposes.
(4) The applicant has not falsely or fraudulently avoided income tax or corporation tax.
(5) Upon presentation of the Exemption Certificate to a payor of domestic source income, the taxpayer records the payor's name, address, office, place of payment of the income, and date of presentation of the Exemption Certificate in its accounting books and records.

Upon presentation of an Exemption Certificate, your clients are not required to collect withholding tax due on your service fees or other covered payments.

The Exemption Certificate is valid for a limited period. After expiration, your clients are liable to collect withholding tax on your service fees or other covered payments. If they fail to do so, penalty tax and interest tax will be imposed on them.

Given the above, it is therefore important to renew Exemption Certificates periodically. The NTA recommends submitting applications for new Exemption Certificates approximately one month before the expiration of the current Exemption Certificate:

Form of Exemption Certificate

外国法人に対する源泉徴収の免除証明書 第　　号

① 外国法人の	本店又は主たる事務所の所在地	アメリカ合衆国〇〇〇州
	名　称	ABC Inc.
② 日本における法人税の納税地にある事務所等の	所　在　地	東京都〇〇区〇〇
	名　称	ABC Inc.

③

上記の者は、所得税法施行令第 304 条に規定する条件を備えていると認められますから、この証明書の発行の日から令和　年　月　日までの間に上記の者に支払う所得税法第161条第１号の２、第１号の３、第２号、第３号、第６号、第７号、第９号又は第10号に掲げる国内源泉所得については、その支払者は所得税法第 212 条第１項の規定による源泉徴収を行う必要はありません。

令和　年　月　日

×× 税務署長　〇〇　〇〇

Q7 Withholding Tax on Dividends and Relief under Tax Conventions

We are a Japanese corporation which is wholly owned by a German corporation, which is actively traded on the Frankfurt Stock Exchange. We are planning to pay a dividend. Is the withholding tax due on that payment either exempt or reduced under the Tax Convention between Germany and Japan?

A:

Under domestic tax law, a withholding tax of 20.42% must be collected at the time of a payment of Dividends by a Japanese corporation to a foreign corporation or non-resident.

However, in the above example, withholding tax on Dividends can be exempt or reduced under the Tax Convention between Germany and Japan if the following conditions are met:

1. your German parent corporation has held 25% or more of your shares for more than eighteen months; and
2. your German parent is a 'qualified person' as defined under the Tax Convention between Germany and Japan.

In order to apply for an exemption from withholding tax in the above example, your German parent must file an 'Application Form for Income Tax Convention' and 'Attachment Form for Limitation on Benefits (Entitlement to Benefits) Article', together with other required documents, such as residency certificate to the competent national tax office at least one day before the date of payment of the Dividends.

Discussion

1. Taxation of Dividends under domestic tax law

Dividends are classified as domestic source income (ITA Article 161(1)(ix)). A person who pays Dividends to a non-resident or a foreign corporation in Japan is required to withhold income tax at the time of payment and pay it to the competent national tax office by the 10th of the following month in which the payment is made (ITA Article 212(1)). The withholding tax rate is 20.42% (ITA Article 213(1)(i)).

2. Withholding tax exemption under the Tax Convention between Germany and Japan

Notwithstanding domestic tax law, withholding tax on Dividends may be exempted under a Tax Convention, such as that between Germany and Japan, if certain conditions are met.

These conditions include the length of time the shares have been held and the percentage of ownership. They can be summarised as follows for a payment of Dividends from a Japanese corporation to a German parent:

(1) The Withholding tax on Dividends is exempted if the beneficial owner of the Dividends is a resident of Germany and is a corporation (other than a partnership) that has owned directly, for the period of 18 months ending on the date on which entitlement to the Dividends is determined, at least 25% of the voting shares of the corporation paying the Dividends.
(2) The Withholding tax rate is 5% if the beneficial owner is a corporation (other than partnership) that has owned directly, for the period of 6 months ending on the date on which entitlement to the Dividends is determined, at least 10% of the voting shares of the corporation paying the Dividends; or
(3) In all other cases, the Withholding tax rate is 15%.

(Tax Convention between Germany and Japan Article 10(2),(3))

In this case, and assuming it has no PE in Japan, as your German parent holds 100% of your shares, if it has done so for more than 18 months it satisfies condition (1) above, and in principle is exempt from withholding tax.

However, in order to qualify for the withholding tax exemption, the German parent must also satisfy the requirements of the Limitation on Benefits clause of the Tax Convention between Germany and Japan.

3. Limitation on Benefits clause in the Tax Convention between Germany and Japan, Article 21

Under Article 21, in order to enjoy the benefits of reduced or exempt withholding tax on certain types of income ('LoB income'), which includes tax-exempt dividends, a taxpayer must, in principle, be a 'qualified person'. A qualified person is a resident who is either:

(1) an individual;
(2) a qualified governmental body;
(3) a corporation, if its principal class of shares is listed or registered and is regularly traded on one or more recognised stock exchanges;
(4) certain pension funds or pension schemes;
(5) a Public Interest Corporation; or
(6) a person other than an individual, if at least 65% of the voting shares or other beneficial interests of the person are owned, directly or indirectly, by residents of Germany that are qualified persons by reason of subparagraphs (1), (2), (3), (4) or (5).

(Tax Convention between Germany and Japan, Article 21(2))

In the above (3), the recognised stock exchanges are

(i) any stock exchange established under the terms of the Financial Instruments and Exchange Law (Law No. 25 of 1948) of Japan;

(ii) any regulated market pursuant to the Markets in Financial Instruments Directive 2004/39/EC (as amended) or any successor Directive;
(iii) Hong Kong Exchanges and Clearing, the NASDAQ System, the New York Stock Exchange, Singapore Exchange, SIX Swiss Exchange and the Taiwan Stock Exchange; and
(iv) any other stock exchange which the competent authorities of the Contracting States agree to recognise for the purposes of this Article.

(Tax Convention between Germany and Japan, Article 21(7)(c))

In this case, the Frankfurt Stock Exchange qualifies as an authorised securities market under the Tax Convention between Germany and Japan (i.e., it is included in the exchanges regulated in accordance with the Markets in Financial Instruments Directive), which means that your German parent satisfies (3) above and is a qualified person.

4. Procedures for obtaining benefits under the Tax Convention between Germany and Japan (Enforcement Order on Act on Special Provisions of the Income Tax Act, the Corporation Tax Act and the Local Tax Act Incidental to Enforcement of Tax Conventions Article 2)

In order to be exempted from withholding tax on Dividends under a Tax Convention, the beneficiary is required to submit 'Application Form for Income Tax Convention' to the competent national tax office through their withholding tax agent no later than the day before the day on which the beneficiary first receives payment (for Dividends deriving from shares held anonymously, an 'Application Form for Income Tax Convention' must be submitted each time a payment is received).

It should also be noted that if the Limitation on Benefits clause applies, 'Attachment Form for Limitation on Benefits (Entitlement to Benefits) Article' must also be submitted. This is valid for a period of three years for a qualified person. Both documents are shown on the following pages.

In addition, when submitting these forms, it is also necessary to submit a residency certificate for your German parent and other documents as reference.

In summary therefore, you will submit the following documents to the competent national tax office on behalf of your German parent to obtain the withholding tax exemption:

(i) Application Form for Income Tax Convention (Form 1).
(ii) Attachment Form for Limitation on Benefits (Entitlement to Benefits) Article (Germany) (Form 17 – Germany).
(iii) Residency certificate.

The tax authorities may also request additional documents after they review the filed documents.

Application Form for Income Tax Convention (Relief from Japanese Income Tax and Special Income Tax for Reconstruction on Dividends)

Form 1

様式 1
FORM

租税条約に関する届出書
APPLICATION FORM FOR INCOME TAX CONVENTION
配当に対する所得税及び復興特別所得税の軽減・免除
Relief from Japanese Income Tax and Special Income Tax for Reconstruction on Dividends

この届出書の記載に当たっては、別紙の注意事項を参照してください。
See separate instructions.

(税務署整理欄 For official use only)
適用；有、無

番号確認

□ 限度税率 ____% Applicable Tax Rate
□ 免税 Exemption

________税務署長殿
To the District Director, ________Tax Office

1 適用を受ける租税条約に関する事項；
Applicable Income Tax Convention
日本国と________________との間の租税条約第____条第____項
The Income Tax Convention between Japan and________________, Article____, para.____

2 配当の支払を受ける者に関する事項；
Details of Recipient of Dividends

氏名又は名称 Full name		
個人番号又は法人番号 Individual Number or Corporate Number (Limited to case of a holder)		
個人の場合 Individual	住所又は居所 Domicile or residence	(電話番号 Telephone Number)
	国籍 Nationality	
法人その他の団体の場合 Corporation or other entity	本店又は主たる事務所の所在地 Place of head office or main office	(電話番号 Telephone Number)
	設立又は組織された場所 Place where the Corporation was established or organized	
	事業が管理・支配されている場所 Place where the business is managed and controlled	(電話番号 Telephone Number)
下記「4」の配当につき居住者として課税される国及び納税地（注8） Country where the recipient is taxable as resident on Dividends mentioned in 4 below and the place where he is to pay tax (Note 8)		(納税者番号 Taxpayer Identification Number)
日本国内の恒久的施設の状況 Permanent establishment in Japan □有(Yes)，□無(No) If "Yes", explain:	名称 Name	
	所在地 Address	(電話番号 Telephone Number)
	事業の内容 Details of Business	

3 配当の支払者に関する事項；
Details of Payer of Dividends

(1) 名称 Full name	
(2) 本店の所在地 Place of head office	(電話番号 Telephone Number)
(3) 法人番号 Corporate Number	
(4) 発行済株式のうち議決権のある株式の数（注9） Number of voting shares issued (Note 9)	

4 上記「3」の支払者から支払を受ける配当で「1」の租税条約の規定の適用を受けるものに関する事項（注10）；
Details of Dividends received from the Payer to which the Convention mentioned in 1 above is applicable (Note 10)

元本の種類 Kind of Principal	銘柄又は名称 Description	名義人の氏名又は名称（注11） Name of Nominee of Principal (Note 11)
□出資・株式・基金 Shares (Stocks) □株式投資信託 Stock investment trust		

元本の数量 Quantity of Principal	左のうち議決権のある株式数 Of which Quantity of Voting Shares	元本の取得年月日 Date of Acquisition of Principal

5 その他参考となるべき事項（注12）；
Others (Note 12)

【裏面に続きます (Continue on the reverse) 】

6　日本の税法上、届出書の「2」の外国法人が納税義務者とされるが、租税条約の規定によりその株主等である者（相手国居住者に限ります。）の所得として取り扱われる部分に対して租税条約の適用を受けることとされている場合の租税条約の適用を受ける割合に関する事項等（注4）；
Details of proportion of income to which the convention mentioned in 1 above is applicable, if the foreign company mentioned in 2 above is taxable as a company under Japanese tax law, and the convention is applicable to income that is treated as income of the member (limited to a resident of the other contracting country) of the foreign company in accordance with the provisions of the convention (Note 4)

届出書の「2」の外国法人の株主等で租税条約の適用を受ける者の氏名又は名称 Name of member of the foreign company mentioned in 2 above, to whom the Convention is applicable	間接保有 Indirect Ownership	持分の割合 Ratio of Ownership	受益の割合＝租税条約の適用を受ける割合 Proportion of benefit = Proportion for Application of Convention
	□	%	%
	□	%	%
	□	%	%
	□	%	%
	□	%	%
合計 Total		%	%

届出書の「2」の外国法人が支払を受ける「4」の配当について、「1」の租税条約の相手国の法令に基づきその株主等である者の所得として取り扱われる場合には、その根拠法令及びその効力を生じる日を記載してください。
If dividends mentioned in 4 above that a foreign company mentioned in 2 above receives are treated as income of those who are its members under the law in the other contracting country of the convention mentioned in 1 above, enter the law that provides the legal basis to the above treatment and the date on which it will become effective.

根拠法令
Applicable law________________　効力を生じる日　年　月　日
Effective date________________

7　日本の税法上、届出書の「2」の団体の構成員が納税義務者とされるが、租税条約の規定によりその団体の所得として取り扱われるものに対して租税条約の適用を受けることとされている場合の記載事項等（注5）；
Details if, while the partner of the entity mentioned in 2 above is taxable under Japanese tax law, and the convention is applicable to income that is treated as income of the entity in accordance with the provisions of the convention (Note 5)

他の全ての構成員から通知を受けこの届出書を提出する構成員の氏名又は名称________________
Full name of the partner of the entity who has been notified by all other partners and is to submit this form

届出書の「2」の団体が支払を受ける「4」の配当について、「1」の租税条約の相手国の法令に基づきその団体の所得として取り扱われる場合には、その根拠法令及びその効力を生じる日を記載してください。
If dividends mentioned in 4 above that an entity at mentioned in 2 above receives are treated as income of the entity under the law in the other contracting country of the convention mentioned in 1 above, enter the law that provides the legal basis to the above treatment and the date on which it will become effective.

根拠法令
Applicable law________________　効力を生じる日　年　月　日
Effective date________________

私は、この届出書の「4」に記載した配当が「1」に掲げる租税条約の規定の適用を受けるものであることを、「租税条約等の実施に伴う所得税法、法人税法及び地方税法の特例等に関する法律の施行に関する省令」及び「復興特別所得税に関する省令」の規定により届け出るとともに、この届出書（及び付表）の記載事項が正確かつ完全であることを宣言します。

In accordance with the provisions of the Ministerial Ordinance for the Implementation of the Law concerning the Special Measures of the Income Tax Act, the Corporation Tax Act and the Local Tax Act for the Enforcement of Income Tax Conventions and the Ministerial Ordinance concerning Special Income Tax for Reconstruction, I hereby submit this application form under the belief that the provisions of the Income Tax Convention mentioned in 1 above is applicable to Dividends mentioned in 4 above and also hereby declare that the statement on this form (and attachment form) is correct and complete to the best of my knowledge and belief.

年　月　日
Date________________

配当の支払を受ける者又はその代理人の署名
Signature of the Recipient of Dividends or his Agent________________

8　権限ある当局の証明（注13）
Certification of competent authority (Note 13)

私は、届出者が、日本国と____________との間の租税条約第____条第____項____に規定する居住者であることを証明します。
I hereby certify that the applicant is a resident under the provisions of the Income Tax Convention between Japan and ____________, Article______, para.______.

年　月　日
Date____________　Signature____________

○　代理人に関する事項　；　この届出書を代理人によって提出する場合には、次の欄に記載してください。
Details of the Agent　；　If this form is prepared and submitted by the Agent, fill out the following Columns.

代理人の資格 Capacity of Agent in Japan	氏名（名称） Full name		納税管理人の届出をした税務署名 Name of the Tax Office where the Tax Agent is registered
□ 納税管理人 ※ Tax Agent □ その他の代理人 Other Agent	住所（居所・所在地） Domicile (Residence or location)	（電話番号 Telephone Number）	税務署 Tax Office

※　「納税管理人」とは、日本国の国税に関する申告、申請、請求、届出、納付等の事項を処理させるため、国税通則法の規定により選任し、かつ、日本国における納税地の所轄税務署長に届出をした代理人をいいます。

※　"Tax Agent" means a person who is appointed by the taxpayer and is registered at the District Director of Tax Office for the place where the taxpayer is to pay his tax, in order to have such agent take necessary procedures concerning the Japanese national taxes, such as filing a return, applications, claims, payment of taxes, etc., under the provisions of Act on General Rules for National Taxes.

○　適用を受ける租税条約が特典条項を有する租税条約である場合；
If the applicable convention has article of limitation on benefits

特典条項に関する付表の添付
"Attachment Form for Limitation on Benefits Article" attached
□有Yes
□添付省略 Attachment not required
（特典条項に関する付表を添付して提出した租税条約に関する届出書の提出日　年　月　日）
Date of previous submission of the application for income tax convention with the "Attachment Form for Limitation on Benefits Article____________

Attachment Form for Limitation on Benefits (Entitlement to Benefits) article (FRG)

(Form 17 – Germany)

様 式 17-独
FORM 17-FRG

特典条項に関する付表（独）

ATTACHMENT FORM FOR LIMITATION ON BENEFITS (ENTITLEMENT TO BENEFITS) ARTICLE (FRG)

記載に当たっては、別紙の注意事項を参照してください。
See separate instructions.

1 適用を受ける租税協定の特典条項に関する事項；
Limitation on Benefits Article of applicable Income Tax Agreement
日本国とドイツ連邦共和国との間の租税協定第21条第1項から第7項
The Income Tax Agreement between Japan and Federal Republic of Germany, paragraph 1 to paragraph 7 of Article 21

2 この付表に記載される者の氏名又は名称；
Full name of Resident

	居住地国の権限ある当局が発行した居住者証明書を添付してください（注5）。 Please Attach Residency Certification issued by Competent Authority of Country of residence. (Note5)

3 租税協定の特典条項の要件に関する事項；
AからCの順番に各項目の「□該当」又は「□非該当」の該当する項目に✓印を付してください。いずれかの項目に「該当」する場合には、それ以降の項目に記入する必要はありません。なお、該当する項目については、各項目ごとの要件に関する事項を記入の上、必要な書類を添付してください。（注6）
In order of sections A, B and C, check the applicable box in each line as "Yes" or "No". If you check any box as "Yes" in sections A to C, you need not fill in the lines that follow. Only the applicable lines need to be filled in and any necessary documents must be attached. (Note6)

A

(1) 個人 Individual □該当 Yes，□非該当 No

(2) 適格政府機関（注7） Qualified Governmental Entity (Note7) □該当 Yes，□非該当 No

(3) 公開会社（注8） Publicly Traded Company (Note8) □該当 Yes，□非該当 No

公認の有価証券市場の名称 Recognised Stock Exchange	シンボル又は証券コード Ticker Symbol or Security Code

(4) 年金基金又は年金計画（注9） Pension Fund, Pension Scheme (Note9) □該当 Yes，□非該当 No
直前の課税年度の終了の日においてその受益者、構成員又は参加者の50%超が日本又はドイツ連邦共和国の居住者である個人であるものに限ります。受益者等の50%超が、いずれかの締約国の居住者である事情を記入してください。
The "Pension Fund" or "Pension Scheme" is limited to those where more than 50% of beneficiaries, members or participants were individual residents of Japan or Federal Republic of Germany as of the end of the prior taxable year. Please provide details below showing that more than 50% of beneficiaries et al. are individual residents of either Japan or Federal Republic of Germany.

(5) 公益団体（注10） Public Service Organization (Note10) □該当 Yes，□非該当 No
設立等の根拠法令 Law for Establishment　設立の目的 Purpose of Establishment　非課税の根拠法令 Law for Tax Exemption

Aのいずれにも該当しない場合は、Bに進んでください。If none of the lines in A are applicable, please proceed to B.

B

(1) 個人以外の者
Person other than an Individual □該当 Yes，□非該当 No
（「個人以外の者」の場合、Aの(1)から(5)までの者であるドイツ連邦共和国の居住者が、議決権の65%以上に相当する株式その他の受益に関する持分を直接又は間接に所有するものに限ります。（注11）
The "Person other than an Individual" is limited to the person, where residents of Federal Republic of Germany who fall under (1),(2),(3),(4) or (5) of A own, either directly or indirectly, shares or other beneficial interests representing at least 65% of the voting shares or other beneficial interests of the person. (Note11)

年 月 日現在の株主等の状況 State of Shareholders, etc. as of (date) / /

株主等の氏名又は名称 Name of Shareholder(s)	居住地国における納税地 Place where Shareholder(s) is taxable in Country of residence	Aの番号 Number in A	間接保有 Indirect Ownership	株主等の持分 Number of Shares owned
			□	
			□	
			□	
			□	
			□	
合計 Total 持分割合 Ratio (%) of Shares owned				(%)

B

(2) ドイツ連邦共和国の居住者 □該当 Yes、□非該当 No
Resident of Federal Republic of Germany

次の(a)又は(b)の要件を満たす者に関する事項を記入してください。
Please provide details following Conditions (a) or (b).

(a) その居住者の議決権のある株式その他の受益に関する持分の 65%以上が、次の(aa)の者に直接又は間接に所有されていること。(注12)
at least 65 per cent of the voting shares or other beneficial interests of the person are owned, directly or indirectly, by persons who meet requirement (aa) (Note12)

(aa) その居住者が日本において取得する所得を直接に取得した場合に日本国とドイツ連邦共和国との間の租税協定(以下「日独租税協定」といいます。)に基づいて同等の又は有利な特典を受けることができる者
If they had derived the item of income in Japan directly, they would, under the Japan－FRG Income Tax Agreement, be entitled to equivalent or more favourable benefits

(b) その居住者の議決権のある株式その他の受益に関する持分の 90%以上が、次の(bb)の者に直接又は間接に所有されていること。(注12)
at least 90 per cent of the voting shares or other beneficial interests of the person are owned, directly or indirectly, by persons who meet requirement (bb) (Note12)

(bb) その居住者が日本において取得する所得を直接に取得した場合に日独租税協定又は日本が他の国との間で締結した租税条約に基づいて同等の又は有利な特典を受けることができる者
If they had derived the item of income in Japan directly, they would, under the Japan－FRG Income Tax Agreement or an income tax agreement between Japan and another State, be entitled to equivalent or more favourable benefits.

株主等の氏名又は名称 Name of Shareholders	株主等の居住地国における納税地 Place where Shareholder(s) is taxable in Country of residence	株主等 Shareholders (a)の場合 (a) (aa)を満たすか Requirement (aa)	株主等 Shareholders (b)の場合 (b) (bb)を満たすか Requirement (bb)	間接保有 Indirect Ownership	株主等の持分 Number of Shares owned
		□はい Yes、□いいえ No	□はい Yes、□いいえ No	□	
				□	
				□	
				□	
				□	
				□	
				□	
				□	
				□	
				□	
			合計 Total (持分割合 Ratio(%) of Shares owned)		(%)

Bに該当しない場合は、Cに進んでください。If B does not apply, proceed to C.

C

次の(a)から(c)の要件をすべて満たす者 □該当 Yes、□非該当 No
Resident satisfying all of the following Conditions from (a) through (c)

居住地国において従事している事業の概要(注13);Description of business in residence country (Note13)

(a) 居住地国において従事している事業が、自己の勘定のために投資を行い又は管理するもの(銀行、保険会社又は証券会社が行う銀行業、保険業又は証券業を除きます。)ではないこと(注14): □はい Yes、□いいえ No
The business in the country of residence is other than that of making or managing investments for the resident's own account (unless the business is banking, insurance or a securities business carried on by a bank, insurance company or securities dealer) (Note14)

(b) 所得が居住地国において従事している事業に関連又は付随して取得されるものであること(注15): □はい Yes、□いいえ No
An item of income is derived in connection with or is incidental to that business in the country of residence (Note15)

(c) (日本国内において行う事業から所得を取得する場合)居住地国において行う事業が日本国内において行う事業との関係で実質的なものであること(注16): □はい Yes、□いいえ No
(If you derive an item of income from a business in Japan) The business carried on in the country of residence is substantial in relation to the business carried on in Japan. (Note 16)

日本国内において従事している事業の概要;Description of Business in Japan.

D 国税庁長官の認定(注17);
Determination by the NTA Commissioner (Note 17)

国税庁長官の認定を受けている場合は、以下にその内容を記載してください。その認定の範囲内で租税協定の特典を受けることができます。なお、上記AからCまでのいずれかに該当する場合には、国税庁長官の認定は不要です。

If you have received authorization from the NTA Commissioner, please describe below the nature of the authorization. The agreement benefits will be granted within the range of the authorization. If any of the above mentioned Lines A through to C are applicable, then authorization from the NTA Commissioner is not necessary.

・認定を受けた日 Date of authorization 年 月 日

・認定を受けた所得の種類
Type of income for which the authorization was received

Q8 Withholding Tax on Dividends and Relief under Tax Conventions (Derivative Benefits Test)

We are a Japanese corporation, which is wholly owned by a Swiss corporation. Our Swiss parent is itself a 100% subsidiary of a US corporation, which is owned by a US resident (Mr A). This shareholding structure has been in place for more than five years.

Will there be withholding tax imposed when we pay Dividends? Can we apply for relief from such withholding tax under a Tax Convention?

A:

Under Japanese domestic law, withholding tax of 20.42% must be withheld at the time of payment of Dividends.

However, if the US corporation, which is the parent of the Swiss corporation, meets certain requirements, the US corporation will be an equivalent beneficiary under the Tax Convention between Japan and Switzerland. As a result, withholding tax on Dividends paid to your Swiss parent will be exempted. If the US corporation does not meet the requirements, the withholding tax can still be reduced to 5%.

In order to obtain the benefits of the Tax Convention between Japan and Switzerland, certain documents, such as the 'Application Form for Income Tax Convention', must be submitted to the competent national tax office by the day before the date on which the Dividends are paid.

Discussion

1. Tax treatment under domestic tax law and exemption from withholding tax under the Tax Convention between Japan and Switzerland

As mentioned in Q7, when paying Dividends to a foreign corporation, the payor is required to collect withholding tax at the rate of 20.42% (ITA Article 161(1)(ix), Article 212(1) and Article 213(1)(i)).

However, under the Tax Convention between Japan and Switzerland, withholding tax on Dividends can be reduced or exempted if certain conditions are met, namely:

(1) The Withholding tax on Dividends is exempted if the beneficial owner of the Dividends is a resident of Switzerland and a corporation that has owned, directly or indirectly, for the period of 6 months ending on the date on which entitlement to the Dividends is determined and holds shares representing at least 50% of the voting power of the corporation paying the Dividends where such corporation is a resident of Japan.

(2) The Withholding tax rate on Dividends is 5% if the beneficial owner of the Dividends is a resident of Switzerland and a corporation that has owned, directly or indirectly, for the period of 6 months ending on the date on which entitlement to the Dividends is determined and holds shares representing at least 10% of the voting power of the corporation paying the Dividends where such corporation is a resident of Japan.

(3) In all other cases, the Withholding tax will be 10%.

(Tax Convention between Japan and Switzerland Article 10(2), (3))

As you have been wholly owned by your Swiss parent for more than five years, and assuming it has no PE in Japan, condition (1) above is satisfied, and the payment of Dividends is, in principle, exempt from withholding tax.

However, in order to qualify for this exemption, the requirements of the Limitation on Benefits clause under the Tax Convention between Japan and Switzerland must also be met.

2. Limitation on Benefits clause in the Tax Convention between Japan and Switzerland, Article 22A

Under Article 22A of the Tax Convention between Japan and Switzerland, in order to enjoy the benefits of reduced or exempt withholding tax on LoB income, which includes tax-exempt dividends, a taxpayer must be a ‘qualified person’. A qualified person is a resident who is either:

① An individual.
② A qualified governmental body.
③ A corporation if its principal class of shares is listed or registered on a recognized stock exchange (specified separately) and is regularly traded on one or more recognised stock exchanges.
④ A bank, an insurance corporation or a securities dealer that is established and regulated as such under the laws of the country of which it is a resident.
⑤ Certain pension funds or pension schemes.
⑥ A person other than an individual, if residents of the country that are qualified persons by reason of the above (1) to (5), own directly or indirectly, shares or other beneficial interests representing at least 50% of the capital or of the voting power of the person.

(Tax Convention between Switzerland and Japan Article 22A(xx))

As your Swiss parent does not satisfy any of the above requirements, it is not a qualified person under the Tax Convention between Japan and Switzerland.

Even in such cases, however, a Swiss corporation may still benefit from the Tax Convention between Japan and Switzerland in respect of LoB income if any of the following tests are met:

(1) Derivative benefits test.
(2) Headquarters corporation test.
(3) Active business test.
(4) Approval from competent authorities.

The derivative benefits test may be met here because a US corporation owns your Swiss parent.

3. Derivative benefits test

Notwithstanding that a corporation that is a resident of a country may not be a qualified person, that resident shall be entitled to the benefits of LoB income if that resident satisfies any other specified conditions for the obtaining of such benefits and s if shares representing at least 75% of the capital or of the voting power of the corporation are owned, directly or indirectly, by seven or fewer persons who are equivalent beneficiaries.

(Tax Convention between Japan and Switzerland Article 22A(2))

An equivalent beneficiary is a resident of a country that has a Tax Convention with another country, from which the resident wishes to claim benefits such that:

(1) that Tax Convention contains provisions for effective exchange of information;
(2) that resident is a qualified person under the limitation on benefits provisions in that convention or, where there are no such provisions in that convention, would be a qualified person when that convention is read as including provisions; and
(3) with respect to an item of income referred to in respective clause that resident would be entitled under that Tax Convention to a rate of tax with respect to the particular class of income for which the benefits are being claimed under this Tax Convention that is at least as low as the rate applicable under this Tax Convention.

(Tax Convention between Japan and Switzerland Article 22A(8)(d))

Moreover:

> The derivative benefit test shall be considered to satisfy the conditions that for the taxable year in which the payment of an item of income is made if such resident satisfies those conditions during the twelve months period preceding the date on which entitlement to the dividends is determined.

(Tax Convention between Japan and Switzerland Article 22A(4)(a)).

Your Swiss parent is wholly owned by a US corporation. Therefore, if the US corporation is an equivalent beneficiary, withholding tax on Dividends paid to your Swiss parent is exempt under the Tax Convention between Japan and Switzerland.

4. Consideration of equivalent beneficiaries

The Tax Convention between Japan and the US will determine whether the US corporation is an equivalent beneficiary or not. In this case:

(1) There are effective information exchange provisions (Tax Convention between Japan and the US, Article 26).
(2) Under Article 22(1) of the Tax Convention between Japan and the US, a qualified person is a resident who falls into one of the following categories:
    (i) an individual;
    (ii) an eligible governmental body;
    (iii) a corporation, if:
        (a) the principal class of its shares, and any disproportionate class of its shares, is listed or registered on a recognized stock exchange specified and is regularly traded on one or more recognized stock exchanges; or
        (b) at least 50 percent of each class of shares in the corporation is owned directly or indirectly by five or fewer residents entitled to benefits under clause (a), provided that, in the case of indirect ownership, each intermediate owner is a person entitled to the benefits of corporation and certain subsidiaries whose principal class of shares is listed, registered and regularly traded on a recognized securities market.
    (iv) Certain public corporation
    (v) Certain pension funds
    (vi) A person other than an individual, if:
        a) residents that are described in the above (i), (ii), (iv) or (v), or clause (a) of the above (iii), own, directly or indirectly, at least 50% of each class of shares or other beneficial interests in the person, and
        b) less than 50% of the person's gross income for the taxable year is paid or accrued by the person in that taxable year, directly or indirectly, to persons who are not residents of either country in the form of payments that are deductible in computing its taxable income in the country of which it is a resident (but not including arm's length payments in the ordinary course of business for services or tangible property and payments in respect of financial obligations to a commercial bank, provided that where such a bank is not a resident of a Contracting State such payment is attributable to a permanent establishment of that bank situated in one of the country).

(Tax Convention between Japan and the US Article 22(1))

As 100% of the shares of the US corporation are held by Mr A, (vi)(a) above is satisfied.

Therefore, as long as the US corporation does not transfer more than 50% of its gross income to residents of third countries, the US corporation will meet the conditions of (vi)(b), and be a qualified person under the Tax Convention between Japan and the US.

(3) Withholding tax on Dividends is exempt for a qualified person who holds 50% or more of the shares in a corporation for at least twelve months before payment of the Dividends (Tax Convention between Japan and the US Article 10(3)). As a result, the withholding tax rate on Dividends to a US resident is the same as the withholding tax rate on Dividends to a Swiss resident under the Tax Convention between Japan and Switzerland, i.e., zero.

In summary, the US corporation should be considered an equivalent beneficiary as long as it does not transfer more than 50% of its gross income to residents of third countries. Additionally, since Mr A has been a US resident for more than five years and owns 100% of the shares of the US corporation, he is considered to have been an equivalent beneficiary for more than twelve months prior to payment of the Dividends.

Therefore, as far as the above conditions are met, the Dividends paid to your Swiss parent will be exempt from withholding tax under the Tax Convention between Japan and Switzerland.

If the US corporation is not an equivalent beneficiary, the withholding tax rate on Dividends will be 5% because your Swiss parent has held at least 10% of your shares for at least six months:

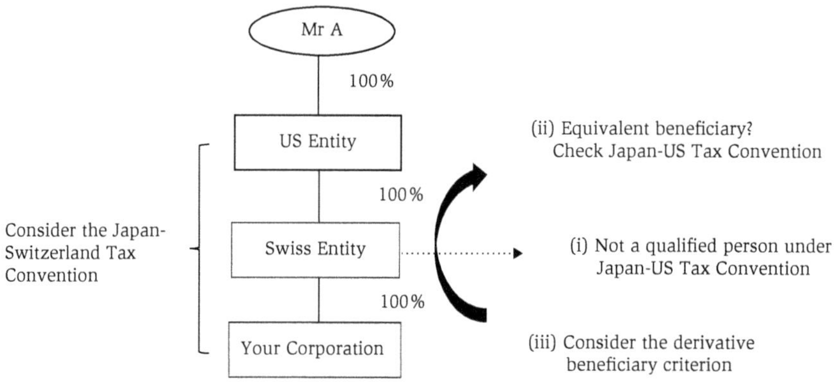

5. Procedures for obtaining benefits under the Tax Convention between Japan and Switzerland (Enforcement Order on Act on Special Provisions of the Income Tax Act, the Corporation Tax Act and the Local Tax Act Incidental to Enforcement of Tax Conventions Article 2)

In order to be exempt from withholding tax on Dividends under a Tax Convention, the beneficiary is required to submit an 'Application Form for Income Tax Convention' to the competent national tax office through its withholding tax agent no later than the day before the day on which the beneficiary first receives payment (in the case of

Dividends on shares with shares held anonymously, an 'Application Form for Income Tax Convention' must be submitted each time a payment is to be received).

If a Limitation on Benefits clause applies, an 'Attachment Form for Limitation on Benefits (Entitlement to Benefits) Article' must also be submitted. This is valid for a period of one year in the case of an equivalent beneficiary.

The 'Attachment Form for Limitation on Benefits (Entitlement to Benefits) Article' of the Tax Convention between Japan and Switzerland is similar to that provided in Q7 for the Tax Convention between Japan and Germany; however, the form for Switzerland (Form 17 - Switzerland) should be used.

When submitting the above forms, a residency certificate of the Swiss parent and other documents as reference must also be provided.

In this case, you will submit the following documents to the competent national tax office on behalf of your Swiss parent:

(i) Application Form for Income Tax Convention (Form 1).
(ii) Attachment Form for Limitation on Benefits (Entitlement to Benefits) Article (Switzerland) (Form 17 - Switzerland).
(iii) Residency certificate.

The tax authorities may also request additional documents after they review the filed documents.

Q9 Withholding Tax on Dividends and Relief under Tax Conventions (Active Business Test)

We are a Japanese corporation wholly owned by a Dutch corporation, which is itself a 100% subsidiary of an Irish corporation. This group structure has been in place for more than five years.

Will withholding tax be imposed when we pay Dividends? Can we obtain relief under a Tax Convention?

A:

Under Japanese domestic law, withholding tax of 20.42% must be collected at the time of payment of Dividends.

However, if your Dutch parent satisfies the 'active business test', this withholding tax will be exempt under the Tax Convention between Japan and the Netherlands. If your Dutch parent does not satisfy the 'active business test', the withholding tax will be reduced to 5%.

In order to obtain benefits under the Tax Convention between Japan and the Netherlands, certain documents, such as an 'Application Form for Income Tax Convention', must be submitted to the competent national tax office by the day before the date of payment of the Dividends.

Discussion

1. Tax treatment under domestic tax law and exemption from withholding tax under the Tax Convention between Japan and the Netherlands

As mentioned in Q7 and Q8, when paying Dividends to a foreign corporation in Japan, the payor is required to collect withholding tax at the rate of 20.42% (ITA Article 161(1)(ix), Article 212(1) and Article 213(1)(i)).

However, under the Tax Convention between Japan and the Netherlands, withholding tax on Dividends can be reduced or exempted if the following conditions are met:

(1) Withholding tax is exempted if the beneficial owner of the Dividends is a resident of the Netherlands and a corporation that has owned, directly or indirectly, at least 50% of the voting power of the corporation paying the Dividends for the period of six months ending on the date on which entitlement to the Dividends is determined.

(2) Withholding tax on Dividends is reduced to 5% if the beneficial owner of the Dividends is a corporation that has owned, directly or indirectly, at least 10% of the voting power of the corporation paying the dividends for the period of six months ending on the date on which entitlement to the dividends is determined.

(3) In all other cases, withholding tax is reduced to 10%.

(Tax Convention between Japan and the Netherlands, Article 10(2), (3))

As the sole shareholder for more than five years, and assuming it has no PE in Japan, your Dutch parent satisfies condition (1) above, such that Dividends paid by you are, in principle, exempt from withholding tax.

However, in order to qualify for the withholding tax exemption, the Limitation on Benefits clause of the Tax Convention between Japan and the Netherlands must also be satisfied.

2. Limitation on Benefits clause of the Tax Convention between Japan and the Netherlands, Article 21

Under Article 21 of the Tax Convention between Japan and the Netherlands, in order to enjoy the benefits of reduced or exempt withholding tax on LoB income, which includes tax-exempt dividends, a taxpayer must be a 'qualified person'. A qualified person for the purposes of the Tax Convention between Japan and the Netherlands is a resident who is one of the following:

(i) An individual;
(ii) A qualified governmental body;
(iii) A corporation, if the principal class of its shares is listed or registered on a recognised stock exchange and is regularly traded on one or more recognised stock exchanges, provided that, if the shares are listed or registered on a recognised stock exchange (specified separately), the primary place of management and control of the corporation is in the Contracting State of which it is a resident;
(iv) Certain pension funds or charitable organisations;
(v) A bank, an insurance corporation or a securities corporation that is established and regulated as such under the Acts of the country of which it is a resident; or
(vi) A person other than an individual, if residents of either country that are qualified persons by reason of (i), (ii), (iii) or (iv) of the above own, directly or indirectly, shares or other beneficial interests representing at least 50 per cent of the voting power of the person.

(Tax Convention between Japan and the Netherlands Article 21)

As your Dutch parent does not fit within any of the above categories, it is not a qualified person under the Tax Convention between Japan and the Netherlands.

However, even if not a qualified person, your Dutch parent may still obtain benefits in respect of LoB income if any of the following tests are satisfied:

(i) Derivative benefits test.
(ii) Active business test.
(iii) Headquarters corporation test.
(iv) Approval from competent authorities.

As the shareholder of your Dutch parent, an Irish corporation, the derivative benefits test cannot be met as Dividends are not exempt under Article 11 of the Tax Convention between Ireland and Japan.

The application of the headquarters corporation test is likely to be difficult given the Dutch corporation only owns your shares. However, the active business test may be satisfied depending on the situation of the Dutch corporation.

3. Active business test (Tax Convention between Japan and the Netherlands, Article 21(5)(a))

Even if not a qualified person, a Dutch resident can obtain benefits in relation to LoB income from Japan if the following conditions are met:

(i) The resident is carrying on business in the country of the resident (other than the business of making or managing investments for the resident's own account, unless the business is banking, insurance or securities business carried on by a bank, insurance corporation or securities corporation).
(ii) The income is acquired in connection with or is incidental to that business.
(iii) The resident satisfies any other specified conditions set out in the Tax Convention.

(Tax Convention between Japan and the Netherlands, Article 21(5))

The following discussion considers the application of the active business test to a Dutch corporation that is a beneficiary of LoB income:

> The business conducted by a partnership in which that person is a partner and the business conducted by persons connected to such person shall be deemed to be conducted by such person. A person shall be connected to another if one owns, directly or indirectly, at least 50% of the beneficial interest in the other (or, in the case of a corporation, shares representing at least 50% of the voting power of the corporation) or a third person owns, directly or indirectly, at least 50% of the beneficial interest (or, in the case of a corporation, shares representing at least 50% of the voting power of the corporation) in each person. In any case, a person shall be considered to be connected to another if, on the basis of all the facts and circumstances, one has control of the other or both are under the control of the same person or persons.

(Tax Convention between Japan and the Netherlands, Article 21(5)(c))

Second, if a Dutch corporation derives LoB income from Japan, the active business test shall be satisfied only if the business conducted in the Netherlands is substantial in relation to the business conducted in Japan. Whether such business is substantial shall be determined based on all the facts and circumstances. For example, if the volume of business in the Netherlands is insignificant in comparison to the volume of business in Japan in terms of the value of assets or amount of income, or if the activities in the Netherlands are negligible in relation to the total business, then this condition is not satisfied.

Taking all of the above into consideration, your Dutch parent will satisfy the active business test if the following conditions are met:

(1) your Dutch parent, or any connected persons, is engaged in business in the Netherlands;
(2) the Dividends are acquired in connection with or incidental to the business in the Netherlands; and
(3) the business in the Netherlands is substantial in comparison to your business in Japan.

If all the conditions of the active business test are met, the Tax Convention between Japan and the Netherlands can be applied and withholding tax on Dividends is exempted. If all conditions are not met, the withholding tax will be reduced to 5% since your Dutch parent has owned more than 10% of your shares for more than six months:

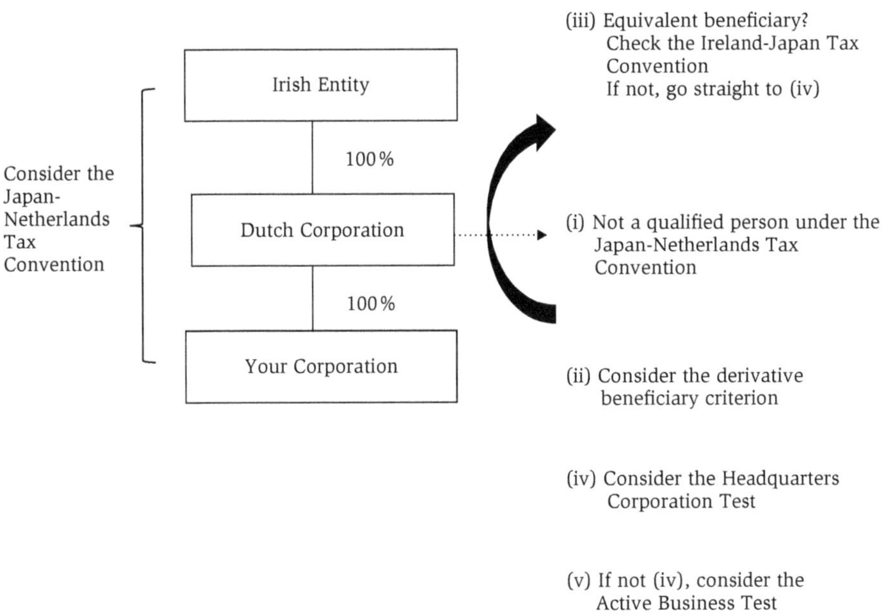

4. Procedures for obtaining benefits under the Tax Convention between Japan and the Netherlands (Enforcement Order on Act on Special Provisions of the Income Tax Act, the Corporation Tax Act and the Local Tax Act Incidental to Enforcement of Tax Convention Article 2)

In order to be exempt from withholding tax on Dividends under a Tax Convention, the beneficiary is required to submit 'Application Form for Income Tax Convention' to the competent national tax office through their withholding tax agent no later than the day before the day on which the beneficiary first receives payment (for Dividends on shares held anonymously, an 'Application Form for Income Tax Convention' must be submitted before each payment is received).

It should also be noted that if a Limitation on Benefits clause applies, an 'Attachment Form for Limitation on Benefits (Entitlement to Benefits) Article' must also be submitted. This is valid for a period of one year in the case of an active business test.

The 'Attachment Form for Limitation on Benefits (Entitlement to Benefits) Article' of the Tax Convention between Japan and the Netherlands is similar to the 'Attachment Form for Limitation on Benefits (Entitlement to Benefits) Article' in the case of the Tax Convention between Japan and Germany mentioned in Q7, but the form for the Netherlands (Form 17 - Kingdom of the Netherlands) should be used.

A residency certificate for the Dutch parent and other documents as reference should be submitted with these forms.

You will therefore submit the following documents for your Dutch parent to the competent national tax office:

(i) Application Form for Income Tax Convention (Form 1).
(ii) Attachment Form for Limitation on Benefits (Entitlement to Benefits) Article (the Kingdom of the Netherlands) (Form 17 - the Kingdom of the Netherlands).
(iii) Residency certificate.

The tax authorities may also request additional documents after they review the filed documents.

Q10 Withholding Tax on Interest Payments and Relief under Tax Conventions

We are a Japanese subsidiary of a US corporation and have received a loan from our US parent. Our US parent is actively traded on the NASDAQ.

Will there be withholding tax on the interest we pay on the loan? If so, can we obtain relief under the Tax Convention between Japan and the US?

A:

Under Japanese domestic law, a withholding tax of 20.42% must be collected at the time of payment of the interest. However, such withholding tax may be exempted or reduced if the conditions under the Tax Convention between Japan and the US satisfy.

In order to obtain the benefits of the Tax Convention between Japan and the US, certain documents, such as the 'Application Form for Income Tax Convention', must be submitted to the competent national tax office by the day before the date of payment of the interest payment.

Discussion

1. Tax treatment under domestic tax law

Interest on a loan to a person conducting business in Japan, which relates to that business is treated as domestic source income (ITA Article 161 (1)(x)).

Accordingly, interest on the loan from your US parent is domestic source income as long as the funds are used for your Japanese business. A person who pays domestic source income to a foreign corporation, such as interest on a loan, is required to collect withholding tax at the time of payment of that interest. The withholding tax should be paid to the competent national tax office by the 10th day of the month following the date of payment of the interest. The withholding tax rate is 20.42% (ITA Article 212(1) and Article 213(1)).

2. Withholding tax exemption under the Tax Convention between Japan and the US

Under the Tax Convention between Japan and the US, interest arises in a country when the payor is a resident of that country, and there is no requirement that the loan to which the interest relates be used for any specific purpose (Tax Convention between Japan and the US Article 11(3)). This creates a difference in the definition of interest for domestic source income purposes between the Tax Convention between Japan and the US and domestic income tax law (which requires the loan to be used in connection with the borrower's business in Japan). Where the definition of domestic source income in a Tax Convention differs from the definition of domestic source income under domestic law as in this case, the definition of domestic source income set out in the Tax Convention is to be adopted (ITA Article 162(1)). Consequently, as long as the payor of the interest is a resident of Japan, the interest is considered to be domestic source income regardless of whether or not it is used in connection with a Japanese business.

As a result, interest paid by you to your US parent should be treated as domestic source income under the Tax Convention between Japan and the US.

Moreover, notwithstanding domestic tax law applies a withholding tax rate of 20.42%; in fact, withholding tax on interest should largely be exempted under the Tax Convention between Japan and the US (the interest that may not be exempted is essentially certain interest covered by US law (Tax Convention between Japan and the US Article 11(2)); thus, all interest paid from Japan to the US should be exempted).

However, in order to obtain the withholding tax exemption, the Limitation on Benefits clause of the Tax Convention between Japan and the US must also be satisfied.

3. Limitation on Benefits clause of the Tax Convention between Japan and the US Article 22

(i) Under Article 22 of the Tax Convention between Japan and the US, in order to enjoy the benefits of reduced or exempt withholding tax on LoB income, a person must be a 'qualified person'. A qualified person for the purposes of the Tax Convention between Japan and the US is a resident who is one of the following:

- (i) an individual;
- (ii) an eligible governmental body;
- (iii) a corporation, if:
  - (a) the principal class of its shares, and any disproportionate class of its shares, is listed or registered on a recognized stock exchange specified and is regularly traded on one or more recognized stock exchanges; or
  - (b) at least 50% of each class of shares in the corporation is owned directly or indirectly by 5 or fewer residents entitled to benefits under clause (i), provided that, in the case of indirect ownership, each intermediate owner is a person entitled to the benefits of this Convention under this paragraph.
- (iv) certain public corporations;
- (v) certain pension funds;
- (vi) a person other than an individual, if:
  - (a) residents that are described in the above (i), (ii), (iv) or (v), or clause (a) of the above (iii), own, directly, or indirectly, at least 50% of each class of shares or other beneficial interests in the person; and
  - (b) less than 50% of the person's gross income for the taxable year is paid or accrued by the person in that taxable year, directly or indirectly, to persons who are not residents of either Contracting State in the form of payments that are deductible in computing its taxable income in the Contracting State of which it is a resident (but not including arm's length payments in the ordinary course of business for services or tangible property and payments in respect of financial obligations to a commercial bank, provided that where such a bank is not a resident of a Contracting State such payment is attributable to a permanent establishment of that bank situated in one of the Contracting States).

(Tax Convention between Japan and the US, Article 22(1))

NASDAQ is a recognised stock exchange as defined in the Tax Convention between Japan and the US Article 22(5)(b). The 'regularly traded' test is satisfied if 'the aggregate number of shares of that class traded on such stock exchange or exchanges during the preceding taxable year is at least is 6% of the average number of shares outstanding during the preceding year' (Protocol on Tax Convention between Japan and the US Article 11).

Therefore, if at least 6% of your US parent's average outstanding shares were traded on the NASDAQ during the preceding taxable year, the conditions of (iii) above are satisfied, and your US parent will be a qualified person under the Tax Convention between Japan and the US.

4. Procedures for obtaining benefits of the Tax Convention between Japan and the US (Enforcement Order on Act on Special Provisions of the Income Tax Act, the Corporation Tax Act and the Local Tax Act Incidental to Enforcement of Tax Convention Article 2)

In order to be exempt from withholding tax on interest under a Tax Convention, the beneficiary is required to submit an 'Application Form for Income Tax Convention' to the competent national tax office through their withholding tax agent no later than the day before the day on which the beneficiary first receives payment. For interest payments, an 'Application Form for Income Tax Convention' must be submitted each time a payment is received unless the loan agreement is provided. In that case, it need only be submitted once.

When submitting the 'Application Form for Income Tax Convention' in relation to interest, it is required to provide the date of conclusion of the loan, the principal amount, the loan period, the amount of interest to be paid during the loan period, and the date(s) of interest payments.

In addition, if there is a change in the above information, unless the change is only an increase or decrease in the amount of principal, or in the loan period, or in the amount of interest, notification of the change by submission of a new 'Application Form for Income Tax Convention' must be made no later than the day before the first day on which payment is received after the change, together with other documents as reference.

The form of the 'Application for Income Tax Convention' in relation to interest (Form 2) is shown on the following page.

In addition, if the Limitation on Benefits clause applies, an 'Attachment Form for Limitation on Benefits (Entitlement to Benefits) Article' must also be submitted, which is valid for three years in the case of a qualified person.

The 'Attachment Form for Limitation on Benefits (Entitlement to Benefits) Article' of the Tax Convention between Japan and the US is similar to the 'Attachment Form for Limitation on Benefits (Entitlement to Benefits) Article' of the Tax Convention between Germany and Japan mentioned in Q7, but the form for the US (Form 17 – US) should be used.

When submitting the above forms, a residency certificate of the US parent and other documents as reference, such as the loan agreement, must also be provided.

The US residency certificate is called Form 6166 (Certification of US Tax Residency). In order to obtain a Form 6166, Form 8802 (Application for United States Residency Certification - Additional Certification Requests) must be submitted to the US tax authorities. As it can take some months for a Form 6166 to be issued, it is recommended to submit Form 8802 as soon as possible.

In this case, you will submit the following documents to the competent national tax office on behalf of your US parent:

(i) Application for Income Tax Convention (Form 2).
(ii) Attachment Form for Limitation on Benefits (Entitlement to Benefits) Article (US) (Form 17 - US).
(iii) Residency certificate (Form 6166).
(iv) Loan contract.
(v) Any other necessary documents.

The tax authorities may also request additional documents after they review the filed documents.

Application Form for Income Tax Convention (Relief from Japanese Income tax and Special Income Tax for Reconstruction on Interest)

Form 2

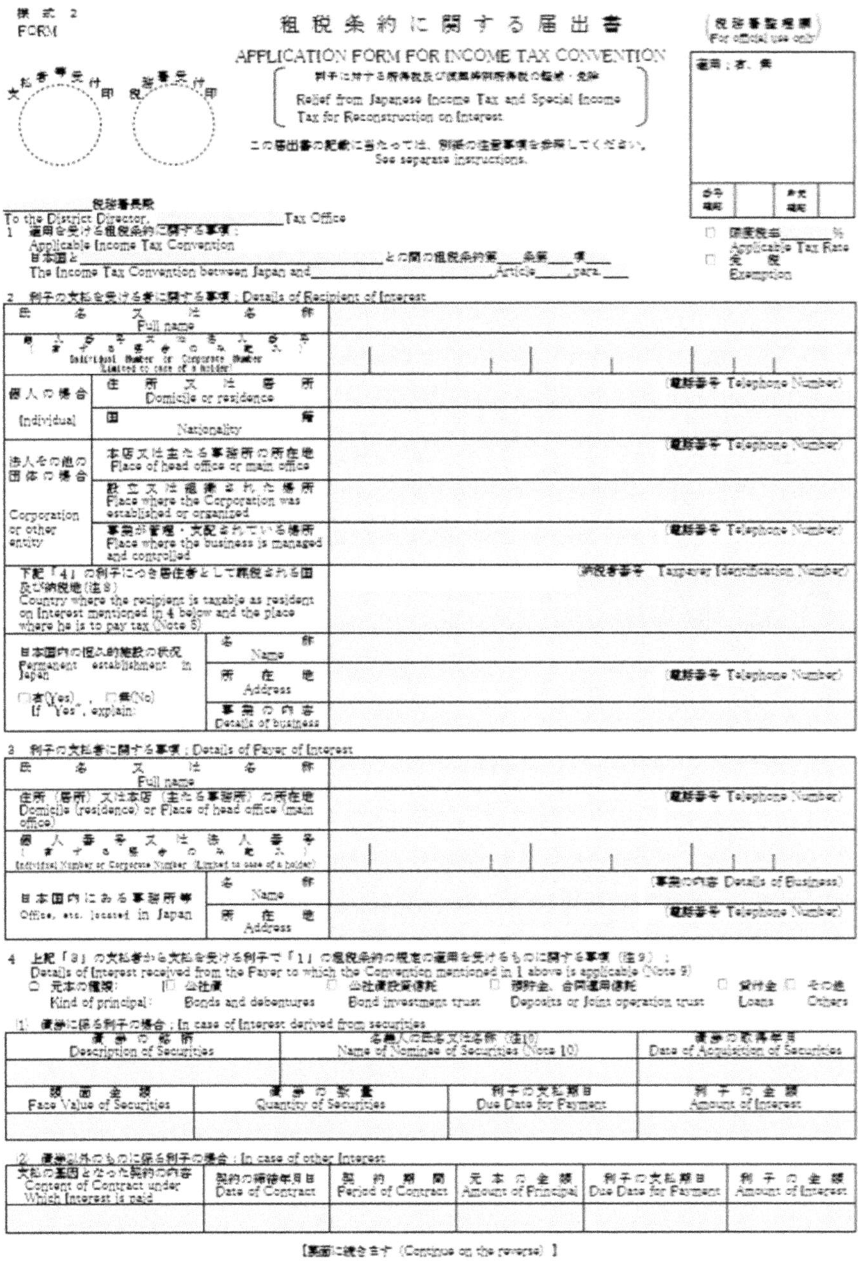

様式 2
FORM

租税条約に関する届出書
APPLICATION FORM FOR INCOME TAX CONVENTION
(利子に対する所得税及び復興特別所得税の軽減・免除
Relief from Japanese Income Tax and Special Income Tax for Reconstruction on Interest)

この届出書の記載に当たっては、別紙の注意事項を参照してください。
See separate instructions.

(税務署整理欄 For official use only)

______税務署長殿
To the District Director, ______ Tax Office

1 適用を受ける租税条約に関する事項；
Applicable Income Tax Convention
日本国と______との間の租税条約第___条第___項___
The Income Tax Convention between Japan and ______, Article ___, para. ___

□ 限度税率 ___%
Applicable Tax Rate
□ 免税
Exemption

2 利子の支払を受ける者に関する事項；Details of Recipient of Interest

氏名又は名称 Full name		
個人番号又は法人番号（有する場合のみ記入） Individual Number or Corporate Number (Limited to case of a holder)		
個人の場合 Individual	住所又は居所 Domicile or residence	(電話番号 Telephone Number)
	国籍 Nationality	
法人その他の団体の場合 Corporation or other entity	本店又は主たる事務所の所在地 Place of head office or main office	(電話番号 Telephone Number)
	設立又は組織された場所 Place where the Corporation was established or organized	
	事業が管理・支配されている場所 Place where the business is managed and controlled	(電話番号 Telephone Number)
下記「4」の利子につき居住者として課税される国及び納税地（注8） Country where the recipient is taxable as resident on Interest mentioned in 4 below and the place where he is to pay tax (Note 8)		(納税者番号 Taxpayer Identification Number)
日本国内の恒久的施設の状況 Permanent establishment in Japan □有(Yes), □無(No) If "Yes", explain:	名称 Name	
	所在地 Address	(電話番号 Telephone Number)
	事業の内容 Details of business	

3 利子の支払者に関する事項；Details of Payer of Interest

氏名又は名称 Full name		
住所（居所）又は本店（主たる事務所）の所在地 Domicile (residence) or Place of head office (main office)		(電話番号 Telephone Number)
個人番号又は法人番号（有する場合のみ記入） Individual Number or Corporate Number (Limited to case of a holder)		
日本国内にある事務所等 Office, etc. located in Japan	名称 Name	(事業の内容 Details of Business)
	所在地 Address	(電話番号 Telephone Number)

4 上記「3」の支払者から支払を受ける利子で「1」の租税条約の規定の適用を受けるものに関する事項（注9）；
Details of Interest received from the Payer to which the Convention mentioned in 1 above is applicable (Note 9)
○ 元本の種類： □ 公社債 Bonds and debentures □ 公社債投資信託 Bond investment trust □ 預貯金、合同運用信託 Deposits or Joint operation trust □ 貸付金 Loans □ その他 Others
Kind of principal:

(1) 債券に係る利子の場合；In case of Interest derived from securities

債券の銘柄 Description of Securities	名義人の氏名又は名称（注10） Name of Nominee of Securities (Note 10)	債券の取得年月日 Date of Acquisition of Securities

額面金額 Face Value of Securities	債券の数量 Quantity of Securities	利子の支払期日 Due Date for Payment	利子の金額 Amount of Interest

(2) 債券以外のものに係る利子の場合；In case of other Interest

支払の基因となった契約の内容 Content of Contract under Which Interest is paid	契約の締結年月日 Date of Contract	契約期間 Period of Contract	元本の金額 Amount of Principal	利子の支払期日 Due Date for Payment	利子の金額 Amount of Interest

【裏面に続きます (Continue on the reverse) 】

5 その他参考となるべき事項（注11）；
Others (Note 11)

6 日本の税法上、届出書の「2」の外国法人が納税義務者とされるが、租税条約の規定によりその株主等である者（相手国居住者に限ります。）の所得として取り扱われる部分に対して租税条約の適用を受けることとされている場合の租税条約の適用を受ける割合に関する事項等（注4）；
Details of proportion of income to which the convention mentioned in 1 above is applicable, if the foreign company mentioned in 2 above is taxable as a company under Japanese tax law, and the convention is applicable to income that is treated as income of the member (limited to a resident of the other contracting country) of the foreign company in accordance with the provisions of the convention (Note 4)

届出書の「2」の外国法人の株主等で租税条約の適用を受ける者の氏名又は名称 Name of member of the foreign company mentioned in 2 above, to whom the Convention is applicable	間接保有 Indirect Ownership	持分の割合 Ratio of Ownership	受益の割合＝租税条約の適用を受ける割合 Proportion of benefit = Proportion for Application of Convention
	□	%	%
	□	%	%
	□	%	%
	□	%	%
	□	%	%
合計 Total		%	%

届出書の「2」の外国法人が支払を受ける「4」の利子について、「1」の租税条約の相手国の法令に基づきその株主等である者の所得として取り扱われる場合には、その根拠法令及びその効力を生じる日を記載してください。
If interest mentioned in 4 above that a foreign company mentioned in 2 above receives are treated as income of those who are its members under the law in the other contracting country of the convention mentioned in 1 above, enter the law that provides the legal basis to the above treatment and the date on which it will become effective.

根拠法令 Applicable law ______________________ 効力を生じる日 年 月 日 Effective date ______________

7 日本の税法上、届出書の「2」の団体の構成員が納税義務者とされるが、租税条約の規定によりその団体の所得として取り扱われるものに対して租税条約の適用を受けることとされている場合の記載事項等（注5）；
Details if, while the partner of the entity mentioned in 2 above is taxable under Japanese tax law, and the convention is applicable to income that is treated as income of the entity in accordance with the provisions of the convention (Note 5)

他の全ての構成員から通知を受けこの届出書を提出する構成員の氏名又は名称 ______________________
Full name of the partner of the entity who has been notified by all other partners and is to submit this form

届出書の「2」の団体が支払を受ける「4」の利子について、「1」の租税条約の相手国の法令に基づきその団体の所得として取り扱われる場合には、その根拠法令及びその効力を生じる日を記載してください。
If interest mentioned in 4 above that an entity at mentioned in 2 above receives are treated as income of the entity under the law in the other contracting country of the convention mentioned in 1 above, enter the law that provides the legal basis to the above treatment and the date on which it will become effective.

根拠法令 Applicable law ______________________ 効力を生じる日 年 月 日 Effective date ______________

私は、この届出書の「4」に記載した利子が「1」に掲げる租税条約の規定の適用を受けるものであることを、「租税条約等の実施に伴う所得税法、法人税法及び地方税法の特例等に関する法律の施行に関する省令」及び「復興特別所得税に関する省令」の規定により届け出るとともに、この届出書（及び付表）の記載事項が正確かつ完全であることを宣言します。

年 月 日
Date ______________

利子の支払を受ける者又はその代理人の署名
Signature of the Recipient of Interest or his Agent

In accordance with the provisions of the Ministerial Ordinance for the Implementation of the Law concerning the Special Measures of the Income Tax Act, the Corporation Tax Act and the Local Tax Act for the Enforcement of Income Tax Conventions and the Ministerial Ordinance concerning Special Income Tax for Reconstruction, I hereby submit this application form under the belief that the provisions of the Income Tax Convention mentioned in 1 above is applicable to interest mentioned in 4 above and also hereby declare that the statement on this form (and attachment form) is correct and complete to the best of my knowledge and belief.

____

8 権限ある当局の証明（注12）
Certification of competent authority (Note 12)

私は、届出者が、日本国と ______________ との間の租税条約第 ____ 条第 ____ 項 ____ に規定する居住者であることを証明します。
I hereby certify that the applicant is a resident under the provisions of the Income Tax Convention between Japan and ______________, Article ________, para. ________.

年 月 日
Date ______________ Signature ______________________

○ 代理人に関する事項 ； この届出書を代理人によって提出する場合には、次の欄に記載してください。
Details of the Agent ; If this form is prepared and submitted by the Agent, fill out the following columns.

代理人の資格 Capacity of Agent in Japan	氏名（名称） Full name		納税管理人の届出をした税務署名 Name of the Tax Office where the Tax Agent is registered
□ 納税管理人 ※ Tax Agent □ その他の代理人 Other Agent	住所（居所・所在地） Domicile (Residence or location)	（電話番号 Telephone Number）	税務署 Tax Office

※ 「納税管理人」とは、日本国の国税に関する申告、申請、請求、届出、納付等の事項を処理させるため、国税通則法の規定により選任し、かつ、日本国における納税地の所轄税務署長に届出をした代理人をいいます。

※ "Tax Agent" means a person who is appointed by the taxpayer and is registered at the District Director of Tax Office for the place where the taxpayer is to pay his tax, in order to have such agent take necessary procedures concerning the Japanese national taxes, such as filing a return, applications, claims, payment of taxes, etc., under the provisions of Act on General Rules for National Taxes.

Q11 Withholding Tax on Inclusion of Interest into Principal

We are a Japanese subsidiary of a foreign corporation. We have a loan from our parent for use in our domestic business. Since we have not paid interest for some time, and since we do not expect to be able to pay interest in the near future, our parent has decided to convert all unpaid interest into the principal amount. What are the tax implications in Japan?

A:

The conversion of accrued interest into principal is subject to withholding tax as if the interest was in fact paid to the lender. The date of 'payment' is the date on which the interest is converted to principal.

Therefore, withholding tax at the rate of 20.42 % will be imposed at the time your parent converts the accrued interest into principal.

However, if there is a Tax Convention between Japan and the country where your parent company is located, that may provide some relief from the withholding tax burden.

Discussion

As stated in Q10, interest on a loan provided to a person engaged in business in Japan, and where that loan is used for the purpose of that business, is treated as domestic source income (ITA Article 161(1) (x)). Consequently, the payment of the interest is subject to withholding tax at the rate of 20.42% (ITA Article 212(1), Article 213(1)).

'Payment' for the purposes of the domestic tax law includes not only actual payment but also any actions that extinguish the obligation for payment, such as conversion of the interest to principal (Income Tax Basic Circular Article 181-223-1).

Accordingly, when your parent converts accrued interest into principal, it is treated as if you had made an interest payment to your parent, and withholding tax at the rate of 20.42 % is imposed.

A Tax Convention between Japan and the country where your parent is located may provide relief from this withholding tax, so it is important to check the applicability of any relevant Tax Convention.

Although not raised in your question, if interest is calculated using the compounding method, accrued interest will be deemed to have been converted into principal, the above payment rule will apply, and thus that converted interest will be subject to withholding tax.

Q12 Withholding Tax on Royalties for Trademarks and Relief under Tax Conventions

We are a wholly owned subsidiary of a Dutch corporation, which is listed and traded on the Amsterdam Stock Exchange. We are conducting business in Japan using a trademark registered by our Dutch parent, and paying royalties for that use.

Will withholding tax be imposed when we pay the royalties? Can we obtain relief under a Tax Convention?

A:

Under domestic tax law, withholding tax at the rate of 20.42% must be collected upon payment of royalties, including those paid for the use of a trademark. However, relief from such withholding tax under the Tax Convention between Japan and the Netherlands may be available if the requirements of that Tax Convention are met. In addition, in order to obtain such benefits, certain documents, such as an 'Application Form for Income Tax Convention', must be submitted to the competent national tax office by the day before the date of the first royalty payment.

Discussion

1. Tax treatment under domestic tax law

The following royalties, or consideration received from persons who conduct business in Japan and which pertains to that business, are considered domestic source income:

(1) Royalty for an industrial property right or any other right concerning technology, a production method involving special technology or any other equivalent right or method, or consideration for the transfer thereof;
(2) Royalty for a copyright (including right of publication, neighbouring right, and any other equivalent right), or consideration for the transfer thereof; and
(3) Royalty for machinery, equipment, or other tools.

(ITA Article 161(1)(xi))

Trademarks are included in industrial property rights as described in (1) above, and therefore royalties for a trademark used for a business in Japan are treated as domestic source income.

Accordingly, the royalties paid by you to your Dutch parent are domestic source income as long as the trademark is used for your business in Japan. In addition, a Japanese resident who pays domestic source income, such as royalties, to a foreign corporation is required to collect withholding tax at the time of payment and remit that withholding tax to the competent national tax office by the 10th day of the following month in which the royalty payment is made. The withholding tax rate is 20.42% (ITA Article 212(1), Article 213(1)(i)).

2. Withholding tax exemption under the Tax Convention between Japan and the Netherlands

Notwithstanding the domestic tax law, withholding tax on royalties may be exempted under the Tax Convention between Japan and the Netherlands Article 12(1).

The term 'royalties' as used in Article 12(1) means: 'payments of any kind received as a consideration for the use of, or the right to use, any copyright of literary, artistic or scientific work including cinematograph films and films or tapes for radio or television broadcasting, any patent, trade mark, design or model, plan, or secret formula or process, or for information concerning industrial, commercial or scientific experience' (Tax Convention between Japan and the Netherland and Japan Article 12(2)).

As can be seen, royalties for the use of a trademark are specifically included in the above definition. As a result, royalties paid by you may be exempted from withholding tax.

However, in order to qualify for the withholding tax exemption, the following Limitation on Benefits clause of the Tax Convention between Japan and the Netherlands must be met.

3. Limitation on Benefits under the Tax Convention between Japan and the Netherlands Article 21

In order to obtain the withholding tax exemption in relation to LoB income, which includes tax-exempt royalties, the recipient of the royalties must be a qualified person under the Tax Convention between Japan and the Netherlands, defined as either:

(i) An individual;
(ii) A qualified governmental body;
(iii) A corporation, if the principal class of its shares is listed or registered on a recognised stock exchange and is regularly traded on one or more recognised stock exchanges, provided that, if the shares are listed or registered on a recognised stock exchange (specified separately), the primary place of management and control of the corporation is in the Contracting State of which it is a resident;
(iv) Certain pension funds or charitable organisations;
(v) A bank, an insurance corporation or a securities corporation that is established and regulated as such under the Acts of the country of which it is a resident; or
(vi) A person other than an individual, if residents of either country that are qualified persons by reason of (i), (ii), (iii) or (iv) of the above own, directly, or indirectly, shares or other beneficial interests representing at least 50 per cent of the voting power of the person.

(Tax Convention between Japan and the Netherlands, Article 21(2))

Since the shares of your Dutch parent are listed on the Amsterdam Stock Exchange, which is one of the recognised exchanges described above, and assuming those shares are regularly traded, the requirements of (iii) will be met.

Note that 'the shares in the principal class of shares of a corporation are considered to be regularly traded on one or more recognised stock exchanges in a taxable year if the aggregate number of the shares in that class traded on such stock exchange or exchanges during the 12 months ending on the day before the beginning of that taxable year is at least 6% of the average number of the shares outstanding in that class during that 12-month period' (Protocol on the Tax Convention between Japan and the Netherlands Article 10).

Consequently, if more than 6% of the total outstanding shares of your parent are traded on the Amsterdam Stock Exchange, it will be a qualified person for the purposes of the Tax Convention between Japan and the Netherlands.

4. Procedures for obtaining benefits under the Tax Convention between Japan and the Netherlands (Enforcement Order on Act on Special Provisions of the Income Tax Act, the Corporation Tax Act and the Local Tax Act Incidental to Enforcement of Tax Convention Article 2)

In order to be exempt from withholding tax on royalties under a Tax Convention, the beneficiary is required to submit an 'Application Form for Income Tax Convention' (*see* below) to the competent national tax office through their withholding tax agent no later than the day before the day on which the beneficiary first receives a payment.

The following must be stated on the 'Application Form for Income Tax Convention':

- Description of the royalties.
- Date of the contract.
- Period of the contract.
- Method of computation for the royalties.
- Due date for payments.
- Amount of the royalties.
- Other items to be referenced.

The relevant royalty contract should also be attached.

If there are any changes to the above information other than that described below, a new 'Application Form for Income Tax Convention' with the revised royalty contract must be submitted at least one day before the date on which the first payment after the change is made.

Notwithstanding the above, changes to the period of the contract or the royalty amount do not require a new 'Application Form for Income Tax Convention' to be submitted.

If the Limitation on Benefits clause applies, an 'Attachment Form for Limitation on Benefits (Entitlement to Benefits) Article' must also be submitted. For qualified persons, this is valid for a period of three years.

The 'Attachment Form for Limitation on Benefits (Entitlement to Benefits) Article' of the Tax Convention between Japan and the Netherlands is the same Form 17 - Kingdom of the Netherlands as in Q9.

When submitting these forms and the royalty contract, it is also necessary to submit a residency certificate of the Dutch parent and other documents as reference.

In this case, you will submit the following documents to the competent national tax office for your Dutch parent:

(i) Application Form for Income Tax Convention (Form 3).
(ii) Attachment Form for Limitation on Benefits (Entitlement to Benefits) Article (Form 17 - Kingdom of the Netherlands).
(iii) Residency certificate.
(iv) Royalty contract.
(v) Other documents as reference.

The tax authorities may also request additional documents.

Application Form for Income Tax Convention (Relief from Japanese Income Tax and Special Income Tax for Reconstruction on Royalties)

Form 3

様式 3
FORM

支払者受付印　　税務署受付印

租税条約に関する届出書
APPLICATION FORM FOR INCOME TAX CONVENTION

（使用料に対する所得税及び復興特別所得税の軽減・免除
Relief from Japanese Income Tax and Special Income Tax for Reconstruction on Royalties）

この届出書の記載に当たっては、別紙の注意事項を参照してください。
See separate instructions.

（税務署整理欄 For official use only）
適用；有、無
番号確認　　身元確認

______税務署長殿
To the District Director, ______ Tax Office

1 適用を受ける租税条約に関する事項；
Applicable Income Tax Convention
日本国と______との間の租税条約第___条第___項___
The Income Tax Convention between Japan and ______, Article ___, para. ___

□ 限度税率 ___%
Applicable Tax Rate
□ 免税（注11）
Exemption (Note 11)

2 使用料の支払を受ける者に関する事項；
Details of Recipient of Royalties

氏名又は名称 Full name		
個人番号又は法人番号（保有する場合のみ記入） Individual Number or Corporate Number (Limited to case of a holder)		
個人の場合 Individual	住所又は居所 Domicile or residence	（電話番号 Telephone Number）
	国籍 Nationality	
法人その他の団体の場合 Corporation or other entity	本店又は主たる事務所の所在地 Place of head office or main office	（電話番号 Telephone Number）
	設立又は組織された場所 Place where the Corporation was established or organized	
	事業が管理・支配されている場所 Place where the business is managed and controlled	（電話番号 Telephone Number）
下記「4」の使用料につき居住者として課税される国及び納税地（注8） Country where the recipient is taxable as resident on Royalties mentioned in 4 below and the place where he is to pay tax (Note 8)		（納税者番号 Taxpayer Identification Number）
日本国内の恒久的施設の状況 Permanent establishment in Japan □有(Yes)，□無(No) If "Yes", explain:	名称 Name	
	所在地 Address	（電話番号 Telephone Number）
	事業の内容 Details of Business	

3 使用料の支払者に関する事項；
Details of Payer of Royalties

氏名又は名称 Full name		
住所（居所）又は本店（主たる事務所）の所在地 Domicile (residence) or Place of head office (main office)		（電話番号 Telephone Number）
個人番号又は法人番号（保有する場合のみ記入） Individual Number or Corporate Number (Limited to case of a holder)		
日本国内にある事務所等 Office, etc. located in Japan	名称 Name	（事業の内容 Details of Business）
	所在地 Address	（電話番号 Telephone Number）

4 上記「3」の支払者から支払を受ける使用料で「1」の租税条約の規定の適用を受けるものに関する事項（注9）；
Details of Royalties received from the Payer to which the Convention mentioned in 1 above is applicable (Note 9)

使用料の内容 Description of Royalties	契約の締結年月日 Date of Contract	契約期間 Period of Contract	使用料の計算方法 Method of Computation for Royalties	使用料の支払期日 Due Date for Payment	使用料の金額 Amount of Royalties

5 その他参考となるべき事項（注10）；
Others (Note 10)

【裏面に続きます (Continue on the reverse)】

6　日本の税法上、届出書の「2」の外国法人が納税義務者とされるが、租税条約の規定によりその株主等である者（相手国居住者に限ります。）の所得として取り扱われる部分に対して租税条約の適用を受けることとされている場合の租税条約の適用を受ける割合に関する事項等（注4）；
Details of proportion of income to which the convention mentioned in 1 above is applicable, if the foreign company mentioned in 2 above is taxable as a company under Japanese tax law, and the convention is applicable to income that is treated as income of the member (limited to a resident of the other contracting country) of the foreign company in accordance with the provisions of the convention (Note 4)

届出書の「2」の外国法人の株主等で租税条約の適用を受ける者の氏名又は名称 Name of member of the foreign company mentioned in 2 above, to whom the Convention is applicable	間接保有 Indirect Ownership	持分の割合 Ratio of Ownership	受益の割合＝租税条約の適用を受ける割合 Proportion of benefit = Proportion for Application of Convention
	□	%	%
	□	%	%
	□	%	%
	□	%	%
	□	%	%
合計 Total		%	%

届出書の「2」の欄に記載した外国法人が支払を受ける「4」の使用料について、「1」の租税条約の相手国の法令に基づきその株主等である者の所得として取り扱われる場合には、その根拠法令及びその効力を生じる日を記載してください。
If royalties mentioned in 4 above that a foreign company mentioned in 2 above receives are treated as income of those who are its members under the law in the other contracting country of the convention mentioned in 1 above, enter the law that provides the legal basis to the above treatment and the date on which it will become effective.

根拠法令 Applicable law ______________________　効力を生じる日 Effective date ______ 年 月 日

7　日本の税法上、届出書の「2」の団体の構成員が納税義務者とされるが、租税条約の規定によりその団体の所得として取り扱われるものに対して租税条約の適用を受けることとされている場合の記載事項等（注5）；
Details if, while the partner of the entity mentioned in 2 above is taxable under Japanese tax law, and the convention is applicable to income that is treated as income of the entity in accordance with the provisions of the convention (Note 5)

他の全ての構成員から通知を受けてこの届出書を提出する構成員の氏名又は名称 ______________________
Full name of the partner of the entity who has been notified by all other partners and is to submit this form

届出書の「2」に記載した団体が支払を受ける「4」の使用料について、「1」の租税条約の相手国の法令に基づきその団体の所得として取り扱われる場合には、その根拠法令及びその効力を生じる日を記載してください。
If royalties mentioned in 4 above that an entity at mentioned in 2 above receives are treated as income of the entity under the law in the other contracting country of the convention mentioned in 1 above, enter the law that provides the legal basis to the above treatment and the date on which it will become effective.

根拠法令 Applicable law ______________________　効力を生じる日 Effective date ______ 年 月 日

私は、この届出書の「4」に記載した使用料が「1」に掲げる租税条約の規定の適用を受けるものであることを、「租税条約等の実施に伴う所得税法、法人税法及び地方税法の特例等に関する法律の施行に関する省令」及び「復興特別所得税に関する省令」の規定により届け出るとともに、この届出書（及び付表）の記載事項が正確かつ完全であることを宣言します。

In accordance with the provisions of the Ministerial Ordinance for the Implementation of the Law concerning the Special Measures of the Income Tax Act, the Corporation Tax Act and the Local Tax Act for the Enforcement of Income Tax Conventions and the Ministerial Ordinance concerning Special Income Tax for Reconstruction, I hereby submit this application form under the belief that the provisions of the Income Tax Convention mentioned in 1 above is applicable to Royalties mentioned in 4 above and also hereby declare that the statement on this form (and attachment form) is correct and complete to the best of my knowledge and belief.

年 月 日
Date ______________

使用料の支払を受ける者又はその代理人の署名
Signature of the Recipient of Royalties or his Agent ______________________

○　代理人に関する事項　；　この届出書を代理人によって提出する場合には、次の欄に記載してください。
Details of the Agent　；　If this form is prepared and submitted by the Agent, fill out the following columns.

代理人の資格 Capacity of Agent in Japan	氏名（名称） Full name		納税管理人の届出をした税務署名 Name of the Tax Office where the Tax Agent is registered
□ 納税管理人 ※ Tax Agent □ その他の代理人 Other Agent	住所（居所・所在地） Domicile (Residence or location)	（電話番号 Telephone Number）	税務署 Tax Office

※　「納税管理人」とは、日本国の国税に関する申告、申請、請求、届出、納付等の事項を処理させるため、国税通則法の規定により選任し、かつ、日本国における納税地の所轄税務署長に届出をした代理人をいいます。

※ "Tax Agent" means a person who is appointed by the taxpayer and is registered at the District Director of Tax Office for the place where the taxpayer is to pay his tax, in order to have such agent take necessary procedures concerning the Japanese national taxes, such as filing a return, applications, claims, payment of taxes, etc., under the provisions of Act on General Rules for National Taxes.

○　適用を受ける租税条約が特典条項を有する租税条約である場合；
If the applicable convention has article of limitation on benefits

特典条項に関する付表の添付　□有Yes
"Attachment Form for Limitation on Benefits Article" attached
□添付省略Attachment not required
（特典条項に関する付表を添付して提出した租税条約に関する届出書の提出日　　年　月　日）
Date of previous submission of the application for income tax convention with the "Attachment Form for Limitation on Benefits Article" ______________

Q13 Application of Tax Conventions to Pass-Through Entities

We have been granted a licence to use a patent owned by a Limited Liability Corporation in the US ('US LLC') for the manufacture of products at our factory in Japan, and we make payments to US LLC under that licence.

The US LLC is owned by Mr B, an individual resident in the US. Mr B has selected pass-through taxation for the US LLC for US tax purposes.

Can we obtain an exemption from withholding tax on the royalty payments under a Tax Convention?

A:

Since Mr B has elected pass-through taxation for the US LLC, the US LLC cannot obtain any exemption from withholding tax under the Tax Convention between Japan and the US. However, the Tax Convention between Japan and the US also applies to income derived from Japan through US entities where that income is treated as the income of beneficiaries, members or participants of that entity under US tax law.

The royalties in question are derived from Japan through US LLC, so they will be treated as the income of US LLC's sole member, i.e., Mr B. Therefore, the Tax Convention between Japan and the US may be available to exempt the withholding tax otherwise due on those royalties.

Discussion

1. Tax treatment under domestic tax law

The following royalties or consideration received from persons who conduct business in Japan and which pertains to that business are considered domestic source income (ITA Article 161(1)(xi)):

(1) Royalty for an industrial property right or any other right concerning technology, a production method involving special technology or any other equivalent right or method, or consideration for the transfer thereof;
(2) Royalty for a copyright (including right of publication, neighbouring right, and any other equivalent right), or consideration for the transfer thereof; and
(3) Royalty for machinery, equipment, or other tools.

(ITA Article 161(1)(xi))

Patents are included in industrial property rights as described in (1), and therefore royalties for patents used for a business in Japan are treated as domestic source income.

Accordingly, the royalties paid by you to US LLC for the use of the US LLC patent are treated as domestic source income, as long as the patent is used for your business in Japan. In addition, a Japanese resident who pays domestic source income, such as royalties, to a foreign corporation is required to collect withholding tax at the time of payment and remit the withholding tax to the competent national tax office by the 10th day of the month following the date of payment. The withholding tax rate is 20.42% (ITA Article 212, Article 213(1)(i)).

2. Withholding tax exemption under the Tax Convention between Japan and the US

Notwithstanding the domestic tax law, withholding tax on royalties may be exempted under the Tax Convention between Japan and the US Article 12(1).

The term 'royalties' as used in Article 12 means 'payments of any kind received as a consideration for the use of, or the right to use, any copyright of literary, artistic or scientific work including cinematograph films and films or tapes for radio or television broadcasting, any patent, trade mark, design or model, plan, or secret formula or process, or for information concerning industrial, commercial or scientific experience' (Tax Convention between Japan and the US Article 12(2)).

Royalties paid for the use of patents are included in the above definition. As a result, royalty payments from you to US LLC may be exempted from withholding tax if the Tax Convention between Japan and the US is applicable.

However, in order to qualify for the withholding tax exemption, the following Limitation of Benefits clause under the Tax Convention between Japan and the US must be met.

3. Residents under the Tax Convention between Japan and the USA

Under Article 4(1) of the Tax Convention between Japan and the US, the term 'resident of a Contracting State' means 'any person who, under the laws of that Contracting State, is liable to tax therein by reason of his domicile, residence, citizenship, place of head or main office, place of incorporation, or any other criterion of a similar nature' (Tax Convention between Japan and the US Article 4(1)).

Any entities subject to pass-through taxation are not taxed in the US, and therefore they are not residents under the above definition. As a result, the Tax Convention between Japan and the US would not apply to income received by such pass-through entities.

However, Tax Convention between Japan and the US provides an exception to permit certain income received by pass-through entities to obtain exemptions from withholding tax.

For example, 'income shall be eligible for the benefits of the Convention that would be granted if it were directly derived by a beneficiary, member or participant of that entity who is a resident of the USA, to the extent that such beneficiaries, members or participants are residents of the USA and satisfy any other conditions specified in the Convention, without regard to whether the income is treated as the income of such beneficiaries, members or participants under the tax laws of Japan;

(1) derived from Japan through an entity that is organized in the USA; and
(2) treated as the income of the beneficiaries, members, or participants of that entity under the tax laws of the USA'.

(Tax Convention between Japan and the US Article 4 (6)(a))

As a result, the Tax Convention between Japan and the US may apply to income received from Japan by a US corporation that is subject to pass-through taxation, where the income is treated as the income of a US resident.

In your case, the sole member of US LLC is Mr A, who is a US resident and is subject to tax in the US. This means that the entire amount of the royalties received by US LLC from you is taxable income to Mr A, and thus is income subject to the Tax Convention between Japan and the US.

However, in order to qualify for the withholding tax exemption, Mr B must also satisfy the requirements of the Limitation on Benefits clause of that Tax Convention.

4. Limitation on Benefits clause in the Tax Convention between Japan and the US Article 22

Under Article 22, in order to enjoy the benefits of reduced or exempted withholding tax, a taxpayer must, in principle, be a qualified person. A qualified person is a resident who is either:

- (i) an individual;
- (ii) an eligible governmental body;
- (iii) a corporation, if:
  - (a) the principal class of its shares, and any disproportionate class of its shares, is listed or registered on a recognized stock exchange specified and is regularly traded on one or more recognized stock exchanges; or
  - (b) at least 50% of each class of shares in the corporation is owned directly or indirectly by 5 or fewer residents entitled to benefits under clause (i), provided that, in the case of indirect ownership, each intermediate owner is a person entitled to the benefits of this Convention under this paragraph
- (iv) certain public corporations
- (v) certain pension funds
- (vi) a person other than an individual, if:
  - (a) residents that are described in the above (i), (ii), (iv) or (v), or clause (a) of the above (iii), own, directly, or indirectly, at least 50% of each class of shares or other beneficial interests in the person, and
  - (b) less than 50% of the person's gross income for the taxable year is paid or accrued by the person in that taxable year, directly or indirectly, to persons who are not residents of either Contracting State in the form of payments that are deductible in computing its taxable income in the Contracting State of which it is a resident (but not including arm's length payments in the ordinary course of business for services or tangible property and payments in respect of financial obligations to a commercial bank, provided that where such a bank is not a resident of a Contracting State such payment is attributable to a permanent establishment of that bank situated in one of the Contracting States).

(Tax Convention between Japan and the US Article 22)

Mr B is an individual and thus falls under (i) above; he is therefore a qualified person.

5. Procedures for obtaining benefits under the Tax Convention between Japan and the US (Enforcement Order on Act on Special Provisions of the Income Tax Act, the Corporation Tax Act and the Local Tax Act Incidental to Enforcement of Tax Convention Article 2)

In order to be exempted from withholding tax on royalties under a Tax Convention, the beneficiary is required to submit an 'Application Form for Income Tax Convention' to the competent national tax office through their withholding tax agent no later than the day before the day on which the beneficiary first receives payment.

The following must be stated on the 'Application Form for Income Tax Convention':

- Description of royalties.
- Date of contract.
- Period of contract.
- Method of computation for royalties.
- Due date for payment.
- Amount of royalties.
- Other items to be referenced.

The relevant royalty contract must also be attached.

If there are any changes to the above, a new 'Application Form for Income Tax Convention' with the revised royalty contract must be submitted at least one day before the date on which the first payment after the change is made. This requirement does not apply if the changes are only to the period of the contract or the royalty amount.

If a Limitation on Benefits clause applies, an 'Attachment Form for Limitation on Benefits (Entitlement to Benefits) Article' must also be submitted. This is valid for a period of three years once for a qualified person.

The 'Attachment Form for Limitation on Benefits (Entitlement to Benefits) Article' of the Tax Convention between Japan and the US is the similar to the 'Attachment Form for Limitation on Benefits (Entitlement to Benefits) Article' under the Tax Convention between Germany and Japan mentioned in Q7, but the form for the US (Form 17 - US) should be used.

A residency certificate of the US beneficiaries and other documents as reference must be submitted with the forms. In the US, a certificate of residency is called Form 6166 (Certification of US Tax Residency). An entity that is subject to pass-through taxation is not a resident for tax purposes; nevertheless, a Form 6166 will still be issued.

In order to obtain Form 6166, it is necessary to submit Form 8802 (Application for United States Residency Certification - Additional Certification Requests) with the US tax authorities. It is recommended to submit Form 8802 as soon as possible, as it generally takes some months for a Form 6166 to be issued.

In this case, you will submit the following documents to the competent national tax office on behalf of US LLC:

(i) Application Form for Income Tax Convention (Form 3).
(ii) Application for Limitation on Benefits (Entitlement to Benefits) (US) (Form 17 - US).
(iii) Residency certificate of US LLC (Form 6166).
(iv) Residency certificate of Mr A (Form 6166).
(v) Royalty agreement.
(vi) Other documents as reference.

The tax authorities may also request additional documents after they review the filed documents.

Q14 Withholding Tax on Fees for Use of Tangible Fixed Assets

We are a Japanese company, and have rented equipment in Italy to manufacture some of our products. Do we need to withhold tax on the fees paid to use this equipment?

A:

Under domestic tax law, a withholding tax of 20.42% is imposed on fees paid for the use of equipment located in Japan. However, under the Tax Convention between Italy and Japan, withholding tax is imposed if the payor of the fees is resident in Japan.

Under this Tax Convention, the withholding tax rate is reduced to 10%. In order to benefit from this reduced tax rate, certain documents, such as an 'Application Form for Income Tax Convention', must be submitted by the day before the first payment of fees.

Discussion

1. Tax Treatment under domestic tax law

The following royalties or consideration received from persons conducting business in Japan are considered domestic source income if those fees are connected to that business:

(1) Royalty for an industrial property right or any other right concerning technology, a production method involving special technology or any other equivalent right or method, or consideration for the transfer thereof;
(2) Royalty for a copyright (including right of publication, neighbouring right, and any other equivalent right), or consideration for the transfer thereof; and
(3) Royalty for machinery, equipment, or other tools.

(ITA Article 161(1)(xi))

Fees for the use of equipment are included in (3) above. For the purpose of this analysis, royalties for business conducted in Japan are royalties corresponding to the portion of the assets that are used for business conducted in Japan (Income Tax Basic Circular Article 161-33). However, since the equipment is used outside Japan (i.e., in Italy), that use is not considered to be related to the business conducted in Japan.

Given this, the fees paid by you for the use of the equipment located in Italy are not domestic source income under domestic tax law, and no withholding tax is required.

2. Treatment under the Tax Convention between Italy and Japan

Under the Tax Convention between Italy and Japan, the term 'royalties' means payments of any kind received as 'consideration for the use of, or the right to use, any copyright of literary, artistic or scientific work including cinematograph films, any patent, trade mark, design or model, plan, secret formula or process, or for the use of, or the right to use, industrial, commercial, or scientific equipment, or for information concerning industrial, commercial or scientific experience' (Tax Convention between Japan and Italy Article 12(2)).

Since fees for the use of equipment are included in the consideration for the use of, or the right to use industrial, commercial, or scientific equipment, they are treated as royalties for Tax Convention purposes.

In addition, under Article 12(4) of the Tax Convention between Japan and Italy, royalties arise in Japan when the payor is a resident of Japan (unless such royalties are received in connection with a PE in Japan) regardless of the location of the equipment.

3. Domestic source income when the definition under a Tax Convention differs from Japanese tax law

As discussed in 1 and 2 above, the definition of domestic source income for royalties/fees for the use of equipment is different under Tax Conventions and Japanese tax law.

In such cases, the definition in the Tax Convention shall, notwithstanding the domestic law, be applied (ITA Article 162(1)). Therefore, as long as the payor is a resident of Japan, such payment is treated as domestic source income regardless of whether it is used for a business in Japan or not. Accordingly, the fees paid for the use of the equipment in Italy by you should be treated as domestic source income.

4. Withholding tax on fees for the use of equipment

A person who pays domestic source income, such as fees for the use of equipment, to a foreign corporation is required to collect withholding tax at the time of payment, and remit it to the competent national tax office by the 10th day of the following the month in which the royalty payment is made (ITA Article 212(1)).

However, the withholding tax rate can be reduced or exempted under a Tax Convention, such as the Tax Convention between Italy and Japan, which reduces the rate to 10% (Article 12(2)). In order to apply for this reduced tax rate, an 'Application Form for Income Tax Convention' must be submitted to the competent national tax office through the withholding tax agent of the beneficiary no later than the day before the day on which the first payment is received.

The following must be stated on the 'Application Form for Income Tax Convention':

- Description of fees paid.
- Date of contract.
- Period of contract.
- Method of computation for fees.
- Due date for payment.
- Amount of fees.
- Other items to be referred.

The relevant contract should also be attached.

Q15 Withholding Tax Refund Claims under Tax Conventions

We paid a dividend to our parent corporation in the US. However, we failed to submit the 'Application Form for Income Tax Convention' and paid withholding tax on the dividend at the rate of 20.42%. We have confirmed that our parent is eligible for the exemption of withholding tax on dividends under the Tax Convention between Japan and the US. Can we claim a refund of the withholding tax already paid?

A:

Assuming your parent qualifies for the exemption on withholding tax on Dividends under the Tax Convention between Japan and the US, they can claim a tax refund by submitting the 'Application Form for Refund of Overpaid Withholding Tax in Accordance with the Income Tax Convention' and other documents as reference.

Discussion

1. Withholding tax on Dividends paid to foreign corporations and relief under Tax Conventions

As mentioned in Q7, Q8 and Q9, when paying Dividends to a foreign corporation in Japan, the payor is required to collect withholding tax at the rate of 20.42% (ITA Article 161(1)(ix), Article 212(1) and Article 213(1)(i)).

However, under Article 10 and Article 22 of the Tax Convention between Japan and the US, this withholding tax may be reduced or exempted if certain conditions are met.

In order to obtain this benefit, the beneficiary is required to submit an 'Application Form for Income Tax Convention' and other documents as reference to the competent national tax office of the beneficiary's withholding tax agent no later than the day before the day on which the Dividends are paid (Enforcement Order on Act on Special Provisions of the Income Tax Act, the Corporation Tax Act and the Local Tax Act Incidental to Enforcement of Tax Convention Article 2). Therefore, if these documents are not submitted by the due date, withholding tax should be collected at the rate of 20.42% under the domestic tax law (ITA Article 212(1), Article 213(1)(i)).

2. Withholding tax refund claim under a Tax Convention

Provided that your parent qualifies for the Tax Convention between Japan and the US, even if withholding tax at the domestic rate has been paid through a failure to submit the necessary documents, a claim may be made for a refund of the difference between the amount of withholding tax paid and the amount reduced or exempted under the Tax Convention. In order to claim the refund, the beneficiary must submit an 'Application Form for Refund of the Overpaid Withholding Tax in Accordance with the Income Tax Convention', as shown on the next page, and other documents as reference to the competent national tax office of the beneficiary's withholding tax agent

(Enforcement Order on Act on Special Provisions of the Income Tax Act, the Corporation Tax Act and the Local Tax Act Incidental to Enforcement of Tax Convention Article 2(8), (9)).

The withholding tax agent should certify the following facts in the 'Application for Refund of Overpaid Withholding Tax':

(i) Category of income.
(ii) Due date for payment.
(iii) Amount paid.
(iv) Withholding tax on (iii).
(v) Date of payment of (iv).
(vi) Tax amount to be withheld under the relevant Tax Convention.
(vii) Amount to be refunded.

In addition, when submitting the 'Application for Refund of Overpaid Withholding Tax in Accordance with the Income Tax Convention', an 'Application Form for Income Tax Convention' and 'Attachment Form for Limitation on Benefits (Entitlement to Benefits) Article' and other documents as reference should also be attached (e.g., residency certificate, as described in Q7) (Enforcement Order on Act on Special Provisions of the Income Tax Act, the Corporation Tax Act and the Local Tax Act Incidental to Enforcement of Tax Convention Article 2 (ix)).

In this case, your US parent should prepare the 'Application for Refund of Overpaid Withholding Tax', 'Application Form for Income Tax Convention' including the 'Attachment Form for Limitation on Benefits (Entitlement to Benefits) Article' and other documents as reference. As your parent's withholding tax agent, you will certify and submit these documents to the competent national tax office.

There is no specific due date for submitting an 'Application for Refund of Overpaid Withholding Tax in Accordance with the Income Tax Convention', but if it is not submitted within five years of the date of the withholding tax payment, the right to claim the refund will be lost.

Application Form for Refund of Overpaid Withholding Tax in Accordance with the Income Tax Convention

Form 11

様式 11
FORM

租税条約に関する源泉徴収税額の還付請求書

（発行時に源泉徴収の対象となる割引債及び芸能人等の役務提供事業の対価に係るものを除く。）

APPLICATION FORM FOR REFUND OF THE OVERPAID WITHHOLDING TAX OTHER THAN REDEMPTION OF SECURITIES WHICH ARE SUBJECT TO WITHHOLDING TAX AT THE TIME OF ISSUE AND REMUNERATION DERIVED FROM RENDERING PERSONAL SERVICES EXERCISED BY AN ENTERTAINER OR A SPORTSMAN IN ACCORDANCE WITH THE INCOME TAX CONVENTION

この還付請求書の記載に当たっては、裏面の注意事項を参照してください。
See instructions on the reverse side.

（税務署整理欄）
For official use only

通信日付印	. .
確認印	
還付金：有、無	
身元確認	身元確認

税務署長殿
To the District Director, ______ Tax Office

1 還付の請求をする者（所得の支払を受ける者）に関する事項；
Details of the Person claiming the Refund (Recipient of Income)

フリガナ Furigana 氏名又は名称（注5） Full name (Note 5)	（納税者番号 Taxpayer Identification Number）
住所（居所）又は本店（主たる事務所）の所在地 Domicile (residence) or Place of head office (main office)	（電話番号 Telephone Number）
個人番号又は法人番号（有する場合のみ記入） Individual Number or Corporate Number (Limited to case of a holder)	

2 還付請求金額に関する事項；
Details of Refund

(1) 還付を請求する還付金の種類；（該当する下記の条項の□欄に✓印を付してください（注6）。）
Kind of Refund claimed; (Check applicable box below (Note 6).)

租税条約等の実施に伴う所得税法、法人税法及び地方税法の特例等に関する法律の施行に関する省令第15条第1項
Ministerial Ordinance of the Implementation of the Law concerning the Special Measures of the Income Tax Act, the Corporation Tax Act and the Local Tax Act for the Enforcement of Income Tax Conventions, paragraph 1 of Article15

□第1号 (Subparagraph 1)
□第3号 (Subparagraph 3)
□第5号 (Subparagraph 5)
□第7号 (Subparagraph 7)

に掲げる還付金
Refund in accordance with the relevant subparagraph

(2) 還付を請求する金額；
Amount of Refund claimed ¥ 円

(3) 還付金の受領場所等に関する希望；（該当する下記の□欄に✓印を付し、次の欄にその受領を希望する場所を記入してください。）
Options for receiving your refund; (Check the applicable box below and enter your information in the corresponding fields.)

受取希望場所 Receipt by transfer to:	銀行 Bank	支店 Branch	預金種類及び口座番号又は記号番号 Type of account and account number	口座名義人 Name of account holder
□ 日本国内の預金口座 a Japanese bank account				
□ 日本国外の預金口座（注7） a bank account outside Japan (Note 7)				
	支店住所（国名、都市名）Branch Address (Country, City):		銀行コード (Bank Code)	送金通貨 (Currency)
□ ゆうちょ銀行の貯金口座 an ordinary savings account at the Japan Post Bank		—		
□ 郵便局等の窓口受取りを希望する場合 the Japan Post Bank or the post office (receipt in person)			—	—

3 支払者に関する事項；
Details of Payer

氏名又は名称 Full name	
住所（居所）又は本店（主たる事務所）の所在地 Domicile (residence) or Place of head office (main office)	（電話番号 Telephone Number）
個人番号又は法人番号（有する場合のみ記入） Individual Number or Corporate Number (Limited to case of a holder)	

4 源泉徴収義務者の証明事項；
Items to be certified by the withholding agent

(1) 所得の種類 Kind of Income	(2) 所得の支払期日 Due Date for Payment	(3) 所得の支払金額 Amount paid	(4) (3)の支払金額から源泉徴収した税額 Withholding Tax on (3)	(5) (4)の税額の納付年月日 Date of Payment of (4)	(6) 租税条約を適用した場合に源泉徴収すべき税額 Tax Amount to be withheld under Tax Convention	(7) 還付を受けるべき金額 Amount to be refunded (4)−(6)
		円 yen	円 yen		円 yen	円 yen

上記の所得の支払金額につき、上記のとおり所得税及び復興特別所得税を徴収し、納付したことを証明します。
I hereby certify that the tax has been withheld and paid as shown above.

年 月 日
Date______________ 源泉徴収義務者
Signature of withholding agent ______________ 印

【裏面に続きます (Continue on the reverse) 】

私は、日本国と＿＿＿＿＿＿＿＿＿＿＿＿との間の租税条約第＿＿条第＿＿項の規定の適用を受ける上記「4」の所得について源泉徴収された税額につき、「租税条約等の実施に伴う所得税法、法人税法及び地方税法の特例等に関する法律の施行に関する省令」及び「復興特別所得税に関する省令」の規定により還付の請求をするとともに、この還付請求書の記載事項が正確かつ完全であることを宣言します。

In accordance with the provisions of the Ministerial Ordinance for the Implementation of the Law concerning the Special Measures of the Income Tax Act, the Corporation Tax Act and the Local Tax Act for the Enforcement of Income Tax Conventions and the Ministerial Ordinance concerning Special Income Tax for Reconstruction, I hereby claim the refund of tax withheld on the Income of 4 above to which subparagraph＿＿＿of paragraph＿＿＿of Article＿＿＿of Income Tax Convention between Japan and＿＿＿＿＿＿＿＿＿＿is applicable and also hereby declare that the above statement is correct and complete to the best of my knowledge and belief.

年　　月　　日
Date＿＿＿＿＿＿＿＿＿＿

還付の請求をする者又はその代理人の署名
Signature of the Applicant or his Agent＿＿＿＿＿＿＿＿＿＿＿＿＿＿

○ 代理人に関する事項 ；この届出書を代理人によって提出する場合には、次の欄に記載してください。
Details of the Agent ; If this form is prepared and submitted by the Agent, fill out the following columns.

代理人の資格 Capacity of Agent in Japan	氏名（名称） Full name		納税管理人の届出をした税務署名 Name of the Tax Office where the Tax Agent is registered
□ 納税管理人 ※ Tax Agent □ その他の代理人 Other Agent	住所（居所・所在地） Domicile (Residence or location)	（電話番号 Telephone Number）	税務署 Tax Office

※ 「納税管理人」については、「租税条約に関する届出書」の裏面の説明を参照してください。

※ "Tax Agent" is explained on the reverse side of the "Application Form for Income Tax Convention".

注意事項

還付請求書の提出について

1 この還付請求書は、還付を請求する税額の源泉徴収をされた所得の支払者（租税特別措置法第9条の3の2第1項に規定する利子等の支払の取扱者を含みます。以下同じです。）ごとに作成してください。

2 この還付請求書は、上記1の所得につき租税条約の規定の適用を受けるための別に定める様式（様式1～様式3、様式6～様式10及び様式19）による「租税条約に関する届出書」（その届出書に付表や書類を添付して提出することとされているときは、それらも含みます。）とともに、それぞれ正副2通を作成して所得の支払者に提出し、所得の支払者は還付請求書の「4」の欄の記載事項について証明をした後、還付請求書及び租税条約に関する届出書の正本をその支払者の所轄税務署長に提出してください。

3 この還付請求書を納税管理人以外の代理人によって提出する場合には、その委任関係を証する委任状をその翻訳文とともに添付してください。

4 この還付請求書による還付金を代理人によって受領することを希望する場合には、還付請求書にその旨を記載してください。この場合、その代理人が納税管理人以外の代理人であるときは、その委任関係を証する委任状及び還付請求をする者（所得の支払を受ける者）のサイン証明書または印鑑証明書を、これらの翻訳文とともに添付してください。

還付請求書の記載について

5 納税者番号とは、租税の申告、納付その他の手続を行うために用いる番号、記号その他の符号でその手続をすべき者を特定することができるものをいいます。支払を受ける者の居住地である国に納税者番号に関する制度が存在しない場合や支払を受ける者が納税者番号を有しない場合には納税者番号を記載する必要はありません。

6 還付請求書の「2(1)」の条項の区分は、次のとおりです。

□第1号…… 租税条約の規定の適用を受ける人的役務の対価としての給与その他の報酬を2以上の支払者から支払を受けるため、その報酬につき「租税条約に関する届出書」を提出できなかったこと又は免税の金額基準が設けられている租税条約の規定の適用を受ける株主等対価の支払を受けるため、その対価につき「租税条約に関する届出書」を提出できなかったことに基因して源泉徴収をされた税額について還付の請求をする場合

□第3号…… 第1号及び第5号以外の場合で、租税条約の規定の適用を受ける所得につき「租税条約に関する届出書」を提出しなかったことに基因して源泉徴収をされた税額について還付の請求をする場合

□第5号…… 特定社会保険料を支払った又は控除される場合において、当該給与又は報酬につき源泉徴収をされた税額について還付の請求をする場合

□第7号…… 租税条約の規定が遡及して適用されることとなったため、当該租税条約の効力発生前に支払を受けた所得につき既に源泉徴収をされた税額について還付の請求をする場合

7 受取希望場所を「日本国外の預金口座」とした場合は、銀行コード（SWIFT コード、ABA ナンバー等）を記載し、送金通貨を指定してください。
なお、欧州向けの場合は、口座番号欄に IBAN コードを記載してください。

INSTRUCTIONS

Submission of the FORM

1 This form must be prepared separately for each Payer of Income who withheld the tax to be refunded (including Person in charge of handling payment of Interest or other payment who prescribed in paragraph 1 of Article 9-3-2 of the Act on Special Measures Concerning Taxation; the same applies below).

2 Submit this form in duplicate to the Payer of Income concerned together with the "Application Form for Income Tax Convention" (Forms 1 to 3, 6 to 10 and 19) prepared in duplicate for the application of Income Tax Convention to Income of 1 above (including attachment forms or documents if such attachment and documents are required). The Payer of the Income must certify the item in 4 on this form and then file the original of each form with the District Director of Tax Office for the place where the Payer resides.

3 An Agent other than the Tax Agent must attach a power of attorney together with its Japanese translation.

4 The applicants who wishes to receive refund through an Agent must state so on this form. If the Agent is an Agent other than a Tax Agent, a power of attorney and a guarantee of signature or seal-impression of the applicant (recipient of income) must be attached together with their Japanese translations.

Completion of the FORM

5 The Taxpayer Identification Number is a number, code or symbol which is used for filing of return and payment of due amount and other procedures regarding tax, and which identifies a person who must take such procedures. If a system of Taxpayer Identification Number does not exist in the country where the recipient resides, or if the recipient of the payment does not have a Taxpayer Identification Number, it is not necessary to enter the Taxpayer Identification Number.

6 The distinction of the provisions of the item 2 (1) on this form is as follows:

□Subpara.1… For the refund of tax on salary or other remuneration for personal services withheld to the benefits of the Income Tax Convention, which was withheld due to the failure to file the "Application Form for Income Tax Convention" because there are more than two Payers of Income. Alternatively, regarding the payment of stockholder value entitled according to the benefits of the Income Tax Convention, which provides an exemption amounts standard, the failure to file the "Application Form for Income Tax Convention" for the value.

□Subpara.3… For the refund of tax on income entitled to the benefits of the Income Tax Convention which was withheld due to the failure to file the "Application Form for Income Tax Convention" in cases other thanSubpara.1 and Subpara.5.

□Subpara.5… For the refund of tax which was withheld at the source from wages or remuneration with which designated insurance premiums were paid or from which said premiums are deducted.

□Subpara.7… For the refund of tax withheld on income paid before the coming into effect of Income Tax Convention when the Convention became applicable retroactively.

7 If you designate a "bank account outside Japan" as the place to receive of your choice, enter the bank code (Swift code, ABA number, etc.) and specify a currency for remittance.
In the case of accounts in Europe, enter IBAN code in the column for the account number.

Q16 Exemption from Withholding Tax for Short-Term Business Travellers under Tax Conventions

We are a Japanese branch of a US corporation. One of our US employees has been on a three-month business trip to Japan. His salary was paid by the US corporation, which then charged that cost, and travel expenses, to us.

Do we have to pay Japanese income tax on his salary during his stay in Japan?

A:

Japanese income tax is imposed on the salary of the US employee during his stay in Japan, and must be withheld and paid to the Japanese tax authorities.

Discussion

1. Tax treatment under domestic tax law

'Salary, compensation, wages, annual allowances, bonuses or any other payment of a similar nature or any other remuneration for the provision of personal services, which arises from provision of personal services such as the service in employment carried out in Japan (including provision of personal services, such as the service in employment outside Japan which is carried out by a person acting as an officer of a domestic corporation)' ('Salary') is treated as domestic source income (ITA Article 161(1)(xii)).

Therefore, if a non-resident travels to Japan on business, they will be taxed on their Salary for the number of days worked in Japan during the business trip.

2. Exemption from withholding tax for short-term business travellers under the Tax Convention between Japan and the US

Under Article 14(2) of the Tax Convention between Japan and the US, Salary derived by a US resident from work performed in Japan shall be taxable only in the US if the following requirements are met:

(i) the recipient is present in Japan for a period or periods not exceeding in the aggregate 183 days in any 12-month period commencing or ending in the taxable year concerned;
(ii) the remuneration is paid by, or on behalf of, an employer who is not a resident of Japan; and
(iii) the remuneration is not borne by a permanent establishment which the employer has in Japan.

Since the Salary of the US employee is recharged to the Japanese branch, the requirement in (iii) above is not met. As a result, the US employee's Salary is treated as domestic source income and is subject to Japanese income tax for the period that the employee worked in Japan.

3. Withholding tax obligations

Under domestic tax law, withholding tax is, in principle, imposed on domestic source income paid to non-residents or foreign corporations if it is paid in Japan. In other words, as far as the payment has been made outside Japan, Japanese withholding tax should not be imposed on such payment.

However, where payment of domestic source income is made outside Japan if the person who makes such payment has *a domicile or residence in Japan or has an office, place of business or any other equivalent place in Japan,* that person is deemed to pay the domestic source income in Japan (ITA Article 212(2)).

Accordingly, although the Salary of the US employee is made by the US head office, it is deemed to have been paid in Japan due to the existence of the Japanese branch. Withholding tax must therefore be collected and remitted to the competent national tax office by the last day of the month following the month in which the Salary is paid (ITA Article 212(2)).

Q17 Withholding Tax on Directors' Remuneration Paid to Non-resident Directors

We are a Japanese subsidiary of a Belgian corporation, and recently appointed a director who is a Belgian resident. The director will work from Belgium, and we will pay director's remuneration. Do we have an obligation to withhold tax on this payment?

A:

Income tax must be withheld at the rate of 20.42% when director's remuneration is paid.

1. Tax treatment under domestic tax law

Salary, compensation, wage, annual allowance, bonus or any other payment of a similar nature or any other remuneration for the provision of personal services, which arises from provision of personal services such as the service in employment carried out in Japan ('Salary') is treated as domestic source income (ITA Article 161(1)(xii)).

Salary paid for work carried out outside Japan is, in principle, treated as foreign source income and, as a result, does not generally incur withholding tax. However, the provision of personal services by a person acting as a director of a domestic corporation is considered domestic source income, even if performed outside Japan (ITA Article 161(1)(xii)).

Withholding tax is imposed on such domestic source income at the rate of 20.42% at the time of payment (ITA Articles 212(1), 213(1)(i)).

2. Treatment of Salary under the Tax Convention between Japan and Belgium

Article 15 of the Tax Convention between Japan and Belgium provides that directors' remuneration 'derived by a resident of Belgium in his capacity as a member of the board of directors, or of a similar organ, of a corporation which is a resident of a Contracting State may be taxed in that Contracting State'. There are no special exemptions from this withholding tax.

Consequently, the Salary paid to your Belgian director is treated as domestic source income for both domestic tax law purposes and for the purposes of the Tax Convention between Belgium and Japan, and income tax must be withheld at a rate of 20.42% at the time of payment of that remuneration.

Q18 Withholding Tax on the Provision of Technical Services by Indian Corporations

We are a Japanese branch of a Singapore corporation. Our Japanese branch provides information technology (IT) consulting services to corporate customers in Japan. In providing these services, we outsourced some of them to a group corporation in India. The outsourced services are performed in India.

Our Singapore head office pays fees to the Indian corporation for these outsourced IT services. However, these fees are charged back to the Japanese branch as an expense.

The Indian corporation does not have any PE in Japan. Is there an obligation to remit withholding tax on the fees paid to the Indian corporation?

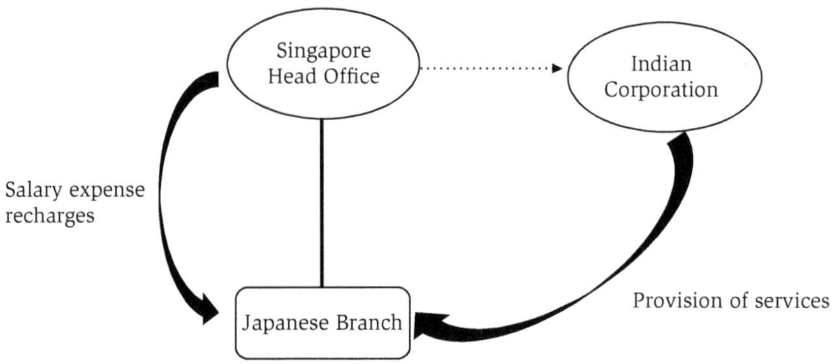

A:

Withholding tax is imposed on the service fees paid to the Indian corporation.

Discussion

1. Treatment under domestic tax law

Any consideration received by a corporation operating a business for which the main activity is the provision of personal services in Japan is treated as domestic source income (ITA Article 161(1)(vi)).

For this purpose, 'personal services' has a broad definition, namely 'a business mainly consisting of the provision of services by a person who has specialized knowledge or special skills in the field of science and technology, business management, or other fields by utilizing such knowledge or skills' (ITAEO Article 282(1)(iii)).

Since the services provided in this case consist of IT consulting services, they should be considered to fall within this definition of 'personal services'.

Having said that, since the IT consulting services are provided by the Indian corporation in India, they should not be treated as domestic source income under the domestic tax law.

2. Treatment of withholding tax under the Tax Convention between India and Japan

Under Article 12(1) of the Tax Convention between Japan and India, 'royalties and fees for technical services arising in a Contracting State [Japan] and paid to a resident of the other Contracting State [India] may be taxed in that other Contracting State [India]'. Further, Article 12(4) defines the term 'fees for technical services' as 'payments of any amount to any person other than payments to an employee of a person making payments and to any individual for independent personal services referred to in Article 14, in consideration for the services of a managerial, technical or consultancy nature, including the provisions of services of technical or other personnel'.

The IT consulting services provided to the Japanese branch would be technical services as defined in the Tax Convention between India and Japan.

Royalties and fees for technical services are deemed to arise in Japan when the payor is a resident of Japan. Where, however, the payor has a PE or fixed base in Japan, whether a resident of Japan or not, and where the liability to pay the royalties or fees for technical services arises from that PE or fixed base, and such royalties or fees for technical services are borne by such permanent establishment or fixed base, then those royalties or fees for technical services are deemed to arise in Japan (Tax Convention between India and Japan Article 12(6)).

The Singapore corporation is the payor of the fees for technical services and has a Japanese branch (i.e., a PE). Moreover, the fees paid to the Indian corporation are for IT consulting services provided to the Japanese branch. Since these fees are recharged to the Japanese branch, those fees are considered to have arisen in Japan and therefore are treated as domestic source income under the Tax Convention between India and Japan.

Where the definition of domestic source income in a Tax Convention differs from the definition of domestic source income under the domestic tax law, the definition in the Tax Convention prevails (ITA Article 162(1)).

Accordingly, the fees paid to the Indian corporation will be considered Japanese domestic source income, even though they are paid by the Singapore corporation.

Domestic source income paid to a foreign corporation is subject to withholding tax at the rate of 20.42%, and is required to be paid by the 10th day of the month following the month of payment (ITA Article 212(1), Article 213(1)(i)).

If domestic source income is paid outside Japan, in principle, no withholding tax will be imposed. However, if the payor has an office or other place of business in Japan, the payment of that domestic source income is deemed to be made in Japan regardless of where it was actually paid, and withholding tax will be imposed (ITA Article 212(2)).

As a result, the payment of the IT consulting services by your Singapore head office to the Indian corporation is subject to withholding tax in Japan. In this case, the due date for payment of the withholding tax is the last day of the month following the month of payment.

In addition, under the Tax Convention between India and Japan, the withholding tax rate on personal services is reduced to 10%. In order to benefit from this reduced rate, an 'Application Form for Income Tax Convention' must be submitted to the competent national tax office by the day before the date of payment.

3. Obligation to submit a corporate tax return

In this situation, the Indian corporation is also required to submit a corporation tax return in Japan. This is because any consideration received by a foreign corporation conducting business for which the main activity is to provide personal services in Japan is also treated as domestic source income for corporation tax purposes (CTA Article 138(1)(iv), CTAEO 179(1)(iii)) and, under the Tax Convention between India and Japan, fees for technical services are deemed to arise in Japan when the payor has a PE in Japan, even if the services are provided outside Japan. As a result, the Indian corporation has domestic source income arising from personal services under domestic tax law.

For corporation tax purposes, a foreign corporation which does not have a PE in Japan is still subject to corporation tax and local corporation tax compliance obligations if it has domestic source income from the provision of personal services (CTA Article 141 (ii)). Thus, it is still required to submit a corporation tax return and a local corporation tax return. Corporate inhabitant tax and corporate enterprise tax are not imposed as the foreign corporation has no fixed place of business nor employees in Japan.

Consequently, the Indian corporation is required to submit a corporation tax return and local corporation tax return. The withholding tax paid by the Singapore corporation should be creditable from the corporation tax amount.

Q19 Withholding Tax on Share-Based Remuneration Granted by Foreign Corporation

We are a Japanese subsidiary of a US corporation, which is listed in the US. The US parent grants share-based compensation (e.g., stock options or restricted stock) to some of our employees. Is withholding tax imposed on this share-based compensation?

A:

Share-based compensation paid to Japanese employees is, in principle, taxable as employment income under Japanese income tax law. However, withholding tax would not be imposed on such share-based compensation, where it is paid by the US parent. As a result, each employee receiving share-based compensation would be required to submit an income tax return and pay the relevant income tax themselves.

The Japanese corporation will also be required to submit a 'Statement of Economic Benefits Provided by a Foreign Parent Corporation to Domestic Directors or Employees' to the competent national tax office to notify the Japanese tax authorities of the individuals who received share-based compensation.

Discussion

1. Treatment of share-based compensation

When stock options are granted to employees, the income tax treatment will differ depending on whether the stock options are tax-qualified or non-tax-qualified. In order to meet the conditions for a tax-qualified stock option, the stock option must be issued under the provisions of the Japanese Companies Act. As a result, stock options granted by a foreign corporation are generally treated as non-tax-qualified stock options for domestic tax law (STMA Article 29-2).

Non-tax-qualified stock options are not taxable at the time of grant; however, the difference between the market price at the time of exercise and the exercise price is taxed as employment income (ITAEO Article 84(3)).

Restricted stock is taxed as employment income at the market value on the day the restrictions on the transfer are released (ITAEO Article 84(1)). Stock is considered restricted for Japanese income tax purposes if it meets the following requirements:

(1) The stock must be subject to restrictions on transfer for a certain period.
(2) The corporation can acquire the restricted stock without consideration, or the stock is forfeited under certain conditions, such as the failure of the employee to meet performance obligations.
(3) The stock is granted in exchange for provision of services by directors or employees.
(4) The stock must be shares of the corporation to which the services are provided or an affiliated corporation.

(ITAEO Article 84(1),(2))

When a director or employee sells stock received after the exercise of a stock option or after restrictions on restricted stock are lifted, the difference between the actual price at which the stock is sold and the market price of the stock at the time of exercise or the lifting of restriction is taxed as capital gain.

2. Withholding tax obligations on share-based compensation

Employers are obliged to withhold income tax on employment income paid to residents in Japan (ITA Article 183). However, since the corporation issuing the share-based compensation in this case is your US parent, it is not the employer and therefore is not obliged to withhold income tax unless it has a PE in Japan. Similarly, since you, as a domestic corporation, did not grant the share-based compensation to your employees, you are also not obliged to withhold income tax.

In this situation, the Japanese employees have employment income which is not subject to withholding tax upon payment, and therefore they will be obliged to submit an income tax return to the competent tax office to pay the income tax due.

As further background, taxpayers in Japan are not generally required to submit an income tax return if they receive employment income from a single employer if the amount of that income is less than JPY 20 million, and if any other taxable income other than employment income or retirement income is less than JPY 200,000 (ITA Article 121). For this reason, most of the directors/employees receiving employment income in Japan do not submit an income tax return.

Due to this, employees may not be familiar with their income tax compliance obligations, including the requirement to submit an income tax return recognising stock options or restricted stock. It is generally recommended that employers issuing stock options or restricted stock inform and remind employees about these obligations, to ensure that they do not fail to submit the required income tax returns.

In addition, if the foreign corporation providing share-based compensation to employees of a Japanese corporation directly or indirectly owns 50% or more of the shares of that subsidiary, the Japanese corporation is required to submit to the tax office a 'Statement of Total Economic Benefits Provided by a Foreign Parent Corporation to Domestic Directors or Employees' and a 'Statement of Economic Benefits Provided by Foreign Parent Corporation to Domestic Directors or Employees' when the share-based compensation is granted, in order to report who and how much stock was granted (ITA Article 228-3-2). *See below* for examples of these forms. The submission due date for these forms is the end of March of the year following the date of grant.

Total Statement of Economic Benefits Provided by Foreign Parent Corporation to Domestic Directors or Employees

税務署受付印

令和　　年分　外国親会社等が国内の役員等に供与等をした経済的利益に関する調書合計表

処理事項	通信日付印		検　収	整理簿登載
	※　・　・		※	※

令和　年　月　日提出	提出者	所在地	電話（　－　－　）	整理番号			
				調書の提出区分（新規=1、追加=2、訂正=3、無効=4）		提出媒体		本店一括	有・無
		法人番号（※）		作成担当者			
税務署長 殿		フリガナ 名称					
		フリガナ 代表者氏名印	㊞	作成税理士署名押印	税理士番号（　　）㊞ 電話（　－　－　）		

外国親会社等（付与会社）	調書の枚数	摘要
	枚	
計		

○　提出媒体欄には、コードを記載してください。（電子=14、FD=15、MO=16、CD=17、DVD=18、書面=30、その他=99）
（注）　平成27年分以前の合計表を作成する場合には、「法人番号」欄に何も記載しないでください。

（用紙　日本産業規格　A 4）

○平成28年1月1日以後提出用

Statement on Economic Benefits Provided by Foreign Parent Corporation to Domestic Directors or Employees

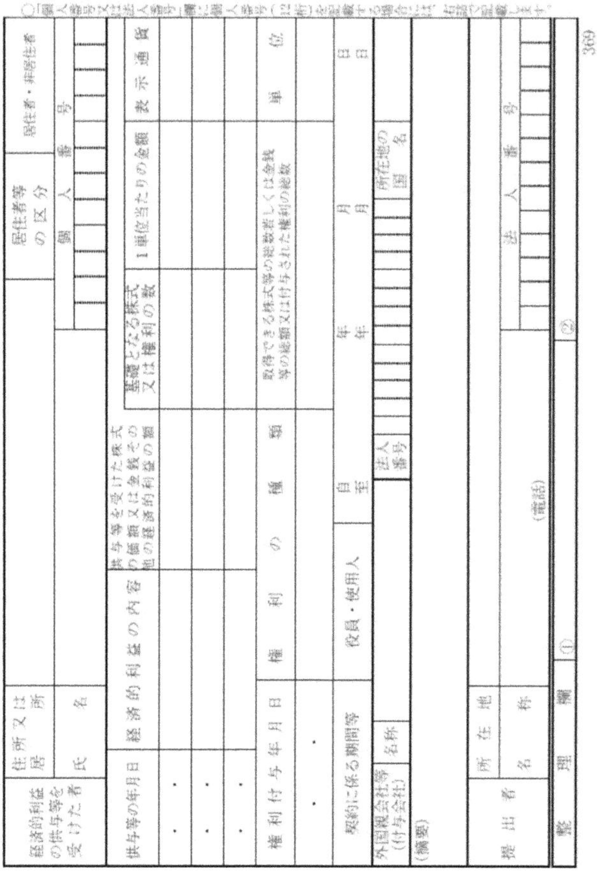

令和　　年分　外国親会社等が国内の役員等に供与等をした経済的利益に関する調書

経済的利益の供与等を受けた者	住所又は居所		居住者等の区分	居住者・非居住者
	氏名		個人番号	

供与等の年月日	経済的利益の内容	供与等を受けた株式の価額又は金銭その他の経済的利益の額	基礎となる株式又は権利の数	1単位当たりの金額	表示通貨
・　・					
・　・					
・　・					

権利付与年月日	権利の種類	取得できる株式等の総数若しくは金銭等の総額又は付与された権利の総数	単位
・　・			

契約に係る期間等	役員・使用人	自　年　月　日 至　年　月　日			
外国親会社等（付与会社）	名称		法人番号	所在地の国名	
（摘要）					
提出者	所在地				
	名称	（電話）	法人番号		
整理欄	①	②			

〇「個人番号又は法人番号」欄に個人番号（12桁）を記載する場合には、右詰で記載します。

369

CHAPTER 3
Corporation Tax

Q20 Blue Form Tax Return Status

We are a foreign corporation which has a Japanese subsidiary. Our Japanese subsidiary has informed us that it will apply for blue form tax return filing status in order to obtain some tax advantages.

What is the blue form tax return status and what are these advantages?

A:

If a taxpayer maintains appropriate accounting and tax books and records and files its tax returns based on these books and records, the taxpayer may be eligible for a blue form tax return, which gives certain advantages when calculating taxable income.

One of the biggest advantages of blue form tax return filing status is the ability to carry tax losses forward, i.e., if the corporation recognises a tax loss in one year, that tax loss can be carried forward for the following ten years. In contrast, taxpayers with white form tax return filing status (i.e., non-blue form tax return filing status) cannot carry forward tax losses.

It is therefore recommended that your Japanese subsidiary applies for blue form tax return filing status.

Discussion

The Japanese corporation tax system is a self-assessment system, whereby taxpayers calculate taxable income and pay tax according to the appropriate tax laws.

In order to do these calculations accurately, and to declare the correct amount of taxable income generated during the fiscal year, the taxpayer must keep a record of their daily income and expense transactions, and preserve the relevant documents produced or received in connection with those transactions.

If a taxpayer maintains appropriate accounting and tax books and records, and submits its tax returns based on these books and records, the taxpayer may be eligible for blue form tax return filing status, which provides certain advantages when calculating taxable income.

A corporation which systematically maintains books of account, records its accounting transactions in an orderly and clear manner in accordance with the principles of double-entry bookkeeping, settles its accounts in accordance with various prescribed procedures, and calculates its accurate profit may, with the approval of the tax authorities, submit a blue form tax return (CTA Article 121). This will entitle the corporation to certain preferential tax treatments as listed below, whereas white form tax return taxpayers (i.e., non-blue form tax return taxpayers) are not so entitled.

The main tax benefits permitted to blue form tax return taxpayers are as follows:

(1) Deduction of reserves for losses on overseas investments (STMA Article 55), for exploration (STMA Article 58), and other reserves under the Special Taxation Measures Act.
(2) Deduction and carry forward of special depreciation for depreciable assets (except for special depreciation of replacement assets in disaster-stricken areas) (STMA Article 43-3).
(3) Special research and development tax credits (STMA Article 42-4).
(4) Tax loss carry forward for a maximum of ten years (CTA Article 57).
(5) Refund of corporation tax through tax loss carry-back (CTA Article 80).
    (The application of tax loss carry-back in fiscal years ended from 1 April 1992 is suspended except for the dissolution period and liquidation period (STMA Article 66-12). However, losses incurred by small- and medium-sized enterprises are permitted to apply tax loss carry-back.
(6) Where a notice of assessment is issued by the Japanese tax authorities, the reason for the assessment must be provided (CTA Article 130(2)).

The above advantages cannot be granted to a corporation with white form tax return filing status. This is particularly important for the ability to carry tax losses forward, which permits a corporation recognising a tax loss in one year to carry that loss forward for the following ten years. It is therefore highly recommended that the Japanese subsidiary applies for blue form tax return filing status. In practice, most corporations in Japan are blue form tax return filers.

In order to become a blue form tax return filer, an 'Application for Approval as a Blue Form Tax Return Filer' must be submitted to the competent national tax office by the day before the start of the fiscal year in which the taxpayer intends to submit a blue form tax return. However, in the case of a corporation whose first fiscal year includes the date of its establishment, the application may be submitted by the day before the earlier of three months after the date of establishment or the end of the first fiscal year.

Q21 Maintenance of Electronic Accounting Books and Records

We are a Japanese subsidiary of a foreign corporation. We currently maintain our accounting books, invoices, and other documents in paper format. However, in order to reduce the costs of document storage, we are considering converting these documents into a soft copy.

It is our understanding that the laws relating to electronic storage of accounting and tax books and records changed recently. What are the current rules?

A:

A taxpayer's books of account and invoices and other related source documents are generally required to be maintained in paper form. However, under the Act on Special Provisions Concerning Preservation Methods for Books and Documents Related to National Tax Prepared by Means of Computers ('Electronic Preservation Law' or 'EPL'), certain accounting books and records, as well as invoices and other source documents, can be maintained electronically.

Discussion

Under the current domestic tax law, the NTA generally requires all taxpayers to maintain their accounting books, and all supporting evidence (e.g., invoices, receipts, etc.) in paper form. Only taxpayers who satisfy certain complicated requirements can maintain their accounting books and supporting evidence in electronic format. The law provides different requirements for three categories of document, namely: (1) tax-related accounting books and records, (2) documents maintained through scanned format, and (3) transactions conducted electronically.

(1) Tax-related accounting books and records

'Tax-related accounting books and records' means the accounting books (e.g., general ledger, journals) and other documents prepared by the corporation itself (e.g., copies of invoices issued to customers).

Tax-related accounting books and records prepared using an electronic system (e.g., some form of accounting software) can be maintained electronically (i.e., in electronic format or as Microfilm output from a computer ('COM')) if certain conditions are met.

In addition, if a taxpayer satisfies certain additional requirements and demonstrates 'excellent electronic tax related accounting books and records', if there are any errors in their tax returns, the penalty tax relating to such errors will be reduced by 5%. Approval from the NTA is required to be classified as a taxpayer with 'excellent electronic tax-related accounting books and records'.

The requirements for maintenance of tax-related accounting books and records electronically are as follows:

Requirements	*Electronic Format*			*COM*		
	Excellent Tax-related Accounting Books	*Tax-related Accounting Books*	*Documents*	*Excellent tax-related Accounting Books*	*Tax-related Accounting Books*	*Documents*
Maintenance of documents for the development of computer processing systems (system outline, system specifications, operation manuals, administration manuals)	◦	◦	◦	◦	◦	◦
Readable devices (computers, programmes, displays, printers and their operation manuals, etc.) and timely output in an orderly format, and clearly displayed electromagnetic records	◦	◦	◦	◦	◦	*1, *2
Able to download electronic records of tax-related accounting books and documents upon request by the NTA based on its rights to question and inspection	Δ *2	◦ *3	Δ *4	Δ *2	◦ *3	Δ *5
Maintenance of documents relating to the process of preparation of the COM				◦	◦	◦

Requirements	*Electronic Format*			*COM*		
	Excellent Tax-related Accounting Books	*Tax-related Accounting Books*	*Documents*	*Excellent tax-related Accounting Books*	*Tax-related Accounting Books*	*Documents*
Provision of COM readable device				◦	◦	◦
Use of a computer processing system by which the facts and contents of corrections/deletions/additions of electronic records can be verified	◦			◦		
Ensuring interrelationship of recorded matter between accounts and books	◦			◦		
Search function capability 1. searchable by transaction date, amount or customer 2. searchable by date or amount range 3. searchable by any combination of two or more record items	Δ *2			Δ *2		*1
Maintenance of an index				◦		
Output the index of recorded matters to COM				◦		

Requirements	*Electronic Format*			*COM*		
	Excellent Tax-related Accounting Books	*Tax-related Accounting Books*	*Documents*	*Excellent tax-related Accounting Books*	*Tax-related Accounting Books*	*Documents*
Parallel preservation of electronic records in the first three years or COM ensuring the search function of the recorded matters of				° *6		

*1 This is a requirement for maintenance of accounting books and records electronically in parallel for an initial period of three years.

2 Where a taxpayer can respond to a 'request for download' from the tax auditors, it is not necessary to have the functions for searching by date range or amount nor for searching by any combination of two or more items.

3 If all requirements to maintain 'excellent tax-related accounting books and records' are met, the requirement to 'respond to download requests' can be ignored.

4 The requirement to 'respond to download requests' can be ignored if the equivalent requirement for search function is met.

5 The requirement to 'respond to download requests' can be ignored if all requirements for 'maintaining an index', 'output of indices to COM', and 'ensuring search functions for COM' are met.

6. If the requirement to 'respond to download requests' is met, a function that allows searching by date range and searching by combining two or more items is not required.

° Necessary.

Δ Necessary with exception.

Tax-related accounting books and records that can be maintained electronically are those that are prepared by the taxpayer using a computer from the initial recording stage. Tax-related accounting books and records originally prepared by hand therefore cannot be maintained electronically.

(2) Documents maintained through scanned format

Tax-related documents, such as invoices received from suppliers or copies of invoices prepared by taxpayers, excluding documents related to settlement of accounts or financial statements can be preserved in electric format after scanning, when certain requirements in relation to the accuracy of the scanning are met. For the purpose of this law, there are three categories of document. 'Important documents' are tax documents other than those related to the closure of accounts or financial statements. 'General documents' are those which are not directly connected or linked to the flow of funds or goods, such as:

(i) contracts with predefined terms and conditions such as insurance contracts, telephone subscription contracts, credit card applications;
(ii) bank transfer forms;
(iii) acceptance certificate and documents confirming receipt prepared by purchasers of inventories;
(iv) purchase orders and quotations;
(v) delivery notes prepared by the taxpayer.

'Past important documents' are important documents prepared or received before the electronic maintenance laws came into effect:

Requirement	*Important Documents*	*General Documents*	*Past important Documents*
Input timing (as soon as possible after receipt of the documents or after the normal period for processing (maximum 2 months) have elapsed)	◦		
Resolution (more than 200 dpi)	◦	◦	◦
Colour gradation (16.77 million colour gradation; each red, green, and blue gradation is required to be more than 256 gradation)	◦	*1	◦
Time stamp by a system provided by an authorised supplier (as soon as possible after receipt of the documents or after the normal period for processing (maximum 2 months) have elapsed)	◦ *2	◦ *3	◦ *3

Requirement	*Important Documents*	*General Documents*	*Past important Documents*
Retention of resolution and colour gradation information	◦	◦	◦
Retention of document size information	◦ *4		◦
Retention of version information (feasible to track delete and revision information)	◦	◦	◦
Feasible to track the information of the input person	◦	◦	◦
Feasible to connect accounting books and the scanned documents	◦	◦	◦
Provision of equipment for legible reading (14'' or larger colour display, 4-point character recognition, etc.)	◦	◦	◦
Orderly and clear printouts (when requested by tax auditor)	◦	◦	◦
Retention of documents for the development of the accounting system	◦	◦	◦
Searching function by date, amount and name of suppliers	◦	◦	◦
Others			*5,*6

*1 'General documents' may be saved in greyscale instead of colour image.

*2 The time stamp requirement may be omitted where it is possible to confirm the following:

(i) tax-related information is input into the system as soon as possible after it is received, and cannot be corrected or deleted, or a record of corrections or deletions is maintained; or

(ii) provided appropriate internal rules for the process from the preparation or receipt of tax-related documents to be input into the system are maintained, and the documents are input into the system within a normal business processing period (generally two months), and cannot be corrected or deleted, or a record of corrections or deletions is maintained.

*3 The time stamp requirement may be omitted if the system does not permit corrections or deletions to input information, or a record of corrections or deletions is maintained.

*4 For documents scanned by the recipient, it is not necessary to maintain information on the size of the document (A4 or smaller).

*5 For 'past important documents', administrative procedures for the creation and maintenance of electronic records (including designation of a person responsible for the relevant procedures) should be maintained as well as maintenance of the electronic records themselves.

*6 For 'past important documents', an application must be submitted to the competent national tax office.

° Necessary.

Where the tax authorities identify fraud in relation to the maintenance of electronic records in scanned format, an additional heavy penalty tax of 10% (i.e., a total tax rate of 45%) will be imposed on the amount of tax related to the fraud.

(3) 'Electronic Transactions' conducted

'Electronic transactions' refers to transactions where the relevant documents or records (e.g., invoices) are exchanged by electronic methods. Therefore, any transaction in which a taxpayer receives an invoice by e-mail would be classified as a transaction conducted electronically.

Electronic transactions must be preserved in electronic format. Consequently, even if the taxpayer prints out the relevant document and maintains it in paper format, the tax authorities may refuse to accept that document as evidence during a tax audit.

In order to maintain documents by 'Electronic Transaction' in electronic format, the following requirements need to be met:

(a) maintenance of documents describing the computer system (where the taxpayer uses a self-developed programme);
(b) maintenance of suitable devices for reading scanned documents;
(c) appropriate search functions; and
(d) one of the following:
  - Documents are received after being timestamped by the sender.
  - The taxpayer timestamps the documents: (i) as soon as possible after their preparation or receipt, or (ii) promptly after the normal business processing period has elapsed (generally two months), provided the relevant corporate procedures are applied.
  - Usage of a system that retains a record of corrections and deletions of data or a system that does not allow corrections and deletions.
  - Maintenance of administrative rules covering the prevention of corrections and deletions.

Q22 Tax Notifications upon Establishment of a Japanese Company

We are a US corporation, and have recently decided to establish a new Japanese subsidiary. What tax notifications must be submitted to the Japanese tax authorities upon establishment?

A:

Upon establishment of a Japanese company, including a Japanese subsidiary of a foreign corporation, the following tax notifications and applications are generally submitted to the tax authorities.

To be submitted to the competent national tax office are the following:

- Notification of establishment of the corporation.
- Application for approval of a blue form tax return filing corporation.
- Application for an extension of due date for filing of corporation tax return.
- Application for an extension of due date for filing of consumption tax return.
- Notification of the inventory cost method.
- Notification of depreciation method.
- Notification of the foreign exchange method.
- Notification of the commencement of a payroll.
- Application for approval for the payment of withholding tax semi-annually.

To be submitted to the competent local tax office are the following:

- Notification of establishment of the corporation
- Application for an extension of due date for filing of corporation tax return.

Discussion

A Japanese subsidiary of a foreign corporation is treated as a domestic corporation if it has its head office in Japan (CTA Article 2(iii)). Thus, there is no difference in the tax notifications and applications that must be submitted to the tax authorities at the time of establishment of a Japanese subsidiary of a foreign corporation or a Japanese corporation.

Having said that, due to additional complexity in the financial reporting processes of multinational groups, there are certain notifications and applications that Japanese subsidiaries of multinational corporations should submit that Japanese corporations may not submit. It is advisable to submit these additional notifications and applications at the time of establishment to avoid overlooking their submission at a later date.

Applications/notifications to be submitted to the competent national tax office are as follows.

1. Notification of establishment of the corporation

This is the notification that provides the basic information about the corporation to the national tax authorities, which must be submitted within two months after the date of establishment. The Articles of Association should be attached to the notification, in order to certify the fiscal year.

2. Application for approval of a blue form tax return filing corporation

The 'application for approval of a blue form tax return filing corporation' must be submitted by the day before the start of the fiscal year in which the corporation intends to submit a blue form tax return. However, in the case of a corporation whose fiscal year includes the date of its establishment, the application must be submitted by the day before the earlier of three months after the date of establishment or the end of the first fiscal year.

The application is deemed to be approved unless the tax authority rejects it by the end of the fiscal year in which the corporation intends to file a blue form tax return.

Please refer Q20 for further details of blue form tax return filing status.

3. Application for extension of the due date for filing of the corporation tax return

The due date for submitting a corporation tax return is two months after the end of the fiscal year (CTA Article 74). However, where the corporation's Articles of Association provide that the ordinary shareholders' meeting for the approval of the financial statements will not be held within two months from the fiscal year end, the filing due date can be extended by one month.

It is generally practically difficult for many multinational corporations to finalise the accounts of their Japanese subsidiary within two months because those accounts are prepared in accordance with the schedule of the parent corporation. The parent corporation is often required to submit its accounts and related information to us relatively early.

However, it often takes time for the parent corporation to approve the contents of its financial accounts and for the parent corporation's independent auditors to audit the consolidated financial statements. In particular, the schedule for approval by the parent corporation and the audit is likely to be based on the statutory closing deadlines of the country in which the parent corporation is located. As the statutory closing period in overseas countries is generally longer than in Japan, the parent corporation or auditor often requires revisions to the Japanese subsidiary's accounts more than two months after fiscal year end. Accordingly, those accounts may not be finalised by the statutory due date for submission of the corporate tax return.

In addition, Japanese subsidiaries of multinational corporations often need to obtain approval from their parent corporation for the submission of tax returns, which can take some time to obtain. Given all of the above, it is usually difficult to submit the corporation tax returns of a Japanese subsidiary within two months after the fiscal year end.

In order to avoid a situation where the financial statements are not completed or the corporation tax return is not approved by the parent corporation by the statutory due date for the corporation tax return filing, it is advisable to submit an 'application for an extension of that due date for the filing of the corporation tax return' (CTA Art 75-2(1)).

It is also advisable to inform the parent corporation of the schedule for the statutory closing of accounts and tax return filing in Japan, in order to avoid exceeding even the extended filing deadline.

The corporation's Articles of Association must also be attached to the application (CTA Article 75-2 (4)); although if the corporation makes this application at the same time it files its notification of establishment, the Articles of Association will already be included in the submission package. The application is deemed to be approved unless the tax authority rejects it within fifteen days from the end of the fiscal year in which the corporation intends to extend the filing due date for its corporation tax return.

4. Application for extension of the due date for filing of the consumption tax return

The due date for submission of the consumption tax return is also two months after the fiscal year end (JCTA Article 45(1)). As Japanese consumption tax returns start from the position recorded in the corporation's financial statements, then similar to the above discussion on corporation tax return filing, it is also recommended to file an 'application for extension of the due date for filing of the consumption tax return'. The application for extension for consumption tax can be submitted after the approval of similar extension for corporation tax.

5. Notification of inventory cost method

Domestic tax law allows multiple inventory cost methods (CTA Article 29(1)). However, unless a 'notification of inventory cost method' is submitted, the last purchase price method, where inventory is valued using the cost of the last unit purchased, must be applied (CTAEO Article 31).

Foreign corporations generally have a global policy for the valuation of inventories, which is unlikely to be the last purchase price method. It is therefore advisable to file a 'notification of inventory cost method' electing the method applied for accounting purposes (CTAEO Article 29) so that accounting and tax inventory valuation methods will be consistent.

For corporations engaged in businesses that do not hold inventories, such as the provision of services, this notification need not be submitted.

6. Notification of depreciation method

Domestic tax law allows multiple depreciation methods (CTA Article 31(1)). However, unless the corporation submits a 'notification of depreciation method', the declining method must be applied other than for certain fixed assets such as buildings (CTAEO Article 53).

On the other hand, most multinational corporation, particularly those adopting the International Financial Reporting Standards (IFRS) apply the straight-line method of depreciation as their group accounting policy.

If there is a difference between the accounting depreciation method and the tax depreciation method, both excess depreciation and shortage depreciation would have to be calculated, which would make management of the fixed asset register very complicated.

Accordingly, it is recommended to submit a 'notification of depreciation method' (CTAEO Article 51) electing to apply the same depreciation method for tax purposes as that applied for accounting, particularly for corporations with voluminous fixed assets.

7. Notification of the foreign exchange method

It is common for multinational corporations to hold assets and liabilities denominated in foreign currencies at the fiscal year end due to the existence of transactions with group corporations. For Japanese tax purposes, if assets or liabilities denominated in foreign currency are owned at fiscal year end, then depending on the asset or liability in question, they must be converted into Japanese yen either at the exchange Article at the time the transaction occurred (accrual method) or at the exchange rate at the end of the fiscal year (year-end method) (CTA Article 61-9(1)(i)).

Specifically, short-term foreign currency-denominated receivables and payables and foreign currency-denominated cash and bank deposits (i.e., those with a maturity date of one year or less from the end of the fiscal year) must be exchanged using the year-end method, while other foreign currency-denominated assets and liabilities must be exchanged using the accrual method (CTAEO Article 122-7).

On the other hand, the group accounting policy of many foreign corporations requires that all foreign currency assets and liabilities be exchanged by applying the year-end method.

It is therefore recommended to submit a 'notification of foreign exchange method' (CTAEO Article 122-5(1)), so that all foreign currency-denominated assets and liabilities can be exchanged by applying the year-end method.

8. Notification of the establishment of payroll

When a corporation commences paying remuneration to its directors or/and employees, a 'notification of establishment of payroll' must be submitted (ITA Article 230). The notification should be submitted within one month from the date of establishment of the payroll.

9. Application for approval for payment of withholding tax semi-annually

Withholding tax must generally be paid to the tax authorities by the 10th day of the month following the month in which the withholding tax was collected. However, corporations paying less than ten salaries at one time are permitted to pay the associated withholding tax to the tax authorities semi-annually (i.e., 10 July and 20 January) (ITA Article 216, 217). For corporations in this category, it is recommended to apply for this special treatment in order to reduce the administrative burden. Semi-annual payments can be adopted from the first withholding tax payment due in the month following the month of submission of the application. The application is deemed to be approved unless the tax authority rejects it by the end of the month following the month of submission of the application.

Withholding tax to which this special treatment is applicable is limited to withholding tax on salaries, severance payments, tax advisors and lawyers. Withholding tax due on other payments, such as withholding tax due on fees for other personal services such as for translators must continue to be paid on a monthly basis.

Notifications/applications to be submitted to the competent local tax office are as follows.

10. Notification of establishment of the corporation

This is the notification which provides the basic information about the corporation to the local tax authorities, which must be submitted within two months after the date of establishment. The contents are largely the same as the 'notification of establishment of the corporation' for national tax purposes. A copy of the legal register must be attached to the notification, as well as the Articles of Association of the corporation.

11. Notification of the approval of an extension of the due date for filing corporation tax return and application for extension of the due date for filing the corporate enterprise tax return

The submission due dates for the corporate inhabitant tax return and corporate enterprise tax return are both two months from the fiscal year end, as for the corporation tax return. The submission due date for the corporate inhabitant tax returns is automatically extended upon approval of the extension of the due date for the corporation tax return. However, the corporation must apply separately for an extension of the filing due date for the corporate enterprise tax return.

Since both corporate prefectural inhabitant tax and corporate enterprise tax are handled by local tax offices, a single combined 'notification of the approval of the extension of the due date for the filing of the corporation tax return and application for extension of the due date for filing of the corporate enterprise tax return' must be submitted to the competent prefectural tax office. If the corporation has offices in two or more prefectures, it must submit this combined form to each prefectural tax office.

For municipal corporate inhabitant tax returns, a separate 'notification of the approval of the extension of the due date for the filing of the corporation tax return' should be submitted.

Q23 Calculation of Corporate Taxation for Japanese Subsidiaries of Multinational Corporation

We are a US corporation intending to establish a subsidiary in Japan. Is there a difference in corporate taxation for corporations if the shareholders are located outside Japan as opposed to in Japan?

Similarly, are there any differences in the calculation of taxable income for corporations whose shareholders are located outside Japan?

A:

There are no particular differences in corporate taxation regardless of where the shareholders of a Japanese corporation are located, although there are specific tax regulations that are more commonly applied to Japanese subsidiaries of multinational corporations (such as thin capitalisation).

In many cases, however, the accounting books and records of Japanese subsidiaries of foreign corporations are maintained under the accounting standards of the parent corporation's jurisdiction, e.g., under US GAAP or IFRS. In such cases, it is necessary to reclassify the financial statements to Japanese GAAP in order to calculate taxable income. Thus, this reclassification is a part of the calculation of taxable income that is specific to Japanese subsidiaries of foreign corporations.

Discussion

Under the domestic tax law, corporations are classified into two categories: domestic corporations and foreign corporations (CTA Article 2(3), (4)). Domestic corporations are subject to corporation tax on all income each fiscal year regardless of the source of that income (worldwide income) (CTA Article 5).

On the other hand, corporation tax for foreign corporations is only levied on all or a part of their domestic source income each fiscal year, although the exact scope of taxation varies depending on whether the foreign corporation has a PE in Japan or not (CTA Article 141).

As such, the scope of taxable income is different between domestic and foreign corporations.

A domestic corporation is defined as a corporation with its headquarters or principal office in Japan, while a foreign corporation is defined as a corporation other than a domestic corporation (CTA Article 2(3),(4)). The headquarters of a corporation established under Japanese law must be located in Japan, so your Japanese subsidiary would be a domestic corporation for Japanese corporation tax purposes. Where the corporation is a domestic corporation, the scope of taxation is the same regardless of the country where the shareholders are located, and thus all domestic corporations, including Japanese subsidiaries of foreign corporations, are taxed on their worldwide income.

Taxable income is defined as the amount of income less the amount of expenses (CTA Article 22(1)). The amount of income or loss shall be calculated in accordance with 'generally accepted accounting principles', except as otherwise provided in the

Corporation Tax Act. These 'generally accepted accounting principles' are considered to be generally in line with Japanese accounting standards.

On the other hand, for Japanese subsidiaries of foreign corporations, the accounting books and records are generally maintained based on the accounting standards of the parent corporation's jurisdiction, e.g., US GAAP or IFRS. In such cases, in principle, those financial statements must be reclassified to financial statements prepared under Japanese GAAP (commonly referred to as a 'GAAP adjustment') before calculating taxable income for Japanese tax purposes.

This process of making GAAP adjustments is specific to the calculation of taxable income for Japanese subsidiaries of foreign corporations:

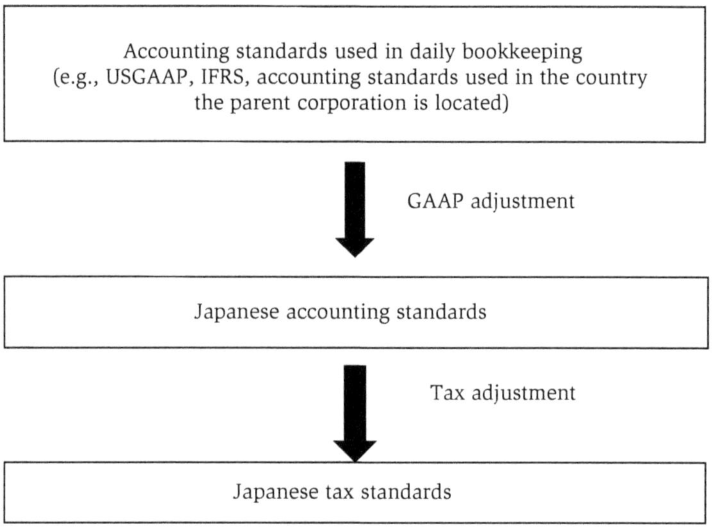

In addition, when performing the deferred tax calculation, both temporary differences from these GAAP adjustments and tax adjustments will be included in deferred tax assets and liabilities. This makes the deferred tax accounting for Japanese subsidiaries of foreign corporations more complex than for other Japanese corporations.

Q24 Calculation of Corporate Tax for Japanese Branches of Foreign Corporations

We are a foreign corporation, and have established a branch in Japan. How is the taxable income of this branch calculated?

A:

The domestic source income for foreign corporation will be divided into taxable income attributable to the PE and taxable income not attributable to the PE. Total corporation tax is the amount of corporation tax calculated for each of these categories of taxable income.

Discussion

A branch is a form of PE (CTA Article 2(xii-xix) (a)). Therefore, the taxable income of a foreign corporation with a PE in Japan is classified as income attributable to the PE (CTA Article 141(1)(i)(a)) and domestic source income other than that attributable to the PE (CTA Article 141(1)(i)(b)).

The calculation of the total taxable income of a foreign corporation with a PE in Japan is demonstrated in the following diagram:

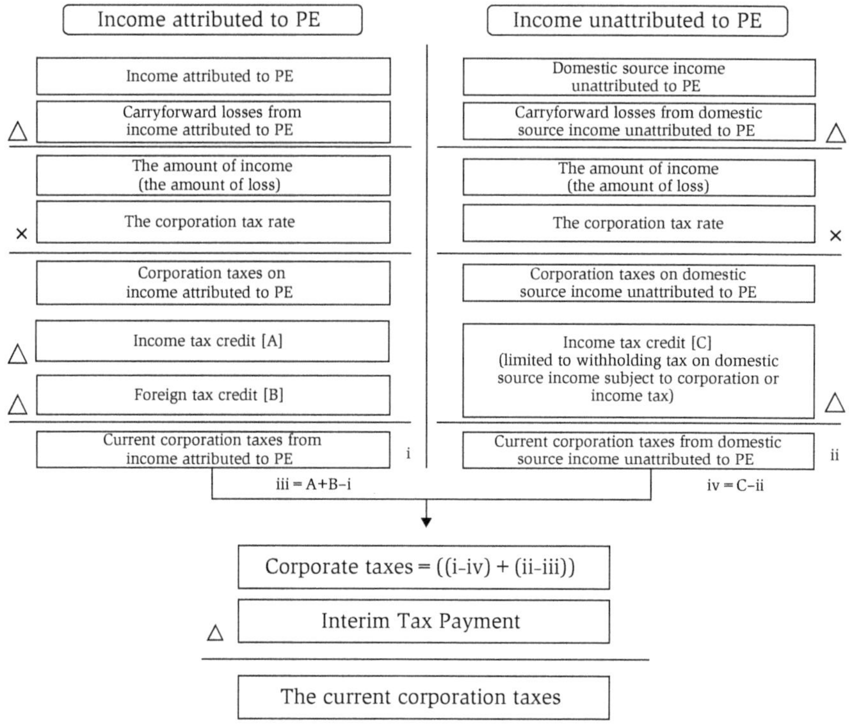

Note: A foreign corporation with a PE in Japan must calculate its corporation tax liability through classification of income attributable to the PE and income other than that attributable to the PE. Tax losses should also be calculated according to this classification, and should be offset against the relevant taxable income of each classification.

(*Source*: National Tax Agency, translation of 'Revision of International Taxation Principles to Align with the Attribution Principle')

1. Income attributable to the PE

The taxable income to be attributed to a PE should be the income that would be earned if the PE were assumed to be conducting business separately and independently from its foreign head office. In making this analysis, consideration should be given to the functions performed by the PE, the assets used by the PE, and any internal transactions ('dealings') between the PE and its headquarters or other PEs of the same foreign corporation (CTA Article 138(1)(i)). In other words, although the PE is legally a part of the foreign corporation, the taxable income attributable to the PE shall be calculated as if the PE were an independent enterprise.

The taxable income attributable to a PE is calculated as the revenue and other income relating to the business conducted through the PE, minus the expenses and losses relating to the business conducted through a PE for the fiscal year of the foreign corporation (CTA Article 142(1)). For the specific calculation of the 'revenue and other income relating to the business conducted through the PE', and the 'expenses and losses relating to the business conducted through the PE', the same provisions regarding the base of corporation tax for a domestic corporation for each fiscal year should be applied with exceptions for provisions not to apply to PE. The examples of such provisions are the following (CTA Article 142(2)):

(1) Exclusion of gains on gifts from 100% affiliated companies (CTA Article 25-2).
(2) Exclusion from gross revenue of tax refunds (CTA Article 26).
(3) Exclusion from deductible expenses of donations to 100% affiliated companies (CTA Article 37(2)).
(4) Exclusion from gross expenses of foreign tax to be credited against the amount of Japanese corporation tax (CTA Article 41).
(5) Profits or losses in devaluation of assets when commencing a consolidated tax return filing (CTA Subsection 5 Division 5).
(6) Profits or losses in transactions between corporations in a 100% shareholding relationship (CTA Subsection 5 Division 6).

In addition to the above, the following provisions relate solely to the calculation of income attributable to a PE.

(1) Recognition of taxable income from dealings (CTA Article 138(2))

The taxable income attributable to a PE is calculated as if the PE were an independent enterprise. Therefore, this income includes income arising from dealings between the PE and its head office or with other PEs of the same foreign corporation. 'Dealing' means any fact, such as the transfer of assets or the provision of services between the PE and its foreign head office or another PE, which would be considered the sale or purchase of assets, the provision of services, or any other legal transaction, if the same fact existed between third parties.

Having said that, there are a few points to note when recognising income or expenses from dealings, for example:

(i) Guarantees of obligations related to the borrowing of funds and the underwriting of reinsurance are excluded from dealings (CTA Article 138 (2), CTAEO Article 181).
(ii) Selling, general and administrative expenses for which the obligation has not yet been determined are included in the amount of deductible expenses if they arise through a dealing (CTA Article 142(3)(i)).
(iii) The provision of funds by a head office to establish a PE and the remittance of any surplus from the PE to the head office are treated as capital transactions and no income is generated from them (CTA Article 142(3)(iii)).
(iv) If the amount of the consideration for the dealing differs from the arm's-length price, which results in an understatement of income attributable to

the PE, the income shall be calculated as if the dealing had been carried out at arm's length (transfer pricing taxation on dealings, STMA Article 66-4-3).

(v) Documentation of dealings is required in the same way as for transaction between a Japanese company and its foreign-related parties (CTA Article 146-2(2)). Please refer to Q25 for more information on the issue of documentation.

(2) Deductibility of head office expenses (CTA Article 142(3)(ii), Article 142-7(1), CTAEO Article 184(2))

Selling, general and administrative expenses incurred for both the business conducted through a PE and other businesses of a foreign corporation shall be deductible in the PE if they are appropriately allocated to the PE, and documents describing the basis of that allocation are maintained.

(3) Exclusion from gross expenses of interest on indebtedness corresponding to capital to be attributed to a PE (CTA Article 142-4)

As PEs do not have capital, an amount of deemed capital attributable to the PE is calculated. If the net assets recognised in the PE are less than the deemed capital, interest expense corresponding to the difference is not deductible.

2. Domestic source income other than income attributable to the PE

Domestic source income, other than income attributable to a PE, which is subject to taxation under the Corporation Tax Act, is defined as the following domestic source income (CTA Article 141 (ii), CTA Article 138(1)(ii)-(vi)):

(1) Income arising from the use and holding of assets located in Japan
(2) Income arising from the transfer of assets located in Japan
(3) Consideration received by a corporation which conducts business for which the main activity is to provide personal services in Japan
(4) Consideration for the lease of real property located in Japan, any right on real property located in Japan
(5) Other domestic source income.

Income from such domestic sources is to be calculated in accordance with the calculation of income attributable to the PE (CTA Article 142-10).

The taxation of domestic source income other than the above will be completed by withholding at source.

The table below summarises the taxation implications for foreign corporations with a PE in Japan:

【An Abstract Regarding Taxation on Foreign Entities】

Classification / Income types			Foreign corporation with PE: Income attributed to PE	Foreign corporation with PE: Income unattributed to PE	Foreign corporation without PE	With-holding tax
Domestic Source Income	(Operating Income)		1. Income attributed to PE 【Corporation Tax】			None
	(1) Income arising from the use and holding of assets located in Japan			【Corporation Tax】	【Corporation Tax】	None None
	(2) Income arising from the transfer of assets located in Japan (only the case on the right side)	Transfer of real estate located in Japan				None (Note 1*)
		Transfer of rights on real property in Japan				
		Felling or transfer of forests located in Japan				None
		Transfer of shares in certain domestic corporations				
		Transfers of shares in domestic corporation similar to business transfer				
		Transfer of shares in real estate related domestic corporation				
		Transfer of shares in legal entities involved in the ownership and management of golf courses in Japan				
	(3) Compensation for personnel services rendered in Japan					20.42%
	(4) Rentals of domestic real estate					20.42%
	(5) Other domestic source income					None
	(6) Interests on Bonds			【Withholding tax only】	【Withholding tax only】	15.315%
	(7) Dividends					20.42%
	(8) Interests on Loan					20.42%
	(9) Royalties					20.42%
	(10) Rewards for advertisement					20.42%
	(11) Pension based on life insurance					20.42%
	(12) Compensation money for periodic deposit					15.315%
	(13) Profit from silent Partnership (TK/ Tokumei Kumiai)					20.42%
Income other than domestic source income			out of scope			None

Note 1: 10.21% of withholding tax on the transfer of land.

2: the above 7-14. refers to only Income tax law, and there is no distinction under corporation tax regulation.

3: withholding tax rates in here shows a sum of income tax and special income tax for reconstruction (Income tax * 102.1%).

(*Source*: National Tax Agency, translation from 'Revision of International Taxation Principles to align the Attribution Principle')

Q25 Documentation Obligations for PEs

We are a Japanese branch of a foreign corporation. We understand that we must prepare certain documents for corporation tax purposes. What kind of documents does this include?

A:

In addition to its obligation to maintain appropriate accounting books and records, and other documents to support the transactions recorded in its tax return (e.g., invoices, receipts, etc.), a Japanese branch is also required to prepare and maintain the following documents for corporation tax purposes:

(1) Documents describing transactions with third parties (i.e., transactions with third parties attributable to the PE).
(2) Documents describing dealings with the head office or other PEs.
(3) Documents relating to head office expense allocations.

Discussion

A branch is a form of PE (CTA Article 2(xii-xix) (a)). Therefore, the calculation of taxable income of a Japanese branch of a foreign corporation requires calculating the income attributable to that PE out of the total income earned by the foreign corporation.

The income attributable to a PE should be determined as if the PE were a business enterprise operating separately and independently from the foreign corporation, considering the functions performed and assets used by the PE, and any dealings between the PE and its head office or other PEs (CTA Article 138(1)(i)). In order to prove such calculation, a Japan PE is required to prepare and maintain the following documents:

(1) Documents describing transactions with third parties (i.e., transactions with third parties attributable to the PE).
(2) Documents describing dealings with the head office or other PEs.
(3) Documents relating to head office expense allocations.

1. Documents describing transactions with third parties attributable to the PE (CTA Article 146-2(1), CTAER Article 62-2)

Where a foreign corporation conducts business through a PE, the income attributable to the PE shall be the income that would be attributable to the PE if the PE were an enterprise conducting business independently from the foreign corporation, considering the functions performed by the PE, assets used in the PE, dealings between the PE and its head office, and any other relevant circumstances (CTA Article 138(1)(i)). For this reason, the portion of income arising from transactions conducted by a foreign corporation with third parties that is attributable to the PE shall be determined based on an analysis of the functions, assets and risks of the PE and its head office or other PEs (i.e., a functional analysis).

As a starting point, a foreign corporation with a PE is required to prepare and maintain the following documents describing transactions with third parties, where the income arising from those transactions is attributable to the PE:

(1) Documents describing the external transactions attributable to the PE.
(2) A statement of the assets and liabilities of the PE and its head office or other PEs in relation to these external transactions.
(3) Documents describing the functions performed by the PE and the head office or other PEs for these external transactions, and the risks associated with those functions.
(4) Documents describing the departments of the PE and its head office or other PEs relevant to the functions performed in relation to these external transactions, and the business of those departments.

2. Documents describing dealings (CTA Article 146-2(2), CTAER Article 62-3)

As the PE and its head office are the same legal entity, transactions between them are not legally transactions. For tax purposes, however, they are deemed to be as such, but are referred to as dealings, for clarification. Given the lack of legal effect, this makes the documentation of dealings more important, as they can materially affect the calculation of taxable income, as thus are liable to be scrutinised closely by the tax authorities.

The specific documentation requirements for dealings are as follows (CTAER Article 62-3):

(1) Order forms, contracts, invoices, receipts, quotations, other documents equivalent thereto or copies thereof stating the transfer of assets, provision of services or other facts.
(2) Details of assets and liabilities used by PE and head office in dealings.
(3) Statement of the functions performed by the PE and the head office and other PEs in dealings and the risks associated with those functions.
(4) Documents describing the departments relevant to the functions fulfilled by PE and the head office and other PEs in dealings and the nature of the business of those departments.
(5) Other documents evidencing the occurrence of facts related to the dealings.

3. Documents describing the allocation of head office expenses (CTA Article 142-7, CTAER Article 60-10)

Selling, general and administrative expenses incurred for both the business conducted through a PE and other businesses of a foreign corporation shall be deductible in the PE if they are appropriately allocated to the PE and documents describing the allocation process are maintained.

The following documents are required to be prepared and maintained in relation to head office expense allocations (CTAER Article 60-10):

(1) An explanation and description of the expenses, and confirmation that they were incurred for both the business carried out through the PE and other businesses
(2) Documents setting out the allocation method
(3) A statement of the reasons why the allocation method is reasonable.

Q26 Fiscal Year for Japanese Tax Purposes

We are a Japanese subsidiary of a US corporation. Our parent corporation's fiscal year end is the last Saturday in December. Is it possible to adopt the same fiscal year as our US parent?

A:

Some foreign corporations, particularly those headquartered in the US, have fiscal year ends on a specific day of the week, rather than on a fixed date such as the 31st of a month.

However, if the fiscal year end is determined on a specific day of the week, this may result in a fiscal year of more than one calendar year.

For corporate tax purposes, the fiscal year cannot exceed one calendar year. If it does, the taxable year should be divided into two periods of one calendar year and the remaining days. Therefore, from the Japanese tax perspective, it is not possible to set your fiscal year end for a specific day, such as the last Saturday in December.

Discussion

A fiscal year is defined as the period for calculation of assets and liabilities, and profits and losses, as specified in the articles of association of a corporation (CTA Article 13). However, if the fiscal year exceeds one calendar year, the tax year shall be divided into periods of one calendar year from the beginning of the fiscal year (or, if the last period is less than one calendar year, a period of less than one calendar year).

If your fiscal year end is the last Saturday in December, your fiscal year may be longer than one calendar year in some years.

It is therefore not possible to adopt such a fiscal year for tax purposes.

If such a fiscal year were adopted for accounting purposes, for example, the last Saturday in December 2021 would be 25 December and the last Saturday in December 2022 would be 31 December. For tax purposes, the 2022 fiscal year would therefore be separated into two fiscal periods: 26 December 2021 to 25 December 2022 and 26 December 2022 to 31 December 2022.

On the other hand, the 2023 accounting year would be from 1 January 2023 to 30 December 2023, which does not exceed one calendar year and would therefore be acceptable for tax purposes.

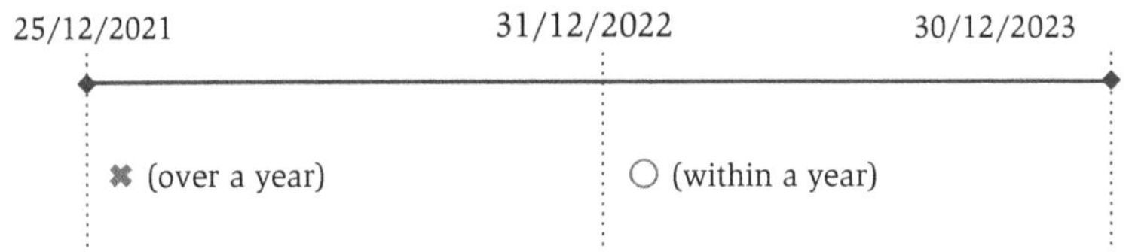

Q27 Tax Treatment of Small- and Medium-Sized Enterprises (SMEs)

We are a Japanese subsidiary of a foreign corporation, and have registered capital of JPY 1 million. Are there any special tax treatments for SMEs under the corporate tax?

A:

Even where a foreign parent corporation or corporate group is very large, its Japanese subsidiary is often similar in size to a Japanese SME. As there are specific corporate tax treatments applicable to SMEs, it is necessary to determine whether the Japanese subsidiary is classified as an SME under the corporate tax law. Moreover, as the definition of SME differs by tax provision, it is necessary to determine the Japanese subsidiary's classification under each separate law.

In addition, the size of the parent corporation is one factor in determining whether a corporation is an SME or not. Accordingly, although it may not be common practice elsewhere, it is important for a Japanese subsidiary to be aware of the relevant capital information of its parent corporation.

Discussion

SMEs are defined differently under different provisions of the corporate tax law. However, for a Japanese subsidiary operating as either a *kabushiki kaisha* ('KK', ordinary corporation) or *godo kaisha* ('GK', limited liability corporation), there are two main categories.

1. Corporations classified as an SME and which are not controlled by a large corporation with a capital of JPY 500 million or more

For the purpose of this provision, an SME is defined as a corporation with registered capital of JPY 100 million or less as of each fiscal year end, and which does not have a controlled relationship (i.e., is not wholly owned) with one or more large corporations (CTA Article 66(2), (6)).

In this case, a large corporation is a corporation with registered capital of JPY 500 million or more [when converting the registered capital of a foreign corporation denominated in foreign currency, the telegraphic transfer mid (TTM) rate on the last day of the fiscal year shall be used (Corporation Tax Basic Circular Article 16-5-2)].

The following special tax provisions can be applied to SMEs categorised as above.

(1) Exemption from additional corporation tax for family corporations (CTA Article 67)

The additional corporation tax for family corporations (*see* Q51) does not apply.

(2) Reductions in corporate tax rate (CTA Article 66(2), STMA Article 42-3-2)

SMEs are entitled to a reduced corporate tax rate of 15% on taxable income of JPY 8 million or less per year and 23.2% on taxable income in excess of JPY 8 million per year.

[The 15% rate is increased to 19% for corporations whose average taxable income for the three fiscal years preceding the fiscal year in question exceeds JPY 1.5 billion.]

(3) Special provision for bad debt reserves (STMA Article 57-9, CTA Article 52(1)(i)(a))

Bad debt reserves are generally not deductible for corporation tax purposes. SMEs are exempted from this non-deductible treatment.

(4) Special provision for entertainment expenses (STMA Article 61-4(2))

Apart from some limited exceptions, entertainment expenses are generally not deductible for corporation tax purposes. However, SMEs are able to deduct entertainment expenses of up to JPY 8 million.

(5) Exemption from limitation of carried forward tax losses (CTA Article 57 (1))

Tax losses carried forward can only be offset against current year taxable income up to a limit of 50% (*see* Q41). SMEs have no restriction on the amount of current year taxable income that can be offset by carry forward losses.

(6) Exemption from tax loss carry-back suspension (STMA 66-12)

Tax losses can be carried back by all corporations; however, this provision is currently suspended (other than for some limited exceptions).

SMEs are not subject to suspension and can carry losses back.

2. Corporations classified as an SME and which are not controlled by a large corporation with a capital of more than JPY 100 million

SMEs as defined in the following provisions are corporations with registered capital of JPY 100 million or less at each fiscal year end, other than the following corporations:

(1) Excluded corporations, i.e., corporations whose average taxable income for the three fiscal years preceding the fiscal year in question exceeds JPY 1.5 billion.
(2) Corporations in which more than 50% of their shares or capital contribution is owned by a single 'major corporation' (*see below* definition).
(3) Corporations where two-thirds or more of their shares or capital contributions are owned by a group of major corporations.'

'Major corporation' is defined as:

(i) Corporations with registered capital exceeding JPY 100 million.
(ii) Corporations with no registered capital but with more than 1,000 employees.
(iii) Corporations in a 100% controlled relationship with one single or multiple large corporations, which themselves have registered capital of JPY 500 million or more.

The following examples of special provisions can be applied to SMEs categorised above:

(1) Accelerated depreciation or tax credits on the acquisition of new equipment (STMA Article 42-6)

When SMEs acquire or manufacture new machinery or equipment, and which is used for certain designated businesses in Japan, such as manufacturing or construction, accelerated depreciation or a tax credit can be applied for the fiscal year that includes the date on which that machinery or equipment was put into use.

(2) Tax credit for increased salaries (STMA Article 42-12-5)

When a corporation increases the salaries paid to employees, and when certain conditions are met, 15% of the increase (25% if additional requirements are met) can be creditable against corporation tax.

(3) Deductible small assets (STMA Article 67-5)

When SMEs acquire depreciable assets with an acquisition cost of less than JPY 300,000, and use those assets for business purposes, the acquisition cost is deductible subject to certain conditions.

Q28 Revenue Recognition for Tax Purposes

We are a wholly owned subsidiary of a foreign corporation. We have recently concluded a contract to provide IT consulting services to a Japanese customer. Our services are customised to the IT system of each specific customer.

Under the terms of the contract, one of our employees will work at the customer's premises for one year to provide support for the system and to respond to ad hoc requests from the customer. We do not provide any deliverables under this contract, although we will submit monthly reports of the work performed to the customer.

The fee for the support services is a monthly fixed amount; however, it is invoiced as a single lump sum at the time of conclusion of the contract and is therefore received in advance.

When should this revenue be recognised for corporation tax purposes? We apply the Japanese GAAP revenue recognition standard for accounting purposes.

A:

Under the Japanese GAAP revenue recognition standard, the support services provided by you should be recognised over the period of the contract. The corporation tax law applies the same treatment.

Discussion

1. Overview of Japanese GAAP revenue recognition standard

The Japanese GAAP revenue recognition standard is effective for fiscal years beginning on or after 1 April 2021, and is aligned with IFRS 15.

Application of the Japanese GAAP revenue recognition standard is optional for SMEs under the 'Guidelines on Accounting for SMEs'. These guidelines are applied to all *kabushiki kaisha* (i.e., ordinary corporations) except for: (1) corporations subject to the Financial Instruments and Exchange Act (e.g., listed corporation), their subsidiaries and related corporations and (2) corporations having statutory accounting auditors (e.g., with registered capital of JPY 500 million or more, or with total liabilities of JPY 20 billion or more).

Under the Japanese GAAP revenue recognition standard, an entity shall recognise revenue over a specified period if it is considered to satisfy a performance obligation for or transfer control of an asset to a customer over that period because any of the following conditions are met (Revenue Recognition Standard Article 38):

(1) the customer simultaneously receives the benefits provided by the entity's performance as the entity performs.
(2) the entity's performance creates or enhances an asset that the customer controls as the asset is created or enhanced.
(3) All the following requirements must be met:;
    (i) the entity's performance does not create an asset with an alternative use to the entity; and

(ii) the entity has an enforceable right to payment for performance completed to date.

2. Overview of corporation tax law for revenue recognition

For corporation tax purposes, unless otherwise provided, profits are recognised in the fiscal year that includes the date of delivery of the goods or provision of the services generating the profit (CTA Article 22-2(1)).

However, if revenue is recognised based on the Japanese GAAP revenue recognition standard for accounting purposes, the same treatment should be applied for corporation tax purposes (CTA Article 22-2(2)).

Where services are provided over a certain period, the date of the provision of the services is each date in 'the period when the performance obligation is fulfilled' (Corporation Tax Basic Circular Article 2-1-21-2). 'The period when the performance obligation is fulfilled' is as follows.

(1) Where a deliverable is provided

From the date when services are commenced to the date on which the services are completed and the deliverable is delivered to the customer.

(2) Where no deliverable is provided

From the date when services are commenced to the date when the services are completed.

A performance obligation is fulfilled over a period if it satisfies one of the following conditions (Corporation Tax Basic Circular Article 2-1-21-4):

(1) The customer simultaneously receives the benefits provided by the entity's performance as the entity performs.
E.g., routine or recurring services, such as cleaning services.
(2) The entity's performance creates or enhances an asset that the customer controls as the asset is created or enhanced.
(3) All the following requirements are met:
 (i) the entity's performance does not create an asset with an alternative use to the entity;
 (ii) the entity has an enforceable right to payment for performance completed to date.

As explained above, when the corporation applies the Japanese GAAP revenue recognition standard, corporation tax law adopts the same treatment.

3. IT consulting services provided by you

Your IT consulting services can be categorised as follows:

(1) Your customer simultaneously receives the benefits provided by the performance of the services at the time your employee performs those services.
(2) The performance of the services creates or enhances an asset that your customer controls as the asset is created or enhanced.
(3) The performance of the services does not create an asset with an alternative use to the entity, given they are customised for your customer's specific IT system, and you have an enforceable right to payment for performance completed to date.

Given the above, as your IT consulting services meet the above conditions, the timing of revenue recognition is over a period under the Japanese GAAP revenue recognition standard. Similarly, for corporation tax purposes, the timing of revenue recognition is over a period.

Q29 Non-refundable Revenue Received in Advance

We provide software maintenance services to our customers in Japan.

When we provide these services, we receive a full year's revenue payment in advance from the customer upon conclusion of the contract. Under the terms of the contract, the revenue received is non-refundable under any circumstances, including termination of the services before the end of the contract period.

We treat such income as revenue received in advance on the date of receipt, and recognise it as income over the contract period. Is this treatment acceptable for corporation tax purposes? Note that for accounting purposes, we apply the Japanese GAAP revenue recognition standard.

A:

It is common practice for companies providing software maintenance services in Japan to receive payment for those services in advance from customers upon conclusion of the contract, which payment is non-refundable under any circumstances.

Under these contracts, the revenue received in advance has generally all been recorded as income at the time of receipt for corporation tax purposes.

However, if the revenue received in advance is a consideration for the provision of services during a specific period, and that revenue is recognised over a specific period for accounting purposes, that revenue received in advance may also be recognised as income over a specific period for corporation tax purposes.

Discussion

1. Treatment under Japanese GAAP revenue recognition standard

Under the Japanese GAAP revenue recognition standard, when an entity receives a non-refundable payment from a customer, it is necessary to determine whether the payment is related to a transfer of goods or the provision of services immediately, or at some time in the future. If it is not related to an immediate transfer of goods or services, the entity should recognise the revenue when it provides the goods or services in the future (Guidance on Revenue Recognition Standard Article 57, 58).

The one-year maintenance fee received by you is related to the provision of services in the future, as no services have been provided at the time the fees are received.

Therefore, for accounting purposes, the payment should be treated as the receipt of revenues in advance (i.e., a liability) and should not be treated as revenue at the time of receipt.

2. Treatment under corporation tax law

Under corporation tax law, if a corporation receives revenue in advance from a customer upon conclusion of a contract, and the corporation is not required to refund that payment to the customer in any circumstances, such payment should be recognised as revenue in the fiscal year in which it is received (Corporation Tax Basic Circular Article 2-1-40-2).

Examples of revenue received in advance which are not required to be refunded include the following:

(1) Upfront payment received as consideration for the grant of a licence of an industrial property right.
(2) Upfront or down payment received under a contract for the provision of know-how.
(3) Advances, start-up fees or similar payments from customers under contracts for the provision of technical services, other than those which are to be settled later and any surplus refunded.
(4) Admission fees on signing up for membership of a sports club.

On the other hand, if the revenue received in advance is consideration for the provision of services during a specific period and the revenue is recognised over a specific period for accounting purposes, such payment may also be treated as revenue received in advance and recognised as income over the period for corporation tax purposes.

You will provide services to your customer over a specific period of time specified in the contract, and the services fees you will receive correspond to the term of the contract. Therefore, if the revenue is recognised over the contract period for accounting purposes under the Japanese GAAP revenue recognition standard, the same treatment should be accepted for corporation tax purposes.

In order to receive this treatment, however, the written contract terms and conditions must specify that the payment corresponds to the specified contract period and scope of services.

Q30 Deductibility of Reasonably Estimated Provisions

We recognise a bonus provision each fiscal year for accounting purposes. The amount of the bonus provision is reasonably estimated and is approximately the same amount as the actual amount paid in the subsequent year. Is such reasonably estimated provision deductible for corporation tax purposes?

A:

For accounting purposes, it is common practice, particularly for foreign corporations, to recognise various different types of provision allowance, or accrued expense, on an estimated basis. The corresponding liability is determined by the end of the fiscal year at the end of the relevant period.

Such estimated provisions, allowances or accruals are not deductible for corporation tax purposes even if reasonably estimated, as they generally do not meet the requirements for the determination of liabilities under corporation tax act.

Therefore, expenses for bonus provision should generally not be deductible, unless the conditions for special treatment of accrued bonuses are met.

Discussion

For the calculation of taxable income for corporation tax purposes, the amount of deductible expenses for each fiscal year is, in principle, the amount of cost of sales, selling, general and administrative expenses and other expenses and losses (CTA Article 22(3)).

However, selling, general and administrative expenses and other costs, except for depreciation expenses, are limited to those for which the corresponding liability is determined by the end of the fiscal year in question.

Expenses, other than depreciation expenses, for which the corresponding liability has been determined by the end of the fiscal year, are generally defined as those that meet all the following requirements (Corporation Tax Basic Circular Article 2-2-12):

(1) a liability corresponding to such expenses has been established by the end of the fiscal year;
(2) the facts giving rise to the obligation to provide specific benefits for the bonus that the provision is designed to cover have occurred by the end of the fiscal year; and
(3) the amount can be reasonably calculated by the end of the fiscal year.

For accounting purposes, on the other hand, provisions or allowances shall generally be recognised if all the following are fulfilled:

(1) there is a specific future expense or loss;
(2) the expense or loss is attributable to an event occurring before the current period;
(3) the expenses are highly likely to occur; and

(4) the amount can be reasonably estimated.

As set out above, there is difference in the requirements for a provision or allowance for accounting purposes and the requirements for a provision or allowance for tax purposes. In particular, as a provision or allowance for accounting purposes is a specific future expense or loss, it is generally not required to have a corresponding liability for such expense at the end of the fiscal year.

Accordingly, provisions or allowances are not considered to be liabilities for tax purposes, and related expenses are not deductible.

However, in the case of an accrued bonus to employees, the bonus shall basically be deemed to have been paid in the fiscal year in which the notice is given, if all the following conditions are met (CTAEO Article 72-3):

(1) The bonus amount to be paid must be notified to all eligible employees at the same time.
(2) The noticed amount has been paid to all eligible employees within one month after the end of the fiscal year.
(3) The bonus is recorded as an expense for accounting purposes in the fiscal year in which the employees are given notice.

In summary, a bonus provision should generally not be deductible, unless the conditions for special treatment for accrued bonuses are met.

Q31 Tax Treatment of Remuneration for Seconded Directors

The representative director of our corporation is an expatriate seconded from our foreign parent. Our parent pays the director's remuneration directly to the director, but recharges us as salary contribution. The salary contribution charges are the same amount every month. Is this salary contribution charged by our foreign parent deductible for corporation tax purposes?

A:

Directors of Japanese subsidiaries of foreign headquartered corporations are often seconded from a foreign parent or related corporation. Although the foreign corporation pays the director directly, the Japanese subsidiary is usually required to bear the equivalent cost.

Where an amount equal to the amount of remuneration paid to a director is recharged to a Japanese corporation, it may be treated as salary paid directly to the director if it meets the following requirements:

(1) The amount is approved at a general shareholders' meeting.
(2) A secondment agreement has been concluded between the foreign corporation and the Japanese subsidiary, which stipulates the period of secondment and the amount of salary contribution in advance.
(3) The remuneration is paid to the parent corporation in a fixed amount each month.

Discussion

1. Fixed periodical remuneration

Remuneration paid by a corporation to its directors is not deductible for Japanese corporation tax purposes unless the following requirements are met (CTA Article 34(1)):

(1) The remuneration is paid periodically in a fixed amount.
(2) The amount of remuneration is fixed and notified in advance.
(3) The remuneration is performance based.

Notwithstanding the above, any part of the remuneration that is considered unreasonably high will be treated as a non-deductible expense.

For the purposes of this discussion, remuneration does not include the following payments:

(1) Severance payments, which are not performance-based remuneration.
(2) Any portion of the remuneration that is paid as remuneration of an employee, for directors who are also employees.

(3) Remuneration paid to director that is concealed or hidden by the corporation in its accounting books.

Fixed periodical remuneration refers to the following types of payments (CTA Article 34(1), CTAEO Article 69(1)):

- Remuneration paid every month or less ('fixed periodical remuneration'), where the amount of remuneration (with or without withholding tax and social insurance) is the same each payment period in the fiscal year.
- If the fixed periodical remuneration is revised ('revision of remuneration'), the amount of remuneration (with or without withholding tax and social insurance) is the same from the beginning of the fiscal year to the day before the first payment of the revision of remuneration, and is the same from the following day of the last payment period before the revision of remuneration to the fiscal year end.
- Economic benefits provided continually throughout the fiscal year which are fixed each month.

2. Remuneration to seconded directors

It is common practice that a foreign corporation will pay seconded directors directly, and then recharge that cost to the Japanese subsidiary as salary contribution. If the following requirements are met, that salary contribution may be deemed to be remuneration paid to the director for corporation tax purposes (Corporation Tax Basic Circular Article 9-2-46):

(1) the salary contribution is approved at a shareholders' meeting,
(2) the period of secondment and the amount of salary contribution are specified in advance in the secondment contract.

In summary, if all the following requirements are met, the salary contribution you are recharged can be deductible for corporation tax purposes:

(1) A shareholders' meeting resolved that director's remuneration was an amount equivalent to the salary contribution.
(2) There is a secondment agreement between you and your parent executed in advance which specifies the term of the secondment and the amount of the salary contribution.
(3) The same amount of salary contribution is paid to your parent every month.

Q32 Tax Treatment of Net Guaranteed Directors' Remuneration Paid in Foreign Currency

Our director is paid a fixed amount each month, but that amount is denominated in foreign currency. Due to fluctuations in the exchange rate, the monthly amount in Japanese yen fluctuates.

In addition, under a net guarantee agreement with the director, we are liable for taxes and social insurance in Japan. As a result, the gross remuneration varies each month.

Is the amount paid to the director deductible each month?

A:

Directors of Japanese subsidiaries of foreign headquartered corporations are often seconded from the foreign parent or related corporation. Although the foreign corporation pays the remuneration to the director directly, the Japanese subsidiary is generally required to bear the cost.

When the remuneration is paid directly by a foreign corporation, it is often fixed in foreign currency. In addition, remuneration paid to seconded directors is often guaranteed on a net basis.

As a result, the gross Japanese yen-based director's remuneration may not be fixed on a monthly basis but is likely to fluctuate.

However, remuneration denominated in a foreign currency and fixed on a net basis is still considered to be fixed periodical remuneration for corporation tax purposes.

Discussion

1. Directors' remuneration paid in foreign currency

Fixed periodical remuneration paid to directors (paid every month or less) is treated as a deductible expense for the calculation of a corporation's taxable income (CTA Article 34).

However, it is not necessary to fix the amount in Japanese yen. Thus, if the remuneration is denominated and fixed periodically in foreign currency, it can still be treated as fixed for corporation tax purposes.

2. Net guaranteed directors' remuneration

If directors' remuneration is guaranteed at a fixed amount after deducting withholding tax, inhabitant tax and social insurance, the net remuneration is deemed to be fixed (CTAEO Article 69 (2)). Therefore, net guaranteed remuneration that is fixed every month is treated as fixed periodical remuneration.

In summary, directors' remuneration denominated in foreign currency and net guaranteed in a fixed amount paid periodically can be treated as fixed periodical remuneration and therefore deductible for corporation tax purposes.

If the director is seconded from a foreign corporation, the requirements of Q31 must also be met.

Q33 Tax Treatment of Charges for Share-Based Compensation

We are a Japanese subsidiary of a US corporation. Our US parent has granted shares to its directors and employees in the US, which have the following characteristics:

- The shares are not transferable for two years from the date of grant.
- In certain cases, such as retirement during the two-year period, the parent corporation acquires the shares from the director or employee without payment.

Our parent is considering granting shares on similar terms to our directors and employees.

The parent corporation will recharge us for the cost of these shares. Is the recharged expense deductible for corporation tax purposes?

A:

It is common practice for foreign corporations to grant shares as remuneration to directors and employees ('share-based compensation'). The shares granted as remuneration are generally subject to certain restrictions, such as being non-transferable for a certain period.

Share-based compensation is often granted not only to the directors and employees of the corporation issuing the shares but also to the directors and employees of related corporations within the group. If such share-based compensation is granted to an employee of a Japanese subsidiary, the recharged cost may be deductible when the employee is subject to income tax on those shares if they are classified as 'specified restricted shares' under the corporation tax law. In the case of directors, the recharged cost is only deductible if it is classified as fixed monthly remuneration and is notified in advance.

Discussion

1. 'Restricted shares' and 'specified restricted shares'

'Restricted shares' are shares that meet the following requirements (CTA Article 54(1), CTAEO Article 111-2(1)):

(1) The transfer of shares must be restricted, and there must be a restriction period on the transfer.
(2) The reason for allocating shares without consideration (or the reason for forfeiture) by the corporation receiving the services or the corporation that issued or delivered the shares must be specified.

Furthermore, restricted shares that meet the either of following requirements are classified as 'specified restricted shares' (CTA Article 54(1)):

(1) Restricted shares are delivered to an individual in exchange for the performance of services by that individual.
(2) Restricted shares other than (1) are effectively a consideration for the provision of services.

Even if the corporation receiving the services from the individual is not the corporation issuing the specified restricted shares, if the above requirements are met, the shares can be classified as specified restricted shares. Therefore, restricted shares received by directors or employees of a Japanese subsidiary from a foreign corporation will also be treated as specified restricted shares if the above requirements are met.

2. Deductibility of expenses recharged for specified restricted shares

When a corporation receives services from an individual, the cost of the services is deductible if its consideration is specified restricted shares. However, the cost is only deductible at the date the income for the employee is taxed ('salary taxation date') (CTA Article 54(1)).

The salary taxation date is the date on which the restriction on the transfer of specified restricted shares is released (Income Tax Basic Circular Article 23-35 Common 5-3).

The deductible amount is considered to be the amount equivalent to the amount the employee is entitled to in consideration for the provision of services, and which is extinguished upon delivery of the specified restricted shares (CTAEO Article 111-2 (4)). If the salary is stipulated as a fixed number of shares delivered on a predetermined date (CTAEO Article 71-3(1)), the deductible expense will be calculated based on the market price on the date on which the stipulation is made.

Therefore, in principle, the cost of restricted shares charged from your parent will be deductible if it is determined as above.

3. Deductibility of directors' remuneration recharged for specified restricted shares

Expenses for specified restricted shares paid to directors as compensation are only deductible if the requirements for fixed periodic remuneration notified in advance are satisfied (CTA Article 34 (1) (ii)).

If the number of specific restricted shares to be acquired without payment varies for reasons other than the period of service, such shares are not considered fixed periodic remuneration and are therefore not deductible.

Q34 Acquisition Cost of Inventories for Tax Purposes

We import goods from our foreign parent and sell them to our customers in Japan.

The purchase price of the goods is agreed with our parent. In addition to the purchase price, we also bear incidental costs, such as import duties, customs clearance, and transportation costs from the point of importation to our warehouse.

We record such incidental costs as expenses for accounting purposes. Are these costs also deductible for corporation tax purposes?

A:

Japanese subsidiaries of foreign corporations often record incidental costs related to the acquisition of inventories as expenses for accounting purposes.

However, all such costs should be treated as inventory acquisition costs for corporation tax purposes. A tax adjustment must be made in the corporation tax return for the difference between the accounting and the tax treatment.

Discussion

For corporation tax purposes, inventory acquisition costs are the total of the following items (CTAEO Article 32(1)(i)):

- Consideration for the purchase of the inventory, including any costs incurred for the purchase, such as freight, loading costs, transport insurance, procurement commissions, customs duty and any other costs incurred for the purchase.
- Costs directly incurred to consume the inventory or to make it available for sale.

On the other hand, the following may not be included in the cost of acquisition if the total amount is small (approximately 3 % or less of the inventory price) (Corporation Tax Basic Circular Article 5-1-1).

- Costs incurred for such as purchasing administration, inspection, and sorting.
- Freight, packaging and other costs incurred in transferring inventory from one sales location to another.
- Costs incurred in storing inventory for a long period of time, for example, for sale at a special time.

The costs you have incurred and recorded as expenses are import duties, customs clearance, and transportation costs from the point of importation to your warehouse. Foreign corporations often record such incidental costs relating to the acquisition of inventory as expenses for accounting purposes. On the other hand, the corporation tax law requires such incidental expenses to be included in the inventory acquisition cost.

As such, there is difference between your accounting treatment and the required tax treatment, and therefore such expenses must be added back to taxable income in your corporation tax return.

Q35 Tax Depreciation of Fixed Assets

We are a Japanese subsidiary of a US corporation, and our calculation of fixed asset depreciation is based on our group accounting policies. This means that the useful lives of our fixed assets are based on economic estimates and that all assets are depreciated on a straight-line basis.

For corporation tax purposes, what method should we use to depreciate our fixed assets?

A:

Most foreign corporations have accounting policies that depreciate fixed assets using the unified depreciation method and useful life. For corporation tax purposes, depreciation methods and useful lives are defined by statute. Therefore, the deductible depreciation amount for corporation tax purposes must be calculated, and an adjustment be made to the depreciation expenses recorded for accounting purposes. This will create either excess depreciation or a shortage of depreciation.

The excess and shortage of depreciation affect the calculation of deductible depreciation each year, so Japanese subsidiaries of foreign corporations are generally required to carefully manage their fixed asset register every year.

Considering the administrative complexity of this process, it is preferable to match the accounting depreciation calculation with the tax depreciation calculation. However, in practice, it is difficult for foreign corporations to do so. It is recommended to match the depreciation method for accounting and tax purposes (e.g., straight-line method) by submitting a 'Notification of depreciation method'.

Discussion

Under the corporation tax law, 'depreciation expense' is only deductible up to the limit set by the law (CTA Article 31 (1)). Depreciation expense is generally calculated using acquisition cost, depreciated at a rate over a useful life both of which are prescribed under the law for each type of asset.

1. Useful life

Useful life is defined in detail according to the 'type of asset' and 'structure or use' (CTAEO Article 56, Annexes 1 to 6 of the Ministerial Ordinance on Useful Life).

2. Depreciation method

Corporations can choose the straight-line or declining method for depreciation of fixed assets (CTA Article 31(1), CTAEO Article 48). However, some fixed assets, such as buildings and leasehold improvements, may only be depreciated using the straight-line method.

Except for buildings and leasehold improvements for which the depreciation method is prescribed by law, the declining method is deemed to be chosen unless the corporation submits a 'notification of depreciation method' to the competent national tax office (CTA Article 53).

3. Excess or shortage of depreciation

Under the corporation tax law, depreciation expense is deductible to the extent that the corporation recognises it as a depreciation expense for accounting purposes (CTA Article 31(1)).

In addition, if the accounting depreciation expense is less than the depreciation expense limit for tax purposes, the shortage cannot generally be deducted for tax purposes. This shortage is discarded in the calculation of the tax depreciation expense in the following years.

On the other hand, if the accounting depreciation expense exceeds the depreciation expense limit for tax purposes, the excess is not deductible for tax purposes. This excess is added to the book value of the fixed assets for tax purposes (i.e., as a result, there is a difference between the book value of the asset for accounting purposes and the book value for tax purposes). Excess depreciation is deferred and will be deductible in the event of a future shortage of depreciation expense for the same asset.

The calculation of the deductible depreciation expense (including any excess or shortage of depreciation expense) must be determined for each fixed asset.

As discussed above, the calculation of depreciation is very complicated when accounting depreciation expenses differ from tax depreciation expenses. The calculation is further complicated when a corporation has some fixed assets that have excess depreciation and others that have a shortage. As both excess and shortage of depreciation may affect the depreciation calculation in future years, it is necessary to manage each fixed asset every year.

Considering this administrative complexity, it is preferable if the accounting depreciation calculation and the tax depreciation calculation can be aligned. However, in practice, especially for foreign corporations, it is generally difficult to do so, because of the requirement to comply with group accounting policies.

The next best solution is therefore to submit a 'notification of depreciation method' so that the accounting and tax depreciation methods can be consistent. Once this is done, the difference between the two is only the useful life. As the useful life for accounting purposes is generally shorter than the useful life for tax purposes, it is generally only excess depreciation that is calculated for newly acquired assets, which reduces some of the administrative complexity.

Many foreign corporations have difficulty in managing their Japanese fixed asset depreciation. However, there are a number of Japanese software applications that can help to manage this calculation.

Q36 Tax Requirement to Recognise Depreciation Expenses for Accounting Purposes

Under our group accounting policy, we only capitalise assets where the acquisition cost exceeds USD 10,000.

We recently acquired an asset with an acquisition cost of JPY 800,000 and, in accordance with our group accounting policy, we have recorded it as a supply expense.

For tax purposes, we understand that the JPY 800,000 must be added back to fixed assets, and depreciation for corporation tax purposes must be separately calculated and deducted from taxable income (with a statutory useful life of five years).

Is this depreciation expense deductible for tax purposes?

A:

Many foreign corporations have their own criteria for capitalisation of fixed assets under the group accounting policy.

On the other hand, under corporation tax law, assets with an acquisition value of less than JPY 100,000 generally do not have to be capitalised and can be recorded as deductible expenses. However, under the group accounting policy of most foreign corporations, assets of more than JPY 100,000 are often recorded as expenses for accounting purposes. Consequently, there will be a difference between the accounting treatment (i.e., expense) and the tax treatment (i.e., fixed asset). An adjustment must be made for this difference in the corporation tax returns,

In addition, if the corporation records an expense other than depreciation, it will not satisfy the requirement for tax deductibility since the corporation has not recorded a 'depreciation expense' for accounting purposes.

However, as an exception to this rule, if the corporation adds the expense to its fixed assets for tax purposes and calculates tax depreciation in its tax return (Schedule 16), such depreciation expense can be deductible for tax purposes.

Discussion

1. Capitalisation of fixed assets

Under corporation tax law, assets with a useful life of less than one year or with an acquisition cost of less than JPY 100,000 do not need to be capitalised as fixed assets (CTAEO Article 133). Assets with a useful life of more than one year and an acquisition cost of JPY 100,000 or more must be capitalised as fixed assets.

Since the asset purchased by you in this case has an acquisition value of JPY 800,000 and a useful life of five years, it should be recorded as a fixed asset for corporation tax purposes.

2. Accounting for depreciation as a tax-deductible expense

Under corporation tax law, depreciation expense that is deductible for tax purposes is limited to the depreciation expense that is recorded as such for accounting purposes (CTA Article 31).

The depreciation expense charged as such for accounting purposes includes not only the amount of depreciation expense itself but also the following (Corporate Tax Basic Circular Article 7-5-1):

(1) Incidental costs included in the acquisition cost of depreciable assets for tax purposes that are charged to expenses for accounting purposes.
(2) Where the book value of a depreciable asset has been reduced by more than the limit of the advance depreciation amount, the excess amount.
(3) Amounts spent on depreciable assets that were recorded as repair costs for accounting purposes, but are not deductible for tax purposes.
(4) In the case of a depreciable asset acquired free of charge or at a lower cost, if the amount the corporation has accounted for as the acquisition cost is lower than the actual value of the asset at the time of acquisition, the lower value.
(5) The loss on disposal or loss on valuation of depreciable assets not deductible for tax purposes.
(6) In the case that the acquisition cost of a smaller depreciable asset (generally less than JPY 600,000) or a depreciable asset with a useful life of less than three years recorded as supplies for accounting purposes, the amount of the expenses which are treated as supplies.
(7) The amount recorded as research and development expenses which should be capitalised as software.

Assets recorded as supplies do not fall into any of the above categories and are therefore not included in the amount recorded as 'depreciation expenses'.

However, as an exception, if a corporation added such expenses to fixed assets in its tax return (or amended tax return) (i.e., Schedule 16, 'Statement of Depreciation') for the fiscal year in which the corporation has commenced to use the assets for its business, the amount stated in Schedule 16 can be deemed as 'depreciation expenses' for accounting purposes (Corporation Tax Basic Circular Article 7-5-2). As a result, the depreciation to the limit of tax depreciation can be deductible.

Given the above, the assets which you have acquired and recorded as supplies can be deemed as 'depreciation expense' for corporation tax purposes and can be deductible to the limit of tax depreciation if you add such expense to fixed assets for tax purposes, list them in the Schedule 16, and calculate the tax depreciation expense.

Q37 Tax Treatment of Bad Debt Losses

One of our customers, with whom we had been doing business for a long time, has fallen into financial difficulties and has not yet paid our account.

Under our group accounting policy, a bad debt reserve of 50% of the amount of a receivable is established if collection is delayed more than three months. In the event of a delay of more than six months, the full amount of a receivable is recorded as a bad debt loss.

Since the payment from the customer has been delayed for more than six months, we have recorded the full amount of the account as a bad debt loss. Is such bad debt loss deductible for corporation tax purposes?

The payment of our account has been delayed, but our customer has not been subject to bankruptcy, corporate reorganisation or any other legal proceeding.

A:

For corporation tax purposes, there are strict requirements for the recognition of bad debt losses, which are only deductible in certain circumstances, such as legal procedures for bankruptcy. Multinational corporations, on the other hand, generally record bad debt losses in accordance with their group accounting policies. Where those accounting policies do not meet the tax requirements, such bad debt losses should be added back to taxable income for tax purposes.

Discussion

Bad debt losses are deductible under generally accepted accounting principles. However, as it is often very difficult to establish the facts relating to the determination of bad debts, a general standard for the deductibility of bad debt losses is set out in the Corporation Tax Basic Circular.

Under this circular, bad debt losses are divided into three categories and treated as follows.

1. Bad debt losses where a receivable has been waived under the law (legal bad debt losses) (Corporation Tax Basic Circular 9-6-1)

(1) Amounts waived in accordance with the provisions of the Corporate Reorganization Act, Act on Special Measures for the Reorganization Proceedings of Financial Institutions, the Companies Act, and the Civil Rehabilitation Act.
(2) Amounts waived on a reasonable basis at a voluntary meeting of creditors not governed by law, or at a discussion mediated by a government or financial institution.
(3) Amounts waived in writing to the debtor when the debtor has been insolvent for a considerable period and is unable to meet its debts.

2. Bad debt losses where a receivable is effectively uncollectible (factual bad debt) (Corporation Tax Basic Circular 9-6-2)

If it becomes apparent that the creditor is unable to collect the full amount of the debt due to the debtor's lack of assets or inability to pay, the receivables can be treated as uncollectible in the fiscal year in which this state of affairs becomes apparent. However, if there is any collateral related to the receivable, the receivable will not be deemed to be uncollectible until the collateral has been disposed of.

Similarly, where a guarantee has been given, the receivable will not be considered uncollectible until after the guarantee has been fulfilled.

3. Bad debts where a receivable is formally considered uncollectible (formal bad debt losses) (Corporation Tax Basic Circular 9-6-3)

Where any of the following events occurs, the amount of an account receivable less any residual value (generally JPY 1) can be treated as a bad debt loss. Formal bad debt losses are limited to accounts receivable and therefore do not include other receivables, such as loans:

(1) Where a debtor with whom the corporation has had a continuous business relationship ceases to do business due to deterioration in the debtor's assets or inability to pay, at least one year must have elapsed since the latest of the time of the cessation of business and the time of the last payment (except in the case where the receivables are secured by collateral). Note that this treatment does not apply to account receivables from debtors with whom the creditor does not have continuous business relationship, such as real estate transactions.

(2) Where the total amount of accounts receivable from debtors in the same geographical area is less than the collection costs and no payment has been made after reminding the debtors to pay.

As your case does not fall into any of the above categories, it cannot be treated as a bad debt loss for tax purposes.

However, if you cannot collect the account receivable for more than one year from the date of cessation of business with the customer, the amount less the residual value may potentially be treated as a deductible bad debt loss for tax purposes.

The above can be summarised as shown in the following figure:

Classification	Types of accounts receivable	Facts relating to the bad debt	Deductible amount	Fiscal year deductible	Recorded as expense in accounts
1. Legal bad debt	Monetary claims	i. A reorganisation plan under the Corporate Reorganisation Act or Act on Special Measures for the Reorganization Proceedings of Financial Institutions or a rehabilitation plan under the Civil Rehabilitation Law is approved	The amount not collectable as a result of the decision	Fiscal year in which the decision is made	Not necessary
		ii. Special liquidation under the Companies Act			
		iii. Decision made by stakeholders and not governed by statutory provision			
		iv. When the debtor's insolvency has continued for a considerable period and it is considered that the debtor will not be able to repay the monetary claim	The amount of the debt waiver stated in the documents	Fiscal year in which notice is given to the debtor	
2. Factual bad debt		When it is clear that the collection of the entire amount is unlikely due to insolvency or inability to repay for a certain period of time	The total amount of the monetary claim	Fiscal year in which the creditor recognises the uncollectible account	Necessary
3. Formal bad debt	Accounts receivable only	One year or more has passed since transactions with the debtor have ceased (excluding cases where there is collateral)	The total account receivable after deduction of residual value	Fiscal year after one year or more have passed since transactions ceased	
		Total amount of accounts receivable does not cover the costs of collection (e.g., travel expenses), and no repayment has been made after a reminder has been sent		Fiscal year after no repayment has been recognised	

Q38 Timing of Deductibility of Corporate Enterprise Tax

We understand that corporate enterprise tax is deductible for corporation tax purposes. When is it deductible?

A:

In principle, corporate enterprise tax is deductible in the fiscal year in which the corporate enterprise tax return is submitted.

However, there is a special provision that allows corporate enterprise tax for the immediately preceding fiscal year to be deductible even if a corporate enterprise tax return has not been submitted.

It is a unique feature of Japanese corporation tax law that corporate enterprise tax, an income-based tax, is deductible.

Discussion

1. Scope of taxes and dues deductible for tax purposes

The major taxes and dues that are not deductible for corporation tax purposes are as follows (CTA Article 38, Article 39-2, Article 40, Article 41):

(1) Corporation tax, local corporation tax, corporate prefectural inhabitant tax and corporate municipal inhabitant tax.
(2) Additional taxes and surcharges, delinquent taxes (excluding delinquent taxes related to the extension of the due date for local taxes), negligent taxes, and heavy penalty taxes.
(3) Fines and penalties (including those equivalents to fines or penalties imposed by foreign countries or foreign local authorities).
(4) Income tax, special income tax for reconstruction, and foreign income tax to be credited against corporation tax.
(5) Foreign withholding tax on dividends from foreign subsidiaries, which is not included in taxable income.

Taxes and dues other than those mentioned above can be deducted under the corporation tax law.

2. Timing of deductibility of corporate enterprise tax

Since corporate enterprise tax is not included in the above non-deductible taxes and dues, it is deductible for corporation tax purposes.

As corporate enterprise tax is a self-assessed tax, it is generally deductible for the fiscal year that includes the date of submission of the corporate enterprise tax return (Corporation Tax Basic Circular Article 9-5-1). For example, the corporate enterprise tax return for the fiscal year ending 31 December 2022 will be submitted during the fiscal year ending 31 December 2023. As a result, corporate enterprise tax for the fiscal year ending 31 December 2022 will be deductible in the fiscal year ending 31 December 2023.

On the other hand, pursuant to a special provision, corporate enterprise tax for the immediately preceding fiscal year can be deducted even if a corporate enterprise tax return has not been submitted (Corporation Tax Basic Circular Article 9-5-2).

This provision is applied, for example, when a tax audit results in the submission of an amended corporate enterprise tax return for a prior period. In this case, there would be an increase in not only the corporation tax amount for the prior period but also the amount of corporate inhabitant tax and corporate enterprise tax. In accordance with the general rule, this increase in corporate enterprise tax is deductible in the year in which the amended corporate enterprise tax return is submitted. However, with the application of the special provision, it is possible to deduct the increased corporate enterprise tax for the immediately preceding financial year without having to wait for an amended corporate enterprise tax return to be submitted.

This provision is illustrated in the following diagram:

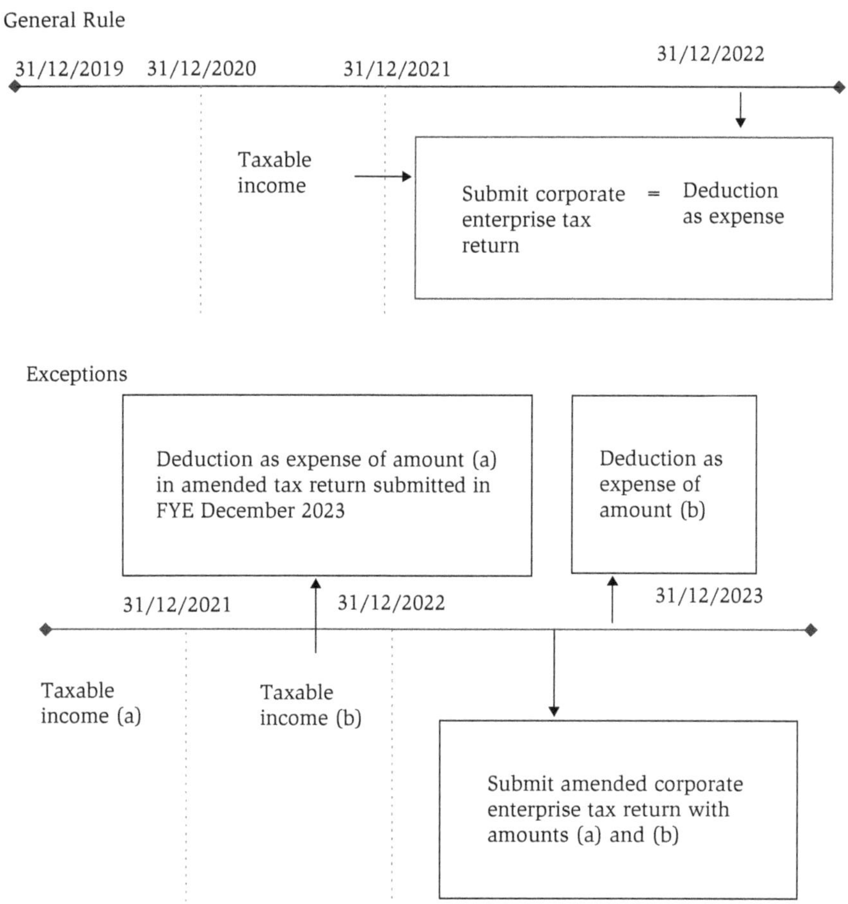

This means that any increase in the amount of corporate enterprise tax resulting from an amended return for the year ending 31 December 2021 will be deductible in the amended return in the year ending 31 December 2022, which is filed during the fiscal year ending 31 December 2023.

In the event of an assessment or decision due to a tax audit, the deductible amount of corporate enterprise tax shall be calculated at the standard corporate enterprise tax rate, and any difference between the actual corporate enterprise tax amount and the deducted corporate enterprise tax shall be included in the taxable income for the fiscal year that includes the date on which the amended corporate enterprise tax return is actually submitted.

Q39 Transfer of Economic Benefit ('Donation') to Foreign-Related Corporation

Our US parent established a new subsidiary in China. As requested by our parent, we have paid consulting fees to third parties related to the establishment of the Chinese subsidiary. Can we deduct these consulting fees for tax purposes?

A:

Consulting fees incurred in relation to the establishment of the Chinese subsidiary should be an expense of that subsidiary, and are not deductible for you. Any deduction would be disallowed by the tax authorities as transfer of economic benefit to the Chinese subsidiary, generally referred to as a 'donation' under domestic tax law.

Discussion

1. Definition of 'donation'

For corporation tax purposes, 'donation' is any amount of money, the value of assets, or the value of other economic benefits transferred by a domestic corporation gratuitously, regardless of whether the word 'donation' or any other term is used (CTA Article 37(vii)). Advertising costs, samples, and other similar costs, as well as entertainment, hospitality, and welfare costs, are excluded from the definition.

Where consideration for the transfer of an asset or provision of services is lower than the actual value, the difference between the consideration and the value is also treated as a donation (CTA Article 37(8)).

In other words, for corporation tax purposes, any transaction conducted by a corporation for which there is no consideration is treated as a donation. In addition, even if there is consideration, if the consideration is lower than the actual value, the difference between the actual value and the consideration will also be treated as a donation.

Consideration here refers to corresponding benefit from the other party to the transaction. Therefore, if there is no such benefit, the transaction will be treated as a donation. Even if there is a corresponding benefit, if the value is less than the corporation's expenditure, the difference will be considered a donation.

When analysing if a donation has been made, it is only necessary that economic value is transferred to the other party without consideration. It is not necessary to determine if the corporation had the intention to make a donation. Consequently, the concept of a donation under domestic tax law is broader than in general use.

Donations other than to the national government, specified public interest incorporated foundation, or authorised non-profit organisation, are deductible to the following limit:

> Deductible donation: [capital and capital surplus for tax purposes * 0.25% + taxable income *2.5%]*0.25

2. Applicability of the donation concept to the consulting fees paid for the Chinese subsidiary

The beneficiary of the consulting fees is the Chinese subsidiary (or, potentially, your US parent, depending on the nature of the consulting services provided). Therefore, the Chinese subsidiary (or US parent) would normally bear the consulting fees.

If you bear an expense like consulting fees, which should normally be borne by another corporation, this will be treated as the transfer of economic benefit to that other corporation and therefore a donation for corporation tax purposes.

In addition, the entire amount of a donation to a foreign-related corporation (i.e., a foreign corporation that has a capital relationship of 50% or more with another corporation or other controlled relationship) is treated as a non-deductible expense (STMA Article 66-4(3)).

As a result, the consulting fees paid for the Chinese subsidiary should be treated as non-deductible expenses for corporation tax purposes.

As mentioned above, a donation for corporation tax purposes is broader in meaning than commonly used, so it may be confusing to see the term 'donation' used in such situations. Nevertheless, 'donation' is commonly used for Japanese tax purposes.

Q40 Deductibility of Entertainment Expenses for Directors of a Foreign Parent Corporation

We are a Japanese subsidiary of a foreign corporation. Our directors and employees of our foreign parent visited Japan for business, and we arranged a dinner for them, which cost more than JPY 5,000 per person. Can we claim a deduction for the dinner expense even though the attendees were directors and employees of our parent?
Is there a difference if the director is also one of our non-executive directors?

A:

Generally, regardless of who is attending, expenses incurred to provide meals or drinks for persons outside the corporation are treated as entertainment expenses ('external entertainment expenses').

If the external entertainment expenses are JPY 5,000 or less per person, they are treated as deductible expenses. On the other hand, if the amount is more than JPY 5,000 per person, 50% of the amount is deductible for corporations with a registered capital of JPY 10 billion or less.

If one of your parent's directors is also one of your non-executive directors, you will need to determine whether the director attended the dinner as a director of your parent or as your non-executive director. If the former, the expenses incurred should be treated as external entertainment expenses.

Discussion

1. Scope of entertainment expenses

Entertainment expenses are expenses incurred for entertainment, by a corporation for the purpose of receiving or entertaining its customers or suppliers, presenting gifts to them, or other similar activities.

Entertainment expenses paid by a corporation each fiscal year beginning on or before 31 March 2022 are not deductible. However, an exception is made for corporations with capital of JPY 10 billion or less, who can deduct 50/100 of their entertainment expenses (STMA Article 61-4(1)).

2. External entertainment expenses

Entertainment expenses mean expenses that are incurred for eating and drinking or other similar entertainment. Expenses incurred for the entertainment of a corporation's directors, employees, or their relatives are excluded from non-deductible entertainment expenses (STMA Article 61-4(6)). These are generally referred to as 'external entertainment expenses'.

Given the above definition, directors of a parent corporation would be considered persons outside the corporation for determining the treatment of entertainment expenses.

If one of the parent corporation's directors is also one of your non-executive directors, you will need to determine whether there is an external entertainment expense based on whether the director attended the event in his position as a director of your parent or in his position as your non-executive director.

For this determination, the reasons for the director's business trip to Japan may be considered.

In addition, the following information must be provided to make it clear that entertainment expenses are external entertainment expenses (STMAER Article 21-18-4).

(1) Date of the event
(2) Names and relationships of customers, suppliers and other persons related to the business who participated in the event.
(3) Number of persons who participated in the event.
(4) The amount of the expense and the name and location of the restaurant or catering service.
(5) Any other information necessary to clarify that the expenditure is for entertainment.

Q41 Limitation of Tax Losses Carried Forward

We are expecting to record a net loss for accounting purposes this year, due to the poor economic environment. As a result, we expect to record a net operating loss for corporation tax purposes as well. How long can this net operating loss be carried forward?

A:

Net operating losses for corporation tax purposes can be carried forward for ten years by corporations having blue form tax return filing status (CTA Article 57). However, generally, only 50% of the tax loss carried forward can be offset against current year taxable income.

Discussion

A corporation that is eligible to carry forward a net operating loss for corporation tax purposes is a corporation that has filed a blue form tax return for the fiscal year in which the net operating loss arose, and has filed tax returns for each subsequent fiscal year continuously (CTA Article 57(1)).

Net operating losses for tax years beginning on or after 1 April 2018 (i.e., for tax years beginning on or after 1 December 2019 in the case of a December year-end corporation) can be carried forward for ten years. Tax losses incurred in earlier years can be carried forward only nine years.

Tax losses carried forward can be offset against the taxable income in the following years, up to a maximum of 50% of each year's taxable income. However, for small- and medium-sized enterprises (*see* Q27), it is possible to offset the entire current year's taxable income against carried forward losses.

An alternative to the carry forward of net losses is the carry-back of losses for tax purposes. A tax loss carry-back allows a corporation to carry back a tax loss to a previous tax year and claim a refund of the corporation tax paid in the previous tax year (CTA Article 80(1)).

Currently, tax loss carry-back refunds are suspended except in the following cases (STMA Article 66-12):

(1) Losses incurred in a liquidation period.
(2) Losses incurred in a dissolution period.
(3) Losses incurred by SMEs (*see* Q27) each fiscal year.

Q42 Exchange Rates for Foreign Currency Transactions

We purchase goods from a foreign-related corporation. All purchase prices for these goods are denominated in foreign currencies.

In accordance with our group accounting policy, all assets and liabilities denominated in foreign currencies held at the end of the fiscal year are converted to Japanese yen using the exchange rate set by our parent corporation ('internal rate').

Is there any tax risk by using our internal rate? We have not submitted a 'notification of foreign exchange method'.

A:

For tax purposes, monetary assets and liabilities denominated in foreign currencies are to be converted using the accrual method or the year-end method. However, unless you have submitted a 'notification of foreign exchange method' by the deadline for submission of your corporation tax return, foreign currency-denominated monetary claims and debts are to be converted using the year-end conversion method.

Therefore, if there is a difference between the rates used in either of these methods and the internal rate used, the difference in conversion should be added to or deducted from taxable income.

Discussion

Monetary assets and liabilities denominated in foreign currencies held at the end of the fiscal year are to be converted using the accrual method or the year-end method (CTA Article 61-9).

The accrual method is the method of converting foreign currency-denominated assets and liabilities into Japanese yen using the exchange rate at the date the transaction occurred.

On the other hand, the year-end method converts foreign currency-denominated assets and liabilities into Japanese yen using the exchange rate at the end of the fiscal year.

However, unless the corporation submits a 'notification of foreign exchange method', short-term foreign currency-denominated receivables and payables and foreign currency-denominated bank deposits (with a maturity date of one year or less from the end of the fiscal year) shall be converted using the year-end method (CTAEO Article 122-7).

The foreign exchange rate at the end of the fiscal year is defined as the middle rate of the telegraphic transfer market ('TTM') on the last day of the fiscal year (Corporation Tax Basic Circular Article 13-2-2-5). In addition, the foreign exchange rate provided by the corporation's primary financial institution should be used for this purpose (Corporation Tax Basic Circular Article 13-2-1-2).

In your case, if there is a difference between the internal rate and the TTM at the end of the fiscal year, the difference in conversion should be added to or deducted from taxable income.

It is common practice for foreign corporations to make such adjustments since there is usually a difference between the exchange rate defined in the tax law and the internal rate.

Q43 Definition of Permanent Establishments (PE)

We are a foreign corporation. We understand that we may be subject to taxation in Japan if we have a PE there. Please explain the tax treatment of PEs in Japan.

A:

A PE is broadly defined as a fixed place in a country at or through which an enterprise carries on any business. The existence of a PE is a very important concept in the determination of income-based taxation.

In some exceptional cases, a fixed place may not constitute a PE, such as where only auxiliary or preparatory activities are carried out. Under the OECD's Base Erosion and Profit Shifting ('BEPS') project, however, the scope of these exceptions has been narrowed.

Where a PE exists, all business income attributable to the PE will be taxed as domestic source income; where no PE exists, only limited domestic income is taxable.

Discussion

A foreign corporation is taxable only on its domestic source income. However, the taxation of domestic source income differs depending on whether the foreign corporation receiving the payment has a PE in Japan or whether the domestic source income is attributable to a PE.

A PE is classified into the following three types (CTA Article 2(12-19); however, if Japan has concluded a tax convention that differs from what is provided below, the provisions under the tax convention shall be applied:

(1) a branch office, factory, or any other fixed place for conducting business which is held by a foreign corporation and is located in Japan;
(2) a place held by a foreign corporation and located in Japan where the foreign corporation carries out construction or installation work or provision of services for directing and supervising such work, or any other place as being equivalent thereto; or
(3) a person assigned to Japan and authorized by a foreign corporation to conclude a contract on behalf thereof or any other person equivalent thereto.

An agent of a foreign corporation is not included in (3) above if the agent performs services relating to the business of the foreign corporation independently of the foreign corporation, and in the ordinary course of the agent's business. However, this exception does not apply if the agent performs services exclusively or mainly on behalf of one or more affiliated corporations (CTAEO Article 4-4(8)). An 'affiliated corporation' means a corporation with which one party has a control relationship, such as directly or indirectly holding more than 50% of the shares or capital contribution of the other corporation.

In determining whether a corporation has a PE in Japan, the functional aspect is more important than the formality aspect. For example, a room in a hotel which is used as a place for conducting business may constitute a PE, whereas mere storage of products should not constitute a PE.

The definition of PE is expanding with the OECD BEPS project. The PE is a very important criterion for determining income-based taxation. In the past, foreign corporations have sometimes made significant profits locally, but managed to avoid creating a PE, thereby reducing the amount of corporate income tax collected in those local countries. For this reason, BEPS Action 7 focused on the artificial avoidance of PEs, and amendments to the definition of PE were recommended by the OECD in 2015.

The current definition of PE in Japan has been amended in accordance with the OECD recommendation.

Q44 Commissionaire Transactions and PE

We sell products manufactured by our foreign parent corporation to customers in Japan. We have entered into a *toiya* contract (a commissionaire or undisclosed principal contract) with our parent under which we sell products to customers in our own name, and remit the entire sales revenue collected from customers to our parent, after deducting a commission for our services. Our parent's role in this transaction is not disclosed to our customers.

We understand that this business structure may need to be changed for tax reasons. What are the relevant tax issues?

A:

You operate in a commissionaire structure. In the past, you, acting as an independent agent, were not treated as a PE of your parent. Many corporations used this structure to reduce the tax payable in Japan, by paying their commissionaire a small commission only.

However, in accordance with the OECD Base Erosion and Profit Shifting ('BEPS') project, the definition of PE has been amended to reduce the opportunity for corporations to reduce their Japan tax base in this way. Under the current domestic law, you, as an agent, could fall under the definition of an agent PE, and thus your foreign parent could be subject to corporation tax in Japan. The definition of an agent PE under Japan's Tax Conventions may also be amended, due to the implementation of the Multilateral Convention to Implement Tax Treaty Related Measures to Prevent BEPS ('MLI') or due to specific amendment of a tax convention itself. It is therefore likely that many multinational groups will reconsider their use of commissionaire structures.

Discussion

1. Sales agents and commissionaire structures

In a sales agent transaction, the sales agent generally concludes a sales contract with customers in the name of a principal. In your case, this would mean concluding the sales contract with customers in the name of your parent, which customers would be aware of. Concluding contracts in this way would make you a PE of your parent (*see* Q43).

In contrast, a commissionaire structure differs in that the commissionaire sells goods owned by the principal in the name of commissionaire, without the customer being aware of the principal's role. This is your existing structure, where you conclude a sales contract with customers in your own name to sell goods owned by your parent. However, although the sales contract is concluded in your name, the owner of the goods is your parent, and as such the income from the sale of the goods belongs to your parent. Your income, the income of the commissionaire, is the commission income you receive from your parent. In Japan, commissionaire transactions are usually carried out using a *toiya* contract as defined in Article 551 of the Commercial Code.

In some cases, the foreign corporation also owns (or leases) a warehouse in Japan to avoid any practical delivery problems.

A commissionaire transaction can be illustrated as follows:

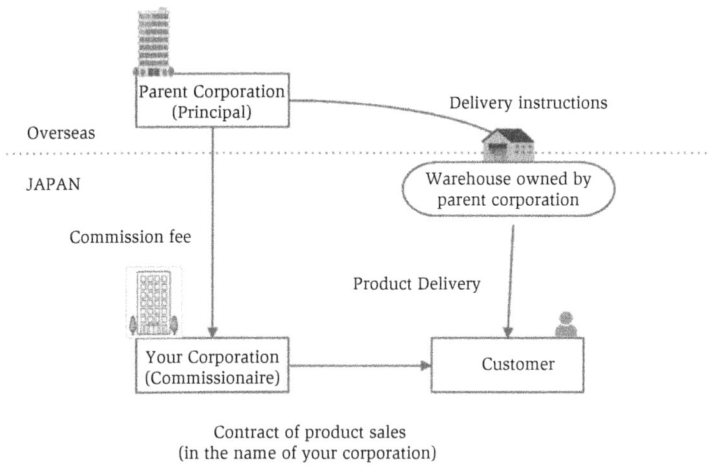

2. Commissionaire transactions and agent PEs

Traditionally, an agent PE was defined as a person who had the power to conclude contracts on behalf of a foreign corporation in relation to the foreign corporation's business and exercised such power continuously or repeatedly (former CTAEO Article 4-4-3(i)). Therefore, in a sales agent transaction in which an agent concluded a contract in the name of a principal, the sales agent could become an agent PE of the foreign corporation, unless the sales agent was an independent agent. The portion of income earned by the principal that was attributable to the PE would then be subject to corporation tax in Japan.

However, since a commissionaire in a commissionaire structure concludes sales contracts in its own name, a commissionaire was not considered to be included in the definition of an agent PE under Japanese corporation tax law. In addition, there was no tax convention that explicitly included a commissionaire in the scope of an agent PE.

Furthermore, even if the principal, the foreign corporation, had a warehouse in Japan for storing inventory, that would not be considered a PE.

As a result of the above, the income of a foreign corporation acting as a principal in a commissionaire structure was not taxed in Japan.

Moreover, given the profit or loss from the sale of goods in Japan belongs to the foreign corporation, and the commissionaire only receives a small commission, the taxable income of the foreign corporation is higher and the taxable income of the commissionaire is lower.

Consequently, the commissionaire structure was sometimes used to keep taxable income in jurisdictions of the commissionaires low.

3. Commissionaire structures and the BEPS project

In order to prevent commissionaire structures being used for tax avoidance, the OECD BEPS project, Action 7, recommended the expansion of the scope of agent PE.

As a result of this recommendation, the definition of agent PE in Japan was also amended, and in principle, the following persons will be treated as agent PEs (CTAEO Article 4-4(7)):

1 A person in Japan who, on behalf of a foreign corporation, repeatedly concludes the following contracts in connection with the foreign corporation's business.

2 A person who repeatedly plays a major role in the conclusion of the following contracts which are routinely concluded by the foreign corporation without material modification:

  (1) Contracts concluded in the name of the foreign corporation;
  (2) Contracts to transfer ownership or grant a right of use in respect of property which the foreign corporation owns or has a right to use;
  (3) Contracts for the provision of services by the foreign corporation.

As a result, even if a commissionaire concludes a contract in its own name, the commissionaire could become an agent PE of a foreign corporation principal, and that principal will be subject to Japanese corporation tax since the commissionaire has concluded a sales contract for goods owned by the principal.

As the provisions of a tax convention generally override the provisions of the domestic tax law, if there is a tax convention between Japan and the jurisdiction of the principal, the definition of agent PE may not yet be changed, and therefore may still not cover commissionaires.

Nevertheless, it is expected that the definition of agent PE will be changed through future amendments to Japan's Tax Conventions (or the new definition will be included in new Tax Conventions going forward). In addition, for countries where the definition of agent PE has been amended by the MLI, the definition of agent PE will be amended as the MLI comes into effect for each of Japan's covered jurisdictions.

It is therefore likely that an increasing number of multinational groups will reconsider their use of commissionaire structures.

Q45 Overview of Transfer Pricing Taxation

We purchase products from our parent corporation located in Germany, and sell them to our Japanese customers. We have been informed that the purchase price of these products should be determined based on transfer pricing principles. What does this mean?

A:

Transfer pricing principles refer to the setting of prices in transactions with foreign-related parties as if those transactions were carried out with third parties (i.e., arm's-length prices). The purpose of these principles is to prevent the transfer of income to foreign countries through transactions with foreign-related parties.

Discussion:

1. Transfer pricing overview

If a corporation sets the price in a transaction with a foreign-related party at an amount different from the price between third parties ('arm's length price'), it is possible to transfer profits from one corporation to the other.

The following is an example of a German parent corporation selling its products to a Japanese subsidiary:

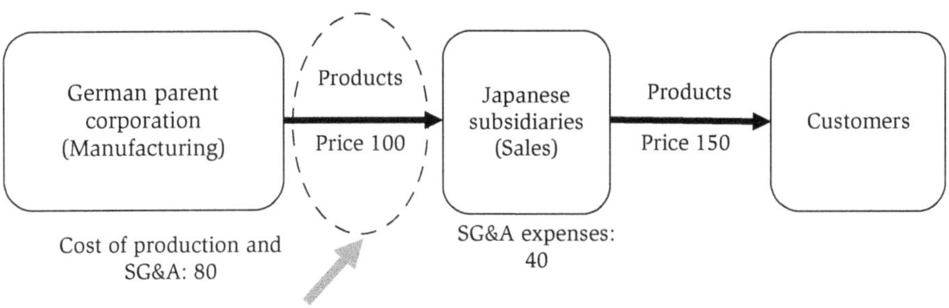

As shown in the table below, it is possible to change the amount of profit before tax in each country by changing the sales price from the German parent to the Japanese subsidiary, without changing the amount of profit before tax for the group as a whole. When there is a difference in the corporate tax rate between the two countries, this will result in a difference in the total amount of profit after tax for the group:

Sales Price *German parent corporation = >* *Japanese subsidiary*	*Germany Profit*	*Japan Profit*	*Group Profit*
80 (lower the selling price)	0	30	30
100 (refer to the above chart)	20	10	30
120 (raise the selling price)	40	▲ 10	30

Since it is easy to change the price in transactions between related parties, there is a possibility that income may be transferred to foreign countries through such transactions. In order to prevent such transfer of income, if the price in a foreign-related party transaction differs from the arm's-length price, taxable income is calculated and taxed as if the transaction had been carried out at an arm's-length price, which is referred to as a transfer pricing adjustment.

It is common for transactions to take place between foreign-related corporations in multinational groups, and therefore transfer pricing will be a key area of focus.

2. Arm's-length price

The arm's-length price is the price that would be charged for a similar transaction between third parties in the same circumstances as between foreign-related parties. Applying transfer pricing principles, taxable income is calculated as if the transaction had been made at an arm's-length price. For this reason, arm's-length pricing is a very important concept for transfer pricing purposes.

There are several methods for calculating the arm's-length price. In Japan, the prescribed methods are as follows, and are consistent with the methods described in the OECD's Transfer Pricing Guidelines (STMA Article 66-4(2)).

(1) The three basic methods:
  (i) Comparable Uncontrolled Price Method (CUP)
  A direct comparison of the transaction price used in a related party transaction with the transaction price used in a third-party transaction that is similar to the related party transaction in nature (comparable transactions).
  (ii) Resale Price Method (RP)
  This method compares the gross profit ratio as a percentage of sales (gross profit margin) on transactions between related parties with the gross profit margin on comparable transactions.
  (iii) Cost Plus Method (CP)
  This method compares the percentage of gross profit as a percentage of cost of sales (markup ratio) of the related party transaction with the markup ratio of the comparator transaction.
(2) Other methods
  (a) Transactional Net Margin Method (TNMM)

This method compares the level of operating profit resulting from transactions between related parties and comparable transactions.

(b) Profit Split method (PS)

The profit split method is a method of calculating the combined profits of the corporations involved in a transaction and allocating the combined profits to each corporation based on a certain method. The following three methods are accepted for the allocation of the combined profits:

(i) Comparative profit split method

The ratio of the division of the profits is determined by reference to the proportion of the profit split between similar independent third parties.

(ii) Contribution-profit split method

The ratio of the division of profits is determined by consideration of the contribution of each corporation to the combined profits.

(iii) Residual profit split method

After deducting the normal profit earned by the parties to the transaction from the combined profit, the ratio of the division of the profits is determined by consideration of the contribution of each corporation in excess of the normal profit.

(c) Discounted cash flow method

The arm's-length price is calculated by discounting the total future cash flow expected from related party transactions using the reasonable discount ratio.

In selecting one of the above pricing methods, the most appropriate method should be chosen, considering the nature of the related party transaction and the functions performed by the parties.

As the pricing methods prescribed in Japan have been determined based on the OECD's Transfer Pricing Guidelines, similar pricing methods are generally accepted in other countries.

3. Actions to be taken by Japanese subsidiaries and Japanese PEs

Transfer pricing principles apply to all transactions between foreign-related parties and foreign headquarters or branches. For this reason, most multinational corporations have group-wide transfer pricing policies, based on arm's-length pricing, and each subsidiary generally follows these policies set by the parent corporation.

It is not common for Japanese subsidiaries to be involved in the determination of the transfer pricing policies. However, it is important to understand the pricing methods applied to your transactions with foreign-related parties based on your group's transfer pricing policies, and to confirm that your transfer pricing has been determined in accordance with those policies.

Q46 Deductibility of Transfer Pricing Adjustment

We import goods from our Swiss parent corporation and sell them to customers in Japan. The purchase price of these goods is fixed during the fiscal year, but at the end of the year, an additional charge is made as a transfer pricing adjustment. What are the tax implications of this adjustment?

A:

Under many transfer pricing methods, in practice, the price in a transaction between related parties is determined based on the profit margin of one of the parties. If the profit margin from transaction falls outside a target range (usually set out in the group's transfer pricing policies), it may be necessary to adjust the profit margin on the transaction by increasing or decreasing the price of the goods purchased during the year.

An adjustment to increase the price of products can be deductible for Japanese corporation tax purposes if certain conditions are met. In addition, price adjustments may also impact customs duties and import consumption tax.

Discussion

1. Transfer pricing adjustments

Since you have purchased products from your Swiss parent, the purchase of those products is subject to transfer pricing principles (*see* Q45 for more information on transfer pricing principles generally).

Under these principles, if the price in a transaction between foreign-related parties is not at arm's-length price, the transaction is deemed to have been conducted at arm's length, and an adjustment needs to be made (STMA Article 66-4(1)). However, since it is very difficult to calculate an actual arm's-length 'price', it is common practice to verify the appropriateness of the pricing in a foreign-related party transaction by comparing the profit margin of one of the parties to the transaction with the profit margins earned by independent third parties engaged in similar transactions. Determining the price in a transaction between foreign-related parties in this way, based on the arm's-length profit margin, is acceptable under transfer pricing principles.

In order to compare the profit margin in the transaction between foreign-related parties with the profit margins of independent third parties, it is general practice to determine a reasonable profit margin range ('target range') rather than a single point.

If the actual profit margin on the transaction between related parties is outside the target range, an adjustment is made to ensure the actual profit margin falls within the target range.

2. Deductibility of pricing adjustments

A pricing adjustment that reduces the profit margin is not always deductible. If a corporation subsequently changes the price in a transaction with foreign-related parties as a pricing adjustment, there must be a reasonable basis for making such a change (Commissioner's Directive on Operation of Transfer Pricing 3-21).

A transfer pricing adjustment will be accepted as an amendment to the price of a transaction between foreign-related parties if the payment is deemed to be made on reasonable grounds after considering all the reasons for the payment, whether the parties had agreed that adjustments would be made, the method and basis of calculation of the adjustment, the date on which the adjustment was decided and the date on which it was paid.

If the transfer pricing adjustment is not deemed to be an amendment of the transaction price, it will be treated as a donation (i.e., a transfer of economic benefit, *see* Q47) to a foreign-related corporation, which is not deductible.

3. Impact on customs valuation

If a transfer pricing adjustment is made subsequently, it means that the transaction price has been changed, and therefore the customs value should also be amended.

For this reason, if you make a pricing adjustment, you will be required to submit an amended customs duty (and import consumption tax) return.

Q47 Donations to Foreign-Related Corporations and Transfer Pricing

Our foreign parent corporation invoiced us for management service fees, which we paid accordingly. We have recently been subject to a tax audit, and the tax examiners determined that this management service fee is not related to our Japanese business.

As a result, management service fees for which we took a deduction in previous years have been assessed as non-deductible donation expenses (i.e., a transfer of economic benefit) to our foreign parent.

We have been asked by our parent why this assessment was made, when the management fees were at arm's length for transfer pricing purposes. What is the difference between transfer pricing and donations to foreign-related parties?

A:

If the tax examiners consider, as in this case, that you did not receive any services for which you paid the management services fee, the payment of that fee is considered a donation (i.e., a transfer of economic benefit) from you to your parent. Under Japanese corporation tax law, donations to foreign-related parties and transfer pricing are treated differently.

Discussion

Transfer pricing principles are applied to transactions with foreign-related parties (STMA Article 66-4 (1)). On the other hand, donations to foreign-related parties are non-deductible expenses (STMA Article 66-4(3)). Therefore, transactions with foreign-related parties need to be considered under both laws.

As discussed in Q39, for Japanese tax purposes, any transaction conducted by a corporation in which there is no consideration is treated as a donation. In addition, even if there is consideration, if it is lower than the actual value, the difference between the actual value and the transaction value is in substance a gift, and will also be treated as a donation.

To determine whether a particular payment is substantially a gift or not, it is only necessary that the economic value is transferred to the other party without consideration. It is not necessary to determine whether the corporation had the intention to make a gift. For this reason, the concept of donation under tax law has a broader concept than that of donation in everyday use.

The following cases are treated as donations to foreign-related parties (Commissioner's Directive on Operation of Transfer Pricing 3-20):

1. Where a corporation sells assets, lends money, provides services or conducts other transactions ('Sale of Assets') to a foreign related corporation and has not recorded any income related to such Sale of Assets, when such Sale of Assets constitutes a gift or gratuitous provision of money or other assets or economic benefits
2. Where a corporation receives a payment from foreign related corporations as consideration for the Sale of Assets, when the consideration for such Sales of

Assets contains the amount in substance of a gift or gratuitous provision of money or other assets or economic benefit

3. Where a corporation makes a payment as consideration for the Sale of Assets to foreign related corporations, when the consideration for such Sales of Assets contains the amount in substance of a gift or gratuitous provision of money or other assets or economic benefit.

Although it is sometimes difficult to distinguish between transfer pricing and donations to foreign-related corporations, in general, the following factors should be considered; (1) whether the donation is a gift in substance, or (2) whether there is consideration. In your case, you have paid management service fees which the tax examiners consider do not have substance. Therefore, the fees paid are treated as the gratuitous provision of economic benefits, and the tax examiners treated them as a donation to a foreign-related corporation.

Donations to foreign-related corporations are not transfer pricing, and, thus, mutual agreement procedures under Tax Conventions are not available to resolve any issue of double taxation arising from the disallowance of such payments.

Q48 Transfer Pricing Documentation Obligations

We have ongoing transactions with various foreign-related parties. What kind of transfer pricing documentation do we need to prepare?

A:

All Japanese corporations and foreign corporations with permanent establishments ('PE') that are a member of a multinational group and where that group has total consolidated revenue of JPY 100 billion or more in the preceding fiscal year must submit a 'Notification of Ultimate Parent Entity', a 'Country-by-Country Report', and a 'Master File' to the national tax authorities through the online national tax return filing and tax payment system ('e-Tax system').

In addition, all corporations must prepare or obtain and preserve documents considered as necessary to calculate arm's-length prices for and transactions with foreign-related parties (i.e., 'Local File') by the deadline for submission of their final corporate income tax return (so-called contemporaneous documentation requirement). However, an exception to the contemporaneous documentation requirement is made in the following cases:

(1) the corporation does not have 'controlled transactions' for which the total value (for the previous fiscal year) is JPY five billion or more, or
(2) the corporation does not have 'controlled transactions' related to intangible property for which the total value (for the previous fiscal year) is JPY 300 million or more.

'Controlled transactions' refer to the sale or purchase of assets, the provision of services, and other transactions conducted by corporations with foreign-related parties.

In the case of a Japanese subsidiary of a multinational group, the parent corporation generally prepares the Master File, which the Japanese subsidiary submits to the Japanese tax authorities without modification. Country-by-Country Reports are not required to be submitted to the Japanese tax authorities as far as the parent corporation submits them to the tax authority in the jurisdiction of the parent corporation. Local Files may or may not be prepared by the Japanese subsidiary directly, depending on the practice of the multinational group.

Discussion

Following the recommendations of the OECD's Base Erosion and Profit Shifting ('BEPS') Project (Action 13: Guidance on Transfer Pricing Documentation and Country-by-Country Reporting), countries, particularly those that are members of the OECD, are becoming more uniform in their transfer pricing documentation requirements. In Japan, the Special Taxation Measures Act was partially revised as part of the 2016 Tax Reform, strengthening the requirements in relation to transfer pricing documentation, in line with the OECD's BEPS recommendations.

All Japanese corporations and foreign corporations with PEs that are a member of a multinational enterprise (MNE) with total consolidated revenue of JPY 100 billion or more in the preceding fiscal year ('Specified MNE Group') must submit a 'Notification of Ultimate Parent Entity', a 'Country-by-Country Report', and a 'Master File' to the competent national tax office through the e-Tax system.

1. Notification of Ultimate Parent Entity

A domestic corporation which is a member of, or a foreign corporation with a PE which is a member of, a Specified MNE Group is required to submit information about the ultimate parent entity of the Specified MNE Group to the competent national tax office through the e-Tax system by the end of the fiscal year for which the information is required to be reported (STMA Article 66-4-4(5)). The fiscal year here refers to the fiscal year of the ultimate parent entity (STMA Article 66-4-4(4)(vii)).

The main information to be submitted is as follows (STMAER Article 22-10-4):

- name of the ultimate parent entity;
- the location of its head or principal office (if the ultimate parent entity resides in a foreign country, the location of its head or principal office or the site where its business is managed or controlled), its corporate number; and
- the name of its representative.

In principle, if there are several Japanese corporations and foreign corporations with a Japanese PE, they all have an obligation to submit such a notification. However, as an exception, one corporation may be designated to submit the notification on behalf of others (STMA Article 66-4-4(6)), *see* Q49.

2. Master File

A domestic corporation which is a member of, or a foreign corporation which has a Japanese PE and is a member of, a Specified MNE Group is required to submit a 'Master File' to the competent national tax office via the e-Tax system within one year from the day following the end of the fiscal year for which the Master File is to be prepared.

In principle, if there are several Japanese corporations or foreign corporations with PEs, they all have an obligation to submit the Master File. However, as an exception, one corporation may be designated to submit the Master File on behalf of the others (*see* Q49).

The detailed list of information to be included in the Master File is included at the end of this section; however, the key items are as follows (STMA Article 66-4-5 (1), STMAER Article 22-10-5):

- a detailed description of the Specified MNE Group's organisational structure,
- a business overview,
- a detailed explanation of research and development activities and intangible assets, and
- an outline of group financing.

As the Master File describes the activities of the whole Specified MNE Group, it is generally prepared by the ultimate parent entity which is responsible for the group's activities. The preparation of the Master File is recommendation of the BEPS project, and thus the contents of the Master File are essentially the same for all countries which have adopted those recommendations. In principle, therefore, the contents of a Master File prepared by an ultimate parent entity as required under the ultimate parent entity's domestic tax law should be consistent with the contents of the Master File required by Japanese tax law.

As a result, most Japanese subsidiaries or Japanese PEs of foreign corporations submit the Master File prepared by the ultimate parent entity without amendment through the e-Tax system. The language of submission of the Master File is either Japanese or English (STMAER Article 22-10-5(2)).

3. Country-by-Country Reports

Japanese corporations that are a member of a Specified MNE Group must submit a Country-by-Country Report ('CbC Report') to the competent national tax office via the e-Tax system within one year of the day following the day when the fiscal year covered by the CbC Report ends (STMA Article 66-4-4 (1)).

In practice, only ultimate parent entities located in Japan submit CbC Reports to the Japanese tax authorities. Japanese subsidiaries or Japanese PEs of Specified MNE Groups generally do not do so.

This is because, in principle, the CbC Report submitted by the foreign ultimate parent entity to the tax authorities in their resident country is provided to the Japanese tax authorities through an automatic exchange of information system.

However, in exceptional cases where the foreign tax authorities of the jurisdiction where the ultimate parent entity is resident are deemed to be unable to provide the CbC Report to the Japanese tax authorities, a Japanese subsidiary or a Japanese PE will be obliged to submit the CbC Report to the competent national tax office (STMA Article 66-4-4(2)). In this case, the deadline for submission is within one year from the end of the fiscal year. If there is more than one subsidiary of PE that is required to submit a CbC Report, one corporation may submit the report on behalf of the others (STMA Article 66-4-4(3)).

The CbC Report should include the following information (STMA Article 66-4-4(1), STMAER Article 22-10-4):

(1) Amount of revenue, profit (loss) before income tax, income tax paid, income tax accrued, registered capital, accumulated earnings, and tangible assets other than cash and cash equivalents, as well as the number of employees.
(2) Names, tax jurisdiction of organisation or incorporation if different from tax jurisdiction of residence, and major business activity(ies) of the group entities.
(3) Other useful information.

4. Local File

Corporations engaged in transactions with foreign-related parties must prepare and preserve documents considered necessary to calculate arm's-length prices for those transactions ('Local File') by the deadline for submission of their final corporation tax returns ('contemporaneous documentation requirement').

The Local File should contain very detailed information about the nature of the transactions with the foreign-related corporations, the functions and risks of each corporation, and the method of calculating the arm's-length price for each transaction (STMA Article 66-4(7), SMAEO Article 22-10(6)). The detailed list of items to be included is attached at the end of this section.

In addition, other documents considered as important to calculate arm's-length prices must also be preserved separately (STMA Article 66-4 (12), STMAER Article 22-10 (11)). These documents should contain the following:

- Information that provides the basis for what is written in the Local File.
- Information related to what is written in the Local File.
- Other documents considered as important when calculating arm's-length prices.

The Local File must be submitted within forty-five days from the date of a request for submission by the tax examiners, while the other documents considered as important to calculate arm's-length prices must be submitted within sixty days of the date of a request for submission by the tax examiners.

Where (1) and (2) below are satisfied, corporations are exempted from the preparation of a Local File:

(1) if the amount of transactions (total of receipts and payments) with each foreign-related corporation during the previous fiscal year (the current fiscal year if there was not a previous one) was less than JPY 5 billion, and
(2) if the amount of transactions of intangibles (total of receipts and payments) with each foreign-related corporation during the previous fiscal year (the current fiscal year if there was not a previous one) was less than JPY 300 million.

However, for corporations that are exempted from preparation of a Local File for the above reason, the other documents considered important for the calculation of arm's-length prices must still be submitted within sixty days of a request for submission by the tax examiners (STMA Article 66-4(14)). Having said that, the other documents considered important for the calculation of arm's-length prices are documents that are equivalent to a Local File (STMAER Article 22-10(12)). Practically speaking, therefore, all Japanese subsidiaries or Japanese PEs engaged in transactions with foreign-related parties should be considered to have an obligation to prepare a Local File.

The below table summarises the above requirements:

Documents	*Prepared by*	*Submitted by*	*Submission to*	*Deadline*
Notification of ultimate parent entity	Domestic corporation or PE of foreign corporation	Domestic corporation or PE of foreign corporation	Japanese tax authority	Fiscal year end of ultimate parent entity
Master File	Foreign parent corporation	Domestic corporation or PE of foreign corporation	Japanese tax authority	Within one year of the day following the day when the fiscal year covered by the Mater File ends
Country-by Country Report (CbC Report)	Foreign parent corporation	Foreign parent corporation, submitted overseas	Tax authority of the jurisdiction where the parent corporation is located	-
Local File	Domestic corporation or PE of foreign corporation	Domestic corporation or PE of foreign corporation	Japanese tax authority	Within 45 or 60 days after being asked to submit on tax audit

(Attachment)

(*Source*: National Tax Agency: Revision of documentation system for transfer pricing)

1. Items of the Master File:

○ Items of the Master File

Article 22.10.5 Paragraph 1 of the Ordinance (excerpts)

Item 1: Names of Constituent Entities of the Specified MNE Group, the location of their head office or principal offices, and a chart illustrating the relationships between the Constituent Entities

Item 2: General description of business of Constituent Entities of the Specified MNE Group, including the following:

(a) Sales, income, and other important sources of profit of Constituent Entities of the Specified MNE Group

(b) Outline of the supply chain for the Specified MNE Group's five major goods, products or services (which refer to the succession of logistic processes that lead up to consumers; this also applies to (c)) as well as of geographical markets in which such goods, products or services are provided

(c) Outline of the supply chain for the Specified MNE Group's goods, products or services that represent 5% of total sales, revenues, or profits in its category or more as well as of geographical markets in which such goods, products and services are provided (excluding the items listed in (b))

(d) List of important agreements on the provision of services between Constituent Entities of the Specified MNE (excluding those related to research and development; this also applies to (d)) and the outline of the agreements (including the outline of policy to set the amount of compensation for the provision of services, that of policy to share the amount of expenses for the provision of services, and that of the functions of major bases where services are provided)

(e) Outline of the major functions fulfilled by Constituent Entities of the Specified MNE Group when creating value added, serious risks assumed by them (possible increases or decreases in profit or loss due to factors such as fluctuations in exchange markets and market interest rates and changes in economic situations), and major roles played by Constituent Entities when creating important assets to be used and other types of value added

(f) Outline of important business mergers, splits, transfers, and other acts involving Constituent Entities of the Specified MNE Group

Item 3: Outline of the Specified MNE Group's comprehensive strategy for research and development, ownership, and use of its intangible fixed assets and other intangible assets (hereinafter referred to as "Intangibles" in sections up to Item 7 below) and the location of major facilities used for research and development of Intangibles and that of sites where such research and development are managed

Item 4: List of important Intangibles used for transactions between Constituent Entities of the Specified MNE Group and of Constituent Entities that possess the Intangibles

Item 5: List of important agreements between Constituent Entities of the Specified MNE Group on the sharing of expenses related to research and development of Intangibles, a list of important agreements on the provision of services for major research and development projects for the Intangibles, a list of important agreements on consent to use of the Intangibles, and a list of other important agreements on Intangibles between Constituent Entities

Item 6: Outline of policy to set the amount of compensation for transactions related to R&D and Intangibles between Constituent Entities of the Specified MNE Group

Item 7: Names of Constituent Entities of the Specified MNE Group which are involved in the transfer of important Intangibles (including equity for the Intangibles; this also applies to the rest of this item) between them, the location of their head office or principal offices, and the content of the Intangibles transferred, the amount of compensation, and other details of the transfer between the Constituent Entities

Item 8: Outline of methods for Constituent Entities of the Specified MNE Group to procure funds (including the outline of important agreements on fund procurement from entities other than the Constituent Entities)

Item 9: Names of those of Constituent Entities of the Specified MNE Group which fulfill pivotal financial functions in the group and the location of their head office or principal offices (including the name of the country or territory where laws and ordinances that govern the establishment of the Constituent Entities are enacted and that of the country or territory where sites are located in which their business is managed and controlled)

Item 10: Outline of policy to set the amount of compensation for financing between Constituent Entities of the Specified MNE Group

Item 11: Profits/losses and financial condition included in the consolidated financial statements of the Specified MNE Group (documents stating the profits/losses and financial condition of the Specified MNE Group if consolidated financial statements are not available)

Item 12: Outline of arrangement for the method to calculate the amount of compensation for transactions between Constituent Entities of the Specified MNE Group that reside in different countries and other items related to the allocation of income between such Constituent Entities if such arrangement is made only by the competent authorities in the country where one of the Constituent Entities resides

Item 13: Items that are useful for those listed in the Items above

2. Documents in Local File:

○ Documents in the Local File

Article 22.10 Paragraph 1 of the Ordinance (excerpts)

Item 1: Documents describing the content of controlled transactions as stipulated in Article 66.4 Paragraph 1 of the Act (hereinafter referred to as "Controlled Transactions" in this paragraph), including the following:

- (a) Documents describing details of assets and the content of services related to the Controlled Transactions
- (b) Documents describing items related to the functions fulfilled by corporations as stipulated in Article 66.4 Paragraph 1 of the Act and foreign-related parties related thereto (which refer to foreign-related parties as stipulated in the same paragraph; this also applies to the rest of this paragraph) in the Controlled Transactions and risks (which refer to possible increases or decreases in the profits or loss of the Controlled Transactions due to fluctuations in exchange markets and market interest rates, changes in economic situations, and other factors; this also applies to the rest of this paragraph) assumed by the corporations and the foreign-related parties in the Controlled Transactions (If, due to the restructuring of the corporations' or foreign-related parties' business (which refers to mergers, splits, transfer of businesses or important business assets, and changes in business structure for other reasons; this also applies to the rest of (b)), a change takes place to the functions fulfilled by the corporations or the foreign-related parties in the Controlled Transactions or the risks assumed by the corporations or the foreign-related parties in the Controlled Transactions, the documents must include a description of the content of the business restructuring and that of changes in the functions and the risks)
- (c) Documents describing the content of intangible fixed assets and other intangible assets used by corporations as stipulated in Article 66.4 Paragraph 1 of the Act or foreign-related parties related thereto in the Controlled Transactions
- (d) Agreements related to, or documents describing the content of agreements on, the Controlled Transactions
- (e) Documents describing details of the amount of compensation received or paid by corporations as stipulated in Article 66.4 Paragraph 1 of the Act from or to foreign-related parties related thereto in the Controlled transactions, the method to set the amount of compensation received or paid, and the content of negotiations about such setting, as well as documents describing the method to calculate arm's length prices (which refer to those stipulated in the same paragraph; this also applies to the rest of this article) for the amount of compensation received or paid and the content of arrangement of items related to the Controlled transactions (including other transactions closely related thereto) if such arrangement is made by the competent authorities in countries or territories other than Japan (excluding cases in which such arrangement is made by the regional commissioner of the regional taxation bureau or the district director who has jurisdiction over the place where the corporations pay income tax)
- (f) Documents describing details of profits/losses for corporations as stipulated in Article 66.4 Paragraph 1 of the Act and foreign-related parties related thereto in the Controlled Transactions and the process in which the amount of profits/losses is calculated
- (g) Documents describing analyses of markets (including analyses of the effects of the characteristics of the markets on the amount of compensation and profits/losses in the Controlled Transactions) related to the sale or purchase of assets, the provision of services, and other transactions in the Controlled Transactions and other items related to the markets
- (h) Documents describing the content of business, business policy, and organizational structure of corporations as stipulated in Article 66.4 Paragraph 1 of the Act and foreign-related parties related thereto
- (i) Documents describing whether there are other transactions closely related to the Controlled Transactions as well as the content of the transactions and the circumstances under which the transactions are closely related to the Controlled Transactions

Item 2: Documents for corporations as stipulated in Article 66.4 Paragraph 1 of the Act to calculate arm's length prices for Controlled Transactions, including the following:

- (a) Documents describing the calculation method stipulated in Article 66.4 Paragraph 2 of the Act which is selected by the corporations, important prior conditions for such selection, and the reasons for such selection as well as other documents prepared by the corporations to calculate arm's length prices (excluding those listed in (b) to (e) below)
- (b) Documents describing items related to the selection of Comparable Uncontrolled Transactions used by the corporation for the Controlled Transactions (transactions in which sellers and buyers without special relationships with each other as stipulated in Article 66.4 Paragraph 2 Item 1(a) of the Act trade inventory assets similar to those related to Controlled Transactions under similar circumstances to those for the Controlled Transactions, Comparable Uncontrolled Transactions as stipulated in Article 39.12 Paragraph 6 of the Order, Comparable Uncontrolled Transactions as stipulated in Paragraph 7 of the same article, Comparable Uncontrolled Transactions as stipulated in Paragraph 8 Item 1(a) of the same article, Comparable Uncontrolled Transactions as stipulated in (c)(1) of the same item, Comparable Uncontrolled Transactions as stipulated in Item 2 of the same paragraph, Comparable Uncontrolled Transactions as stipulated in Item 3 of the same paragraph, Comparable Uncontrolled Transactions as stipulated in Item 4 of the same paragraph, and Comparable Uncontrolled Transactions as stipulated in Item 5 of the same paragraph; this also applies to the rest of this item) (including transactions equivalent to Comparable Uncontrolled Transactions related to the similar method listed in Article 66.4 Paragraph 2 Item 1(d) of the Act, transactions equivalent to Comparable Uncontrolled Transactions related to the method listed in Article 39.12 Paragraph 8 Item 6 of the Order, and transactions equivalent to Comparable Uncontrolled Transactions related to the method stipulated in Article 66.4 Paragraph 2 Item 2 of the Act; hereinafter referred to as "Comparable Uncontrolled Transactions" in the rest of this item) and details of the Comparable Uncontrolled Transactions (including financial information on the Comparable Uncontrolled Transactions)
- (c) Documents for the corporations to calculate the amount computed as one that belongs to the corporations and the foreign-related parties related thereto using the method listed in Article 39.12 Paragraph 8 Item 1 of the Order or the one listed in Item 6 of the same paragraph (limited to methods similar to the one listed in Item 1 of the same paragraph) if the method is selected by the corporations (excluding the documents listed in (b) and (e))
- (d) Documents describing the reason the corporations consider several Controlled Transactions as a single one and calculate an arm's length price for the transaction and the content of each transaction if they make such a calculation
- (e) Documents describing the reason differences are adjusted for Comparable Uncontrolled Transactions (adjustments as stipulated in Article 66.4 Paragraph 2 Item 1(a) of the Act, necessary adjustments as stipulated in Article 39.12 Paragraph 6 of the Order, necessary adjustments as stipulated in Paragraph 7 of the same article, necessary adjustments as stipulated in Paragraph 8 Item 1(a) of the same article, necessary adjustments as stipulated in (c)(1) of the same item, necessary adjustments as stipulated in Item 2 of the same paragraph, necessary adjustments as stipulated in Item 3 of the same paragraph, necessary adjustments as stipulated in Item 4 of the same paragraph, and necessary adjustments as stipulated in Item 5 of the same paragraph; this also applies to the rest of this item) (including adjustments equivalent to difference adjustments for the similar methods listed in Article 66.4 Paragraph 2 Item 1(d) of the Act, adjustments equivalent to difference adjustments for the method listed in Article 39.12 Paragraph 8 Item 6 of the Order, and adjustments equivalent to difference adjustments for the method stipulated in Article 66.4 Paragraph 2 Item 2 of the Act; hereinafter referred to as "Difference Adjustments" in the rest of this item) and the method to adjust such differences if such adjustments are made

Q49 Notification of Ultimate Parent Entity

We are a Japanese subsidiary of a US corporation with group-wide sales in excess of JPY 100 billion. We also have a wholly owned subsidiary in Japan. We understand that we are required to submit the 'Notification of Ultimate Parent Entity', but do we need to submit it every year? Also, is it possible to submit one such notification for all Japanese companies together?

A:

As a general rule, the 'Notification of Ultimate Parent Entity' must be submitted by the end of each fiscal year. In addition, in principle, if there are several Japanese corporations and foreign corporations with Japanese PEs that must submit such notifications, all of them have the duty to submit. However, as an exception, one corporation may be designated to submit the notification on behalf of the others.

Discussion

Japanese corporations or foreign corporations with Japanese PEs that are members of a Specified MNE Group must submit a 'Notification of Ultimate Parent Entity', which includes information on the ultimate parent entity, to the competent national tax office via the e-Tax system by the day when the fiscal year covered by the notification ends (STMA Article 66-4-4 (5)).

Therefore, the notification must be submitted annually.

In principle, if there are several Japanese corporations and foreign corporations with Japanese PEs that must submit a 'Notification of Ultimate Parent Entity', all of them have the duty to submit it. However, as an exception, one corporation may be designated to submit the notification on behalf of the others (STMA Article 66-4-4 (6)).

The key items to be submitted are as follows (STMAER Article 22-10-4 (10)):

- Name of the corporation that submits the notification on behalf of others, the location of its head and other offices, its corporate number, the name of its representative, etc.
- Names of corporations other than the one that submits the notification, the location of their head and other offices, their corporate numbers, the names of their representative:

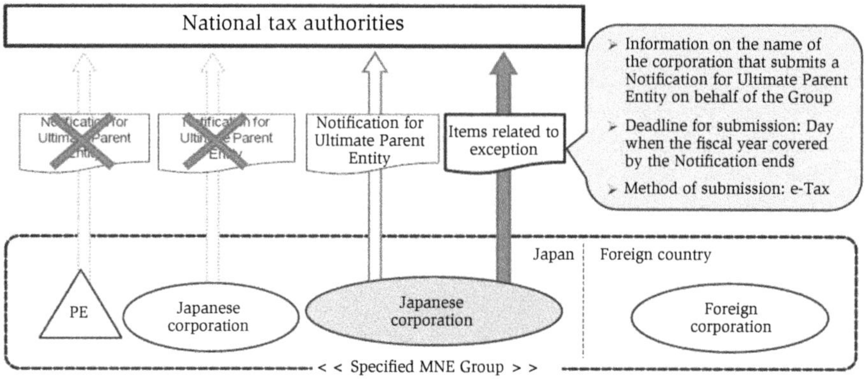

(Source: National Tax Agency: Revision of documentation system for transfer pricing)

Similar requirements, as well as the exception for a single filing, can be applied to the submission of the Master File (STMA Article 66-4-5(2)).

Q50 Transfer Pricing and Hidden Profit Distributions

During a tax audit, the deductibility of management service fees that we paid to our foreign parent was denied, and the fees were treated as donations (or transfers of economic benefit, *see* Q47) to a foreign-related corporation. As a result, we were required to pay additional corporation tax. Our parent has asked us whether we are also liable for additional withholding tax if the donation is considered a hidden profit distribution.

A:

The concept of hidden profit distributions is sometimes found in foreign countries, where certain payments from a subsidiary to its parent are deemed as distributions of profit for tax purposes. Under this concept, transfers of economic benefit, including transfer pricing, may also be treated as hidden profit distributions.

In Japan, the concept of hidden profit distributions has not been adopted, and therefore no withholding tax will be imposed on any transfer pricing adjustments or donations (i.e., transfers of economic benefit) in relation to foreign-related corporations.

Discussion

The concept of a hidden profit distribution is sometimes found in foreign countries. Under this concept, the transfer of income from a subsidiary to a parent corporation is treated as a dividend (whereas the transfer of losses is treated as a hidden contribution). However, as there is no legal procedure for profit distributions, this is referred to as 'hidden' profit distributions.

Under this principle, the transfer of income from a subsidiary to a parent corporation is subject to two types of taxation:

(1) Transfer of income from a subsidiary to a parent corporation is not deductible as it is a profit distribution.
(2) Transfer of income from a subsidiary to a parent corporation is a dividend and is therefore subject to withholding tax:

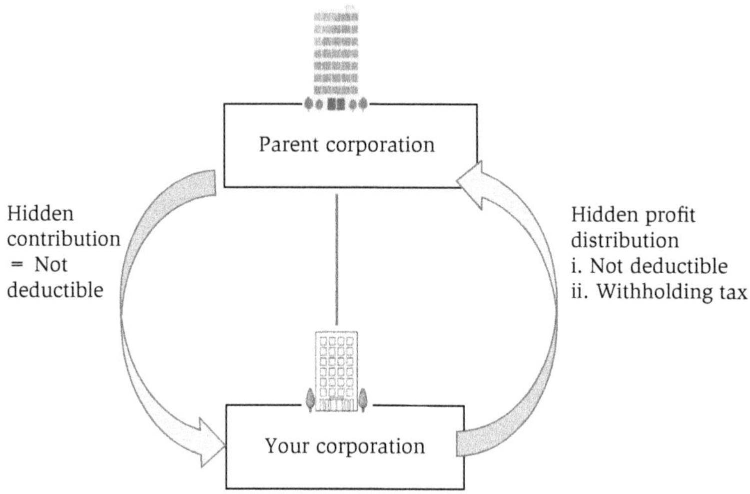

In Japan, this concept of hidden profit distribution has not been adopted, and therefore no withholding tax will be imposed on the disallowance of the management fees paid to your parent.

Q51 Additional Corporation Tax under the Family Corporation Tax Regime

All equity interests in our parent corporation are owned by the individual founder and representative director of our parent corporation. We understand there is a special 'family corporation' tax regime for this type of ownership structure in Japan. Do we fall within this regime and need to pay additional corporation tax?

A:

If your registered capital is over JPY 100 million, you would meet the definition of 'specified family corporation' and would be subject to additional corporation tax under the family corporation tax regime.

Discussion

When a corporation meets the definition of 'specified family corporation' under Japanese tax law, that corporation is subject to additional corporation tax on its retained income (CTA Article 67(1)).

If a Japanese corporation is directly or indirectly controlled by one or more shareholders, it is called a 'controlled corporation'. For the purpose of the application of this rule, the corporation is controlled by a shareholder or a group of shareholders if more than 50% of the issued shares or voting rights are owned by a shareholder or a group of shareholders. A group of shareholders mean the relatives of a shareholder, a corporation controlled by a shareholder, or a corporation commonly controlled by a person who controls a shareholder.

A 'specified family corporation' is a Japanese corporation, which is still a controlled corporation even if its shareholders that do not fall within the definition of 'controlled corporation' are excluded at the time of the analysis.

In general, a foreign corporation meets the definition of a 'specified family corporation' if its ultimate shareholders are related individuals.

Small- and medium-sized corporations, i.e., those corporations with registered capital less than JPY 100 million, are excluded from the definition of 'specified family corporation' (CTA Article 67(1), *see* Q27).

For determining family corporation status, the ultimate shareholders of the corporation are not limited to Japanese residents. Therefore, as in your case, even if the ultimate shareholders are non-resident, the corporation may meet the definition of a 'specified family corporation'.

1. Calculation of taxable retained income

Additional corporation tax payable by 'specified family corporations' is calculated based on the amount of taxable retained income multiplied by the applicable tax rate. Taxable retained income is retained income for the current period less certain deductions from retained income (CTA Article 67(1)).

(1) Retained income for the current period (CTA Article 67(3))

Retained income is calculated by adding or deducting certain amounts to or from taxable income for the current period. There are a number of items that can be added or deducted, but the Japanese subsidiary of the foreign corporations are typically required to add or deduct the following items: (a) dividends received are not included in taxable income; (b) directors' remuneration, not deducted; (c) entertainment expenses, not deducted; (d) donations, not deducted; (e) delinquent taxes, not deducted; (f) income tax, foreign corporation tax and refunds of corporation tax due to loss carry-back, not included in taxable income; (g) tax loss carry-forwards, deducted; and (h) excess interest, included in deductible expenses.

Retained income for the current period is calculated by adjusting the retained income derived through the above adjustments for: (i) dividends paid and (ii) corporation tax and corporate inhabitant tax paid.

(2) Deductions from retained income

Deductions from retained income are the highest of the following amounts (CTA Article 67(5)):

(i) Taxable income for the period x 40%.
(ii) JPY 20 million * number of months in the current year / 12.
(iii) Registered capital at fiscal year end * 25% – Profit reserve at fiscal year end.

As noted above, taxable retained income is retained income for the current period less the deductions from retained income.

2. Calculation of additional corporation tax

The additional corporation tax to be paid is the total of the following (CTA Article 67(1)):

(1) Amounts less than or equal to JPY 30 million * 10%.
(2) Amounts exceeding JPY 30 million to JPY 100 million *15%.
(3) Amount exceeding JPY 100 million *20%.

If the current fiscal year is less than twelve months, the calculation above should be adjusted by the number of months in the current fiscal year.

As specified, family corporations are subject to this additional corporation tax on their retained income; dividend payments may be considered to ensure that the retained income does not trigger such additional tax. However, since withholding tax is generally imposed on Dividends, the Dividends strategy for specified family corporations should be considered from both the additional corporation tax and additional withholding tax perspectives.

Q52 Foreign Tax Credits

Our UK parent corporation has recently established a new subsidiary in China, which operates a factory. To set up the factory, we sent one of our employees to China for about a month to provide technical support. We invoiced the Chinese subsidiary for these services; however, the payment we received was reduced by Chinese withholding tax.

Can we get a foreign tax credit for the withholding tax paid in China? We do not have any business in China other than this technical support.

A:

The Chinese withholding tax deducted from your technical support services fee cannot be used as a foreign tax credit. However, such withholding tax can be treated as a deductible expense in the fiscal year in which the withholding tax payment is made.

Discussion

Under a foreign tax credit regime, foreign corporation tax can be credited against Japanese corporation tax subject to certain limitations (CTA Article 69). Foreign corporation tax means taxes imposed under the laws of foreign countries, which is equivalent to Japanese corporation tax. However, where the amount of foreign corporation tax imposed in a foreign country with which Japan has concluded a tax convention exceeds the amount of tax due or exempted under the provisions of that tax convention, the excess amount cannot be taken as a foreign tax credit (CTA Article 69(1), CTAEO Article 142-2(8)(v)).

Under the tax convention between China and Japan, income from business conducted in China by a Japanese corporation is not taxable in China unless the business is conducted in China through a permanent establishment ('PE') situated in China (Tax Convention between China and Japan Article 7). A Japanese corporation is deemed to have a PE in China if it provides consultancy services through employees or other personnel for a period or periods totalling more than six months within a twelve-month period (Tax Convention between China and Japan Article 5).

Therefore, your technical support services fees should not be subject to withholding tax in China, as you have no PE in China and your staff were only in China for a month or so. Accordingly, such Chinese tax should be treated as excess foreign corporation tax under the Tax Convention between China and Japan and is not eligible for a foreign tax credit.

On the other hand, you should be able to claim a refund of this withholding tax in China since it should not have been imposed in China. If the refund cannot be made, the excess foreign corporation tax can be treated as a deductible expense in the fiscal year in which the payment is made, as it does not fall under the category of non-deductible foreign tax (CTA Article 41, CTA Article 22(iii)2).

Q53 Taxation on the Transfer of Shares of a Japanese Corporation

Since our establishment over ten years ago, we have been a wholly owned Japanese subsidiary of a US corporation. Recently, however, our US parent transferred all our shares to a Singapore corporation in our group by cash. Is there any taxation in Japan on this transfer of shares? Our US parent qualifies for benefits under the Tax Convention between the US and Japan.

A:

In general, shares in a Japanese subsidiary of a multinational group may be sometimes transferred from one corporation to another within the group as a result of a group reorganisation, or transferred to a third party outside the group as a result of a spin-off or sale.

If shares in a Japanese subsidiary of a foreign corporation are transferred, the foreign corporation will be subject to Japanese corporation tax on any capital gain, even if the transfer occurs outside Japan, if the following conditions are met:

1) the foreign corporation held 25% or more of the shares in the Japanese subsidiary at any time within three years prior to the end of the fiscal year in which the transfer occurs; and
2) the foreign corporation transferred 5% or more of those shares within a single fiscal year.

However, under the Tax Convention between the US and Japan, US residents are exempt from taxation in Japan on gains from the transfer of shares in Japanese corporations if certain conditions are met.

Discussion:

1. Tax treatment under the domestic tax law

Under the domestic tax law, foreign corporations are taxed on their domestic source income (CTA Article 4(3)). Foreign corporations that do not have a permanent establishment in Japan are subject to corporation tax only on the following domestic source income (CTA Article 141(2), Article 138(1)):

(1) Income arising from the use and holding of assets located in Japan
(2) Income arising from the transfer of assets located in Japan
(3) Consideration received by a corporation which conducts business for which the main activity is to provide personal services in Japan
(4) Consideration for the lease of real property located in Japan, any right on real property located in Japan
(5) Other domestic source income.

The transfer of assets specified in (2) above includes transfer of the following (CTAEO Article 178(1)):

i. Income from the transfer of real estate located in Japan.
ii. Income from the logging or transfer of forests located in Japan.
iii. Income from the transfer of shares in a domestic corporation purchased in such a way that the exchange requires the purchase to be reported and the shares are transferred using the owner's status.
iv. Income from the transfer of shares in a domestic corporation by a non-resident who is a specially-related shareholder of the domestic corporation.
v. Income from the transfer of shares in a real estate-related corporation.
vi. Income from the transfer of golf club memberships in domestic golf courses.

The transfer of shares in (iv) above is limited to the following cases: (CTAEO Article 178(6)):

a) Specially-related shareholders of the domestic corporation have held 25% or more of the total number of issued shares of the domestic corporation at any time within three years prior to the end of the fiscal year of transfer.
b) Specially-related shareholders of a domestic corporation, including a foreign corporation, have transferred 5% or more of the total number of shares issued by the domestic corporation in the fiscal year of transfer.

Specially related shareholders are the shareholders themselves, their relatives, and any partnerships in which they are members.

If you do not own any real estate, you do not qualify as a real estate-related corporation under (v) above. However, the transfer of your shares by your parent satisfies all of the requirements under (iv). Therefore, your parent will in principle be liable for Japanese corporation tax on any capital gain realised on the sale of those shares. If your parent does not have a Japanese permanent establishment, only corporation tax and local corporation tax will be imposed, while local tax will not.

2. Treatment under Tax Convention

Under Article 13 of the Tax Convention between the US and Japan, capital gains on the transfer of shares other than real estate-related corporations are taxable only in the country of residence of the transferor. Since your parent satisfies the limitation of benefits provisions and is a qualified person under the Tax Convention between the US and Japan, it is able to take advantage of the benefits of that Tax Convention. Therefore, notwithstanding the provisions of the Japanese domestic tax law, any capital gain on the transfer of your shares will not be taxed in Japan.

In order to apply for these benefits, your US parent must submit an 'Application Form for Income Tax Convention' to the competent national tax office in Form 15, 'Application Form for Income Tax Convention (Relief from Japanese Income Tax or Corporation Tax for Japanese Source Income to Report)'. This must be submitted within two months of the day following the end of your parent's fiscal year end (Act on Special Provisions of the Income Tax Act, the Corporation Tax Act and the Local Tax Act Incidental to Enforcement of Tax Conventions Article 9-2). It should be noted that an 'Attachment for Limitation on Benefits Article' (Form 17) as well as residency certificate of your parent must also be submitted.

The application form is shown on the next and subsequent pages.

Form 15

Application Form for Income Tax Convention (Relief from Japanese Income Tax or Corporation Tax for Japanese Source Income to Report)

様式15
FORM

租税条約に関する届出書

APPLICATION FORM FOR INCOME TAX CONVENTION

（税務署整理欄 For official use only）

適用；有、無

税務署受付印

（申告対象国内源泉所得に対する所得税又は法人税の軽減・免除
Relief from Japanese Income Tax or Corporation Tax
for Japanese Source Income to report）

この届出書の記載に当たっては、別紙の注意事項を参照してください。
See separate instructions.

前回提出年月日：（注6）　　年　月　日
Date of Previous Submission (Note 6) ________

番号確認 | 身元確認

________税務署長殿
To the District Director, ________ Tax Office

1 適用を受ける租税条約に関する事項；
Applicable Income Tax Convention
日本国と________との間の租税条約第____条第____項____
The Income Tax Convention between Japan and ________, Article ____, para.____

□ 限度税率____%
Applicable Tax Rate
□ 免除
Exemption

2 申告対象国内源泉所得を有する者に関する事項；
Details of Recipient of Japanese Source Income to Report

氏名又は名称 Full name		
個人番号又は法人番号（有する場合のみ記入） Individual Number or Corporate Number (Limited to case of a holder)		
個人の場合 Individual	住所又は居所 Domicile or residence	（電話番号 Telephone Number）
	国籍 Nationality	
法人その他の団体の場合（注4） Corporation or other entity (Note 4)	本店又は主たる事務所の所在地 Place of head office or main office	（電話番号 Telephone Number）
	設立又は組織された場所 Place where the Corporation was established or organized	
	事業が管理・支配されている場所 Place where the business is managed and controlled	（電話番号 Telephone Number）
居住者として課税される国及び納税地（注9） Country where the recipient is taxable as resident on the income, and the place where he is to pay tax (Note 9)		（納税者番号 Taxpayer Identification Number）
日本において事業を行っている場合、その事業の概要 Description of business in Japan, if any		
日本において所得税又は法人税の申告書を提出している場合、その納税地 Place where he is to pay tax in Japan, if tax return is filed in Japan		（電話番号 Telephone Number）

3 申告対象国内源泉所得のうち「1」の租税条約の規定の適用を受けるもの（条約適用所得）に関する事項（注10）；
Details of Japanese Source Income to report to which the Convention mentioned in 1 above is applicable(Applicable Income) (Note10)

条約適用所得の種類及びその概要 Type and Description of applicable Income	____税法第____条第1項第____号に規定する国内源泉所得 Japanese Source Income prescribed in Subparagraph____ of Paragraph 1 of Article____ of ____Tax Act （　　　）
	____税法第____条第1項第____号に規定する国内源泉所得 Japanese Source Income prescribed in Subparagraph____ of Paragraph 1 of Article____ of ____Tax Act （　　　）
	____税法第____条第1項第____号に規定する国内源泉所得 Japanese Source Income prescribed in Subparagraph____ of Paragraph 1 of Article____ of ____Tax Act （　　　）

4 「1」の租税条約の規定の適用を受ける条約適用所得の支払者に関する事項（注11）；
Details of Payer of Applicable Income to which the Convention mentioned in 1 above is applicable (Note11)

所得の種類 Type of Income	氏名又は名称 Full name	住所（居所）又は本店（主たる事務所）の所在地 Domicile (residence) or place of head office (main office)
		（電話番号 Telephone Number）
		（電話番号 Telephone Number）
		（電話番号 Telephone Number）

5 その他参考となるべき事項（注12）；
Others (Note12)

【裏面に続きます（Continue on the reverse)】

6　「2」の外国法人の株主等である者の所得として取り扱われる部分に対して「1」の租税条約の規定が適用される場合の記載事項（注13）；
Details of Members of Foreign Company etc. If the Convention mentioned in 1 above is applicable to Part of Income treated as Income of Members of Foreign Company mentioned in 2 above (Note 13)

(1)　「1」の租税条約の相手国の法令に関する事項（注14）；
Law in the other contracting country of the convention mentioned in 1 above (Note 14)
(__________ ; __________第____条第____項)
(__________ ; __________, Article ____, para.____)

(2)　外国法人の株主等である者の各人別の申告対象株主等所得の金額に関する事項（注15）；
Amount of Japanese Source Income to report of respective Members (Note 15)

外国法人の株主等の氏名又は名称 Full Name of Member of Foreign Company	申告対象株主等所得の金額 (a) Amount of Japanese Source Income to report	軽減又は免除を受ける金額 (b) Amount applicable to the Relief of Convention
	(　%)	
	(　%)	
	(　%)	
合計 Total	(100.0%)	
申告対象株主等所得に係る国内源泉所得のうち、外国法人の株主等である者に係る国において その法令に基づきその者の所得として取り扱われる金額（申告対象株主等所得を除きます。） Amount of income that is treated as income of the members of the foreign corporation in their country regarding Japanese source income pertaining to Japanese source income to report (excluding Japanese source income to report)		

7　「2」の非居住者又は外国法人が構成員となっている相手国団体の所得として取り扱われるものに対して「1」の租税条約の規定が適用される場合の記載事項（注16）；
Details of Entity, etc., if the Convention mentioned in 1 above is applicable to Income treated as Income of the Entity of which Non-resident or Foreign Corporation mentioned in 2 above is a Member (Note 16)

(1)　「1」の租税条約の相手国の法令に関する事項（注17）；
Law in the other contracting country of the convention mentioned in 1 above (Note 17)
(__________ ; __________第____条第____項)
(__________ ; __________, Article ____, para.____)

(2)　相手国団体に関する事項；
Entity in the other contracting country

団体の名称 Name of entity	
本店又は主たる事務所の所在地 Place of head office or main office	（電話番号 Telephone Number）
設立又は組織された場所 Place where entity was established or organized	
事業が管理・支配されている場所 Place where business is managed and controlled	（電話番号 Telephone Number）
申告対象相手国団体所得の金額 Amount of income of the entity to report	

私は、この届出書の「3」に記載した申告対象国内源泉所得（「6」の(2)に記載した申告対象株主等所得又は「7」の(2)に記載した申告対象相手国団体所得）が「1」に掲げる租税条約の規定の適用を受けるものであることを、「租税条約等の実施に伴う所得税法、法人税法及び地方税法の特例等に関する法律の施行に関する省令」の規定により届け出るとともに、この届出書及び付表の記載事項が正確かつ完全であることを宣言します。

In accordance with the provisions of the Ministerial Ordinance for the Implementation of the Law concerning the Special Measures of the Income Tax Act, the Corporation Tax Act and the Local Tax Act for the Enforcement of Income Tax Conventions, I hereby submit this application form under the belief that the provisions of the Income Tax Convention mentioned in 1 above are applicable to the Japanese source income to report mentioned in 3 above (Japanese source income of members to report in 6(2) above or Japanese source income of entity to report in 7(2) above). I also hereby declare that the above statement is correct and complete to the best of my knowledge and belief.

年　月　日
Date________________

申告対象国内源泉所得を有する者の署名
Signature of the Recipient of Japanese Source Income to report ________________

○　代理人に関する事項；この届出書を代理人によって提出する場合には、次の欄に記載してください。
Details of Agent ; If this form is prepared and submitted by the Agent, fill out the following columns

代理人の資格 Capacity of Agent in Japan	氏名（名称） Full name		納税管理人の届出をした税務署名 Name of the Tax Office where the Tax Agent is registered
□ 納税管理人 ※ Tax Agent □ その他の代理人 Other Agent	住所（居所・所在地） Domicile (Residence or location)	（電話番号 Telephone Number）	税務署 Tax Office

※　「納税管理人」とは、日本国の国税に関する申告、申請、請求、届出、納付等の事項を処理させるため、国税通則法の規定により選任し、かつ、日本国における納税地の所轄税務署長に届出をした代理人をいいます。

※　"Tax Agent" means a person who is appointed by the taxpayer and is registered at the District Director of Tax Office for the place where the taxpayer is to pay his tax, in order to have such agent take necessary procedures concerning the Japanese national taxes, such as filing a return, applications, claims, payment of taxes, etc., under the provisions of Act on General Rules for National Taxes.

Q54 Tax Treatment on Reorganisation of a Parent Corporation

Our 100% parent corporation, a UK corporation, has now merged with its own 100% parent corporation located in the Netherlands (the grandmother corporation from our perspective). The merger was carried out under the laws of the UK and the Netherlands implementing Directive 2005/56/EC of the European Parliament and of the Council of 26 October 2005 and, as a merger between a parent company and a subsidiary, it was without consideration. As a result of this merger, all the shares in our corporation were transferred to the Dutch corporation, and we became a direct subsidiary of the Dutch corporation. Is this group reorganisation subject to tax in Japan?

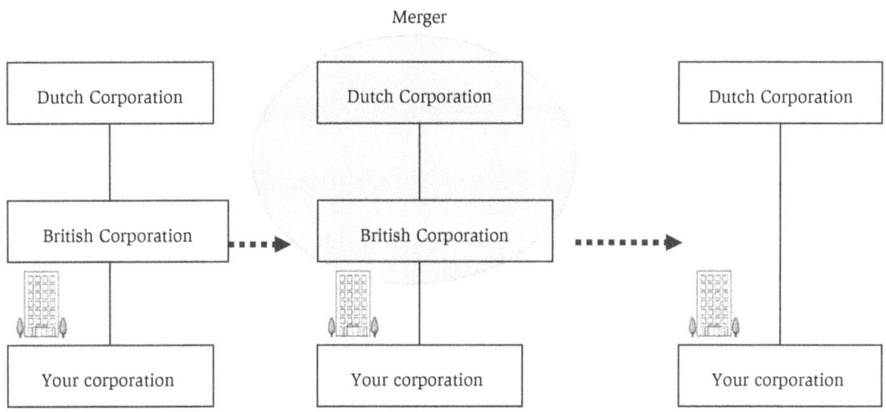

A:

As the shares in your corporation were transferred as part of a qualifying merger between a Dutch corporation and a UK corporation, the transfer is deemed to have taken place at book value, and no gain or loss should be recognised. As a result, there is no corporation tax imposed on the transfer of your shares.

Discussion

1. Capital gain or loss on transfer of shares

When shares are transferred, the capital gain or loss on the transfer is included in taxable income under the domestic law (CTA Article 61-2(1)). However, if assets and liabilities are transferred from a merged corporation to a surviving corporation as a result of a merger, the assets and liabilities are transferred at book value if the merger is classified as a qualified merger (CTA Article 62-2). No capital gains or losses are recorded on transfers arising from qualified mergers, and therefore no corporation tax is imposed.

2. Definition of merger under Japanese tax law

Corporation tax law does not provide a definition of merger. This raises the question of how a merger between two foreign entities should be treated for Japanese tax purposes. Consequently, mergers under Japanese tax law are not limited to mergers defined under the Japanese Companies Act. It is generally understood that in order for a merger between two foreign entities to be treated as a merger under Japanese tax law, it must have the same legal effect as a merger under the Japanese Companies Act.

The Companies Act does not provide a definition of a merger, but generally a merger is considered to be an act which has the following two characteristics:

(1) The entire rights and obligations of the merged corporation are comprehensively succeeded to by the surviving corporation ('comprehensive succession').
(2) The merged corporation is automatically liquidated and ceases to exist without any separate legal procedures ('automatic liquidation').

A merger of two foreign entities will be treated as equivalent to a merger under the Companies Act, and thus will be treated as a merger under domestic tax law if it satisfies these two elements. This applies even if the two foreign entities are in two different jurisdictions ('cross border merger').

The merger of your parent was conducted pursuant to the laws of the UK and the Netherlands implementing 'Directive 2005/56/EC of the European Parliament and of the Council of 26 October 2005' which should have the following legal effects: (i) automatic transfer of all assets and liabilities from the merging entity to the surviving entity (comprehensive succession); and (ii) liquidation of the merging entity without separate legal procedure (automatic liquidation).

Therefore, this merger has the essential elements of a merger under the Companies Act, and will be treated as a merger under corporation tax law.

3. Qualified merger

A qualified merger requires that no assets other than shares of the merging corporation be transferred to the shareholders of the transferor corporation (CTA Article 2(12-8)). A qualified merger may be either:

(1) a merger within a group, where one corporation owns, directly or indirectly, all the shares of the other corporation;
(2) a merger within a group, where one corporation owns between 50% and 100% of the shares of the other corporation, the principal business of the merging corporation is expected to be continued in the surviving corporation, and at least 80% of the employees of the merging corporation are expected to be employed by the surviving corporation; or
(3) a merger to manage a jointly operated business, where the merger is for the purposes of enabling the corporations to jointly conduct a business which satisfies the following criteria:

(a) The jointly operated business is a merger of the principal business of the merging corporation and related business of the surviving corporation.
(b) One of the merged businesses is not disproportionately larger than the other (i.e., sales, employees, capital are not more than five times that of the other), or key directors of both businesses are expected to be key officers in the surviving corporation.
(c) The principal business of the merging corporation is expected to be continued in the surviving corporation, and at least 80 % of the employees of the merging corporation are expected to be employed by the surviving corporation.
(d) If there are fewer than fifty shareholders of the merging corporation, at least 80 % of the shareholders of the merging corporation are expected to continue as shareholders of the surviving corporation.

When the merger is conducted without consideration, the following requirements are also required to be met in order for the merger to be treated as a qualified merger:

i) the surviving corporation holds all issued shares of the merging corporation;
ii) when the merging and the surviving corporations have the same shareholders, the shareholding ratio of each shareholder in the surviving corporation is equal to the shareholding ratio in the merging corporation.

Based on the above, the merger of your UK parent into your Dutch grandparent should be a qualified merger since the surviving corporation (the Dutch corporation) owns 100 % of the shares in the merging corporation (the UK corporation), and the merger has been conducted without consideration.

Therefore, for Japanese tax purposes, your UK parent will be deemed to have transferred your shares to its Dutch parent at book value, and there will be no gain or loss on the transfer. As a result, there is no corporation tax payable on the transfer.

Q55 Deemed Dividend on Capital Reduction

We have been operating in Japan for many years, but our business in Japan has been shrinking. As a result, our capital amount has become too large compared to the current scale of our business, and we have decided to make a capital reduction and return the excess capital to our parent. What are the tax implications of this capital reduction?

A:

A capital reduction may result in deemed Dividends. When deemed Dividends are paid, they will be subject to withholding tax.

Discussion.

1. Treatment of capital reduction with compensation for accounting purposes

Under the Companies Act, where a capital reduction occurs for compensation, the reduction in registered capital is transferred to 'other capital surpluses', followed by a distribution.

The following diagram illustrates 1:

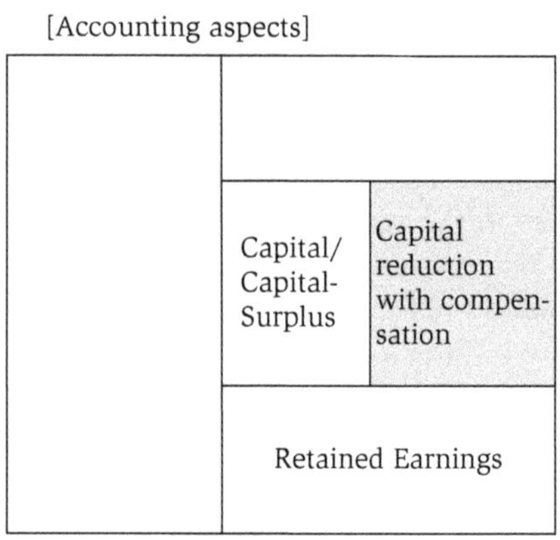

2. Treatment of capital reduction with compensation for tax purposes

For tax purposes, Dividends paid from 'other capital surplus' are treated as a return of capital (CTA Article 24(1)(iv)).

In addition, a return of capital is treated as the combination of a return of capital and a dividend from retained earnings (CTAEO Article 8(18), 9(12)).

The following diagram illustrates 2:

[Tax aspects]

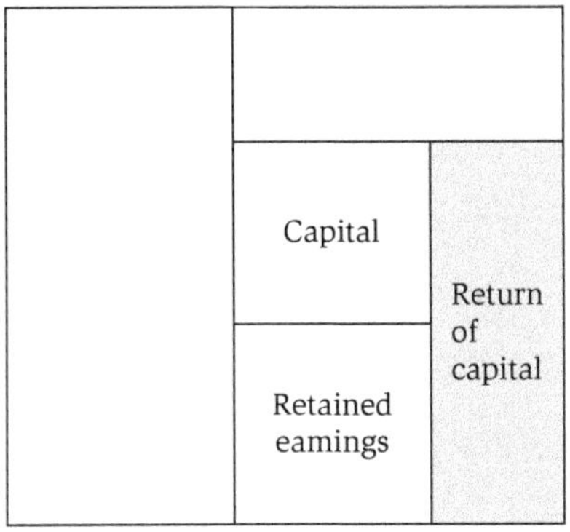

The return of capital from retained earnings is deemed as a dividend for tax purposes (CTA Article 24).

3. Calculation of deemed dividend

The amount of the deemed dividend is calculated according to the following formula (CTA Article 24)

deemed dividend = return of capital – corresponding capital

The 'corresponding capital' for this calculation is as follows (CTA Article 23(1)(iv)):

corresponding capital = capital immediately before the return of capital * reduced capital ratio

Reduced capital ratio = capital surplus reduced by the return of capital / (book value of assets at the end of the previous fiscal year – book value of liabilities at the end of the previous fiscal year)

4. Withholding tax on deemed Dividends

Dividends of surplus, dividends of profit, distribution of surplus or interest on funds ('Dividends') received from a domestic corporation are classified as domestic source income (ITA Article 161(1)(ix)). A person who pays domestic source income, such as Dividends, to a non-resident or foreign corporation in Japan is required to collect income tax at the time of payment and pay it to the competent national tax office by the 10th day of the month following the month in which the collection is made (ITA Article 212(1)).

Deemed Dividends are included in the definition of Dividends, and therefore, in principle, withholding tax is required when a deemed dividend is paid to a foreign parent corporation.

In addition, since the definition of Dividend in Tax Conventions also includes deemed Dividends, it is possible to receive a reduction or exemption from that withholding tax under a Tax Convention, where applicable.

Q56 Thin Capitalisation and Earnings Stripping Rules

We have borrowings from our parent corporation used for our business activities in Japan. Is interest expense on this loan deductible under Japanese tax law?

A:

Interest expense paid to foreign-related corporations is generally subject to both thin capitalisation and earnings stripping rules; whichever is the greater amount is treated as a non-deductible expense.

If earnings stripping is applied, the non-deductible amount may be carried forward for up to seven years.

Discussion

1. Thin capitalisation

Interest expenses on debt paid to controlling foreign shareholders is not deductible to the extent that the average balance of debt on which that interest expense is calculated is more than three times the equity investment of the controlling foreign shareholders (STMA Article 66-5(1)).

Under thin capitalisation, the meaning of each term is as follows.

(1) Controlling foreign shareholders

A controlling foreign shareholder is a non-resident or a foreign corporation that directly or indirectly owns 50% or more of the issued shares of a domestic corporation (STMA Article 66-5(5)(i), STMAEO Article 39-13(12)).

(2) Average balance of debt

The average balance of debt is the amount calculated using a reasonable method as the average balance of the book value of liabilities for the relevant fiscal year (STMAEO Article 39-13(19)).

(3) Equity of controlling foreign shareholders

The equity of controlling foreign shareholders is the remaining amount after deducting the total liabilities from the total assets for accounting purposes (STMAEO Article 39-13(23)(24)). However, if the result is less than the capital amount, the capital amount is treated as the equity of the controlling shareholders.

As your parent is a controlling foreign shareholder, it is necessary to analyse the average balance of debt and equity of those shareholders and determine whether thin capitalisation applies. If the average balance of debt exceeds three times the equity of those, the non-deductible interest expense must be calculated.

2. Earnings stripping

If net interest expense exceeds 20% of a corporation's adjusted income for each fiscal year, the excess interest amount is not deductible in calculating the corporation's income for the relevant fiscal year (STMA Article 66-5-2(1)). Excess interest can be carried forward for seven years and is deductible up to a maximum of 20% of adjusted income in each year (STMA Article 66-5-3(1)).

Under the earnings stripping rule, the meaning of each term is as follows.

(1) Net interest expense (STMA Article 66-5-3 (2))

Net interest expense is calculated as interest expense less corresponding interest income. Interest expense does not include: (i) interest expenses on specified bonds (issued not to the public, but to a limited number of unrelated parties), (ii) interest expenses paid to corporations or individuals subject to Japanese taxation or paid to qualifying public service corporations, and (iii) interest on back-to-back repos. Note that for earnings stripping purposes, it is not necessary that the interest expense be paid to a related party.

In relation to (ii) above, if the recipient of the interest is subject to Japanese corporation tax or withholding tax, that interest expense will not be included in the net interest expense calculation. However, if withholding tax is exempted under a Tax Convention, the interest expense will be included in the net interest expense calculation.

(2) Adjusted income (STMA Article 66-5-2(1), STMAEO Article 39-13-2(1))

Adjusted income is defined as taxable income for corporation tax purposes, adding back items such as tax loss carry-forwards deducted from current taxable income, interest expense, bad debt loss and depreciation expense.

Earnings stripping will not be applied in the following cases (STMA Article 66-5-2(3)):

(a) net interest expense in the fiscal year is JPY 20 million or less,
(b) the aggregated net interest expense on a Japanese corporate group basis (where there is more than a 50% capital relationship) is 20% or less of the aggregated adjusted income on the same group basis.

In order to apply either of these exemptions, a specified form must be attached to the corporation's tax return, and relevant documents must be preserved.

In order to determine whether the earning stripping rules are applicable, it is necessary to calculate the net interest expense and consider whether there is a possibility of applying for an exemption. If an exemption is not available, the non-deductible net interest expense should be determined after calculation of adjusted taxable income.

3. Relationship between the application of thin capitalisation and earnings stripping rules

If a corporation is subject to both thin capitalisation and earnings stripping in a fiscal year, the only greater amount is treated as the non-deductible expense (STMA Article 66-5(4), Article 66-5-2(6)).

If you have any interest expenses, and some or all of it is paid to a controlling foreign shareholder, you will need to calculate the non-deductible amount under both the thin capitalisation and earnings stripping rules to determine which one governs.

Q57 Tax Treatment upon Dissolution and Liquidation of a Japanese *Godo Kaisha* (GK) Subsidiary

We are a Japanese GK with a December fiscal year end, wholly owned by a US corporation. Due to poor market conditions, our parent has decided to withdraw from the Japanese market. This will involve our dissolution and voluntary liquidation, as follows:

- Dissolution: 30 November.
- Expected completion of liquidation: 28 February.

Given this schedule, when do we submit our final corporate tax return?

A:

Japanese subsidiaries of foreign corporations are still treated as domestic corporations as long as their head office or principal business location is in Japan. For this reason, the procedures for dissolution and liquidation of a Japanese subsidiary of a foreign corporation are the same as those for a Japanese resident individual or a Japanese corporation.

In Japan, there are two main categories of corporation. A *kabushiki kaisha* (KK) is the more widely used; however, GKs are also commonly used, especially for Japanese subsidiaries of multinational groups. One of the differences between a GK and a KK is the liquidation procedure.

Upon liquidation, a GK will have a fiscal year ending on the date of dissolution, and then a second fiscal year ending on the date of liquidation. Thus, a GK needs to submit a corporate tax return for both periods.

Discussion

There are no differences in the tax procedures upon liquidation of a corporation, regardless of whether the shareholder is a foreign or domestic individual/corporation.

1. Tax procedures on dissolution of a corporation

(1) Submission of notification of dissolution
A notification of dissolution must be submitted to the competent national and local tax offices without delay.

(2) Submission of corporate tax return for the period ending on the date of dissolution
Upon dissolution, taxable income is calculated for the period from the beginning of the fiscal year to the date of dissolution ('dissolution period') (CTA Article 14(1)(i)).

As you have a December year end, your dissolution period will be from 1 January to 30 November. The calculation of taxable income for the dissolution period is the same as for a normal fiscal year (i.e., revenue minus expenses). However, as the dissolution period is often less than twelve months, some items, such as depreciation, need to be calculated on a monthly basis. In addition, there are certain rules that do not apply for dissolution periods, such as special depreciation and some reserves.

The due date for submission of the corporate tax return for a dissolution period is within two months from the dissolution date, but the general one-month extension can be applied.

If a corporation has a deficit in the dissolution period, the corporation can apply a loss carry-back (CTA Article 80). In such cases, a 'request for tax refund under loss carry-back' must be submitted within one year of the date of dissolution. However, it generally takes several months for the refund to be paid, which may affect the overall liquidation schedule.

2. Fiscal year end

When a GK is dissolved in the middle of the fiscal year and the liquidation process is not finalised within that year, a new fiscal year begins from the day following the date of dissolution to the year-end day specified in the corporation's articles of association. This differs from the treatment for KKs, where the final fiscal year generally commences from the day after the date of dissolution to the day when the residual assets are determined (Companies Act Article 494(1)).

As you are a GK, you will therefore be required to calculate your taxable income, submit a tax return and pay any tax due for the period from 1 to 31 December. The due date for the submission of this return is within two months from the dissolution date, but the general one-month extension can be applied.

3. The period in which residual assets are determined (liquidation period)

(1) Submission of notification of residual assets

After the residual assets are determined (i.e., upon completion of the liquidation), it is necessary to submit a 'notification of residual assets' to the competent national and local tax offices without delay.

(2) Submission of corporate tax return for the period during which residual assets are determined

The period to the date of determination of the residual assets ('liquidation period') is deemed as a fiscal year (CTA Article 14(1)(v)), during which taxable income must be calculated, tax returns submitted and any taxes owing paid.

The tax return for the liquidation period must be submitted by the earlier of the following dates:

(i) The day before the date of final distribution of the residual assets.
(ii) Within one month from the date of completion of liquidation.

There is no extension for submission of the liquidation period tax return.

(3) Distribution of residual assets

Upon completion of the liquidation, the residual assets must be distributed. The residual assets generally constitute an equity component and a retained earnings component. Distributions from retained earnings are deemed to be Dividends. Deemed Dividends paid by a domestic corporation to a foreign parent corporation are domestic source income and are therefore subject to withholding tax. It is possible to apply for relief from this withholding tax under a Tax Convention, if available (refer to Q7).

Q58 Tax Treatment on Dissolution of a Japanese Branch

We are the Japanese branch of a foreign corporation, which has decided to withdraw from the Japanese market and close the branch. What tax procedures are required upon closure?

A:

Although the branch will be closed, the foreign corporation will continue to exist as a legal entity. Upon cessation of operations in Japan, the foreign corporation is required to submit a corporate tax return and pay any corporate tax owing.

However, as the corporate tax return will be submitted after the Japanese branch no longer exists, there will be no one in Japan to handle this procedure. A tax representative will therefore need to be appointed prior to the closure of the branch.

Discussion

For tax purposes, the following procedures are required upon closure of a Japanese branch.

1. Appointment of tax representative

Where a corporate taxpayer will no longer have an office in Japan due to the closure of a Japanese branch, but there are various tax procedures to be completed, such as submission of tax returns, the taxpayer must appoint a tax representative, and notify the competent national and local tax offices before the branch closure (Act on General Rules for National Taxes Article 117(1),(2), Act on General Rules for National Taxes Enforcement Order Article 39).

2. Submission of notification of closure

After the closure of the branch, a 'notification of closure' must be submitted without delay. However, the closure is essentially legally effective upon resignation of the branch representative and therefore, the legal registry will only show the date of resignation of the representative, and not the date of closure.

This may cause problems when reporting the date of closure to the tax offices (especially if the date of closure and the date of resignation of the branch representative are in different fiscal years) since there will be no legal documents to confirm the closure. Accordingly, it is common practice to prepare an affidavit confirming the date of closure, and to submit the affidavit to the tax authorities together with the 'notification of closure'.

3. Submission of a corporate tax return for the closure period

If a permanent establishment of a foreign corporation is closed, the taxable income shall be calculated by deeming the period from the beginning of the fiscal year to the date of closure as a fiscal year ('closure period') (CTA Article 14(1)(viii)).

The calculation of taxable income for the closure period is the same as for a standard fiscal year, i.e., revenue minus expenses. However, as the closure period is often less than twelve months, some items, such as depreciation, need to be calculated on a monthly basis. In addition, there are certain rules that do not apply for the closure period, such as special depreciation and some reserves.

The due date for submission of the corporate tax return for the closure period is within two months from the closure date, but the general one-month extension can be applied.

If a branch has a deficit in the closure period, the branch can apply a loss carry-back (CTA Art 80). In such cases, a 'request for tax refund under loss carry-back' must be submitted within one year of the date of closure. However, it generally takes several months for the refund to be paid after submission of such a request.

CHAPTER 4

Corporate Enterprise Tax

Q59 Factor-Based Taxation for the Japanese Branch of a Foreign Corporation

We are a Japanese branch of a foreign corporation. The registered capital of our head office is equivalent to more than JPY 100 million. Are we subject to factor-based corporate enterprise tax?

A:

If a foreign corporation has a permanent establishment (PE) in Japan and the foreign corporation's registered capital exceeds the equivalent of JPY 100 million at the end of the fiscal year, the PE is subject to factor-based corporate enterprise tax. Therefore, you are subject to factor-based corporate enterprise tax.

Discussion

Corporate enterprise tax is imposed on domestic corporations by the prefecture where the office or place of business is located (LTA Article 72-2(1)). PEs of foreign corporations are treated as offices or places of business for corporate enterprise tax purposes (LTA Article 72-2(6)).

In principle, factor-based taxation is applied to corporations with more than JPY 100 million of registered capital at fiscal year end (LTA Article 72-2(1)(i) (a), (2)).

Factor-based taxation also applies to foreign corporations if they have registered capital equivalent to more than JPY 100 million at fiscal year end. The amount of registered capital refers to the total capital of the corporation (Factor-Based Taxation Notice Article 1-2(1)).

The registered capital of a foreign corporation is converted into Japanese yen using the mid rate of the telegraphic transfer market ('TTM') at fiscal year end (Factor-Based Taxation Notice Article 1-2(2)). In principle, the TTM should be that of the corporation's primary financial institution. However, if the corporation consistently uses a reasonable TTM obtained in the same manner each year, the corporation may use a TTM other than that of their primary financial institution.

In summary, you are subject to factor-based taxation as the registered capital of your head office exceeds JPY 100 million.

Q60 Calculation of Factor-Based Taxation for a Japanese Branch of a Foreign Corporation

We are a Japanese branch of a foreign corporation subject to factor-based taxation as our head office capital exceeds JPY 100 million (*see* Q59). How is factor-based taxation calculated?

A:

Factor-based taxation is based on three factors: an income factor, a value-added factor, and a capital factor. The value-added factor is calculated as the sum of remuneration and salaries, net interest paid, net rent paid, and taxable income for the purpose of calculating domestic source income, all for the current fiscal year.

Capital for the purposes of the capital factor is the amount of capital attributable to the domestic business, which is divided proportionally by the number of employees.

Discussion

1. Calculation of income factor

The tax base for the income tax factor is the taxable income for corporate enterprise tax purposes. The taxable income for corporate enterprise tax purposes for permanent establishment ('PE') in Japan is the same for corporation tax purposes attributed to PE with certain adjustment (Local Tax Act 72-23(1)(ii)).

2. Calculation of value-added factor

The value-added factor is the sum of remuneration and salaries, net interest paid, net rent paid and taxable income for a current fiscal year (LTA Article 72-14). The amounts of remuneration and salaries, net interest paid and net rent paid are, in principle, the amounts included in deductible expenses in the calculation of corporate tax (LTA Article 72-15(1), 72-16(1), 72-17(1)). In addition, taxable income for the current fiscal year is calculated based on domestic source income as defined under the corporation tax law (LTA Article 72-18-1(ii)). In other words, only the sum of remuneration and salaries, net interest paid, and net rent paid, which are deducted from taxable income for corporation tax purposes, and taxable income before the application of any loss carry forward are included in the calculation of the value-added factor.

The credit for employment stability is applied if the amount of salaries (defined above) exceeds 70% of the revenue distribution amount.

3. Calculation of capital factor

The capital of a foreign corporation is used for the entire business conducted by the foreign corporation globally. For this reason, in order to determine the amount of capital for the purposes of corporate enterprise tax, which is imposed only on domestic businesses, the total capital of the corporation should be divided into the portion related to the domestic business and the portion related to businesses outside of Japan (LTA Article 72-22(2), LTAEO Article 20-2-25).

This division is made based on the number of employees, with the capital attributable to the employees involved in the domestic business being the taxable basis for the capital factor, as shown in the following formula:

Taxable capital amount = Total capital of the corporation * number of employees in Japanese branch / total number of employees

CHAPTER 5
Consumption Tax

Q61 Transactions Subject to Consumption Tax

We have decided to set up a wholly owned subsidiary in Japan. What transactions of that subsidiary will be subject to consumption tax?

A:

Consumption tax is a type of value-added tax, broadly similar to European value-added tax, and is in principle applicable to the supply of goods or services in Japan. The consumption tax rate is generally 10%.

'Taxable transactions' for consumption tax purposes are as follows:

(i) the transfer or lease of goods located in Japan and supply of services by a business for consideration in Japan ('Transfer of Assets'), excluding the 'Transfer of Specific Assets' (*see* below);
(ii) 'Specific Purchases' (*see* below); and
(iii) the import of goods.

In general, a service is treated as having been supplied in Japan if such service is provided in Japan or the supplier is based in Japan.

'Non-taxable transactions' include the transfer of certain assets and the provision of certain services, e.g., sales or leases of land, sales of securities, interest on loans, education services, medical services, etc. 'Exempt transactions' are transactions that are taxable, but have a zero consumption tax rate, which are basically the export of goods and the provision of services in Japan to foreign residents/corporations.

Discussion

1. Taxable transactions

Consumption tax is levied on the following transactions:

(1) Transfer of Assets by enterprises in Japan, excluding 'Transfers of Specific Assets' (*see* below).
(2) 'Specific Purchases' (*see* below) by enterprises in Japan.
(3) Foreign goods removed from bonded areas.

The Transfer of Assets includes the transfer of assets, the lending of assets and the provision of services conducted for consideration as a business (JCTA Article 2(1)(viii)).

'Specific Purchases' are the 'Transfer of Specific Assets' (JCTA Article 4(1)). The 'Transfer of Specific Assets' means the provision of services via electronic and telecommunications networks ('provision of electronic services') for enterprises and the provision of 'Specific Services' (JCTA Article 2 (1)(viii-ii)). 'Specific Services' is the provision of services by a non-resident actor or athlete.

The 'provision of electronic services' includes the provision of 'Copyrighted Works' (as defined in the Copyright Act Article 2(1)(i)) via telecommunications lines, including the licensing of such Copyrighted Works (JCTA Article 2 (1)(viii-iii)).

2. Non-taxable transactions

Consumption tax is not imposed on the transfer of certain assets, such as the transfer or leasing of land (JCTA Article 6(1)).

3. Exempt transactions

The export of goods or the provision of services to non-residents is exempt from consumption tax, even if conducted by an enterprise in Japan (JCTA Article 7).

4. Out-of-scope transactions

Transactions that do not fall under the category of Transfer of Assets, such as foreign exchange gains and losses, donations and Transfers of Assets conducted outside Japan, are out-of-scope transactions.

The above can be summarised in the following diagram:

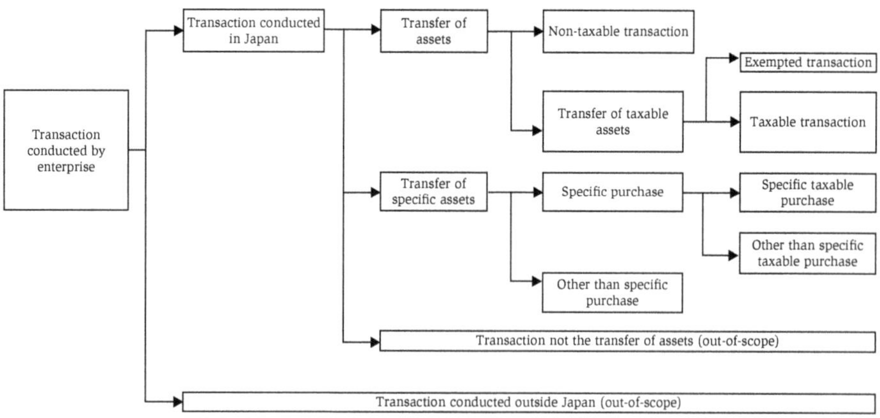

Q62 Reduced Tax Rates

When can we apply consumption tax rates other than the standard 10% rate?

A:

A reduced consumption tax rate of 8% applies to: (i) food and beverages, excluding alcoholic beverages and food services; and (ii) newspapers published more than twice a week (and supplied under a subscription contract). The reduced rate applies not only to enterprises selling such products but also to enterprises purchasing them. Purchases of items subject to the reduced tax rate need to be clearly identifiable in the accounting records.

Discussion

A reduced consumption tax rate of 8% applies to the transfer of the following goods (Supplementary Provision to Act for Partial Revision of the Income Tax Act, No 15 of 2016 Article 34(1)):

1. Food and beverage products (food and beverage products as defined in the Food Labelling Law (excluding alcoholic beverages as defined in the Liquor Tax Act)).
2. Subscriptions of newspapers which feature articles on politics, economics, society and culture, etc., and that are published at least twice a week.

'Food and beverage products' as defined in the Food Labelling Act refers to all foods and drinks for human consumption. 'Food' does not include pharmaceutical products but does include 'additives' as defined in the Food Sanitation Act.

Even if an enterprise does not sell food and beverage products nor newspapers, they may purchase such goods for business use (e.g., tea/coffee for meetings).

When an enterprise purchases goods subject to the reduced 8% rate, it is necessary to account for such transactions separately. In addition, accounting records and documents supporting such transactions must be preserved.

Q63 National and Local Consumption Taxes

How are the overall consumption tax rates determined?

A:

The standard consumption tax rate of 10% is calculated from 7.8% for national consumption tax and 2.2% for local consumption tax. The reduced 8% rate is calculated from 6.24% for national consumption tax and 1.76% for local consumption tax.

The consumption tax return combines the national consumption tax return with the local consumption tax return. The consumption tax return is required to be submitted and paid to the competent national tax office within two months after fiscal year end. A one-month extension can be granted if the filing due date for the corporation tax return is extended.

Discussion

The overall consumption tax rates are calculated from a national consumption tax and a local consumption tax. The standard national tax rate is 7.8% and the reduced national tax rate is 6.24% (JCTA Article 29, Supplementary Provision to Act for Partial Revision of the Income Tax Act, No 15 of 2016 Article 34(2)). The local tax rate is 22/78 of the national tax rate. As a result, the standard local tax rate is 2.2% and the reduced local tax rate is 1.76% (LTA Article 72-83).

These can be summarised in the table below:

Classification	*Standard Tax Rate*	*Reduced Tax Rate*
National consumption tax rate	7.8%	6.24 %
Local consumption tax rate	2.2% (22/78 of national consumption tax)	1.76% (22/78% of national consumption tax)
Total	10.0%	8.0%

The consumption tax return combines the national consumption tax return with the local consumption tax return. The filing due date for the consumption tax return is two months after fiscal year end. A one-month extension may be granted by the competent national tax office by filing an application for extension of the filing due date if the filing due date for the corporation tax return has been extended.

As mentioned above, there is only one consumption tax return (i.e., a single return combining both national and local consumption taxes) submitted, and only one payment is made. However, even if the total amount of consumption tax in a return is correct, if either the national or local component is underpaid, an amended return or request for correction must be submitted (Treatment of Correction of Consumption Tax and Local Consumption Tax and Additional Tax (Administrative Guidelines) Article 2). Penalties and interest will be imposed on the underpaid tax amount.

Q64 Interim Consumption Tax Returns

We paid consumption tax for the first time in the previous fiscal year. Do we need to submit an interim consumption tax return this fiscal year?

A:

If the national consumption tax in the immediate preceding fiscal year is JPY 480,000 or more, interim consumption tax returns are required to be submitted (however, interim returns are not required for shortened taxable periods).

The number of interim returns filed may be one, three or eleven, depending on the national consumption tax in the immediate preceding fiscal year.

There are two methods for calculating interim consumption tax.

1) Prior year method

The interim consumption tax is calculated based on the national consumption tax for the prior year, prorated by months.

2) Provisional calculation method

The interim consumption tax is calculated by making a provisional calculation for the interim consumption tax period.

Taxable enterprises can freely choose their preferred calculation method.

Discussion

1. Number of interim consumption tax returns

An enterprise is required to submit an interim consumption tax return if the consumption tax in the immediate preceding fiscal year exceeds JPY 480,000 (JCTA Article 42). However, interim returns are not required for shortened fiscal years (*see* Q71).

The number of interim returns filed depends on the amount of final national consumption tax for the immediate preceding fiscal year, as follows:

National consumption tax amount immediately preceding tax period	JPY 480,000 or less	JPY 480,000 up to JPY 4 million	Over JPY 4 million up to JPY 48 million	up JPY 48 million
Number of interim Consumption tax return	Not required	1 time	3 times	11 times
Due date for interim Consumption tax return filing and payment		within 2 months after the interim Consumption tax period (6 months from the beginning of the taxable period) e.g., The end of August in case of December fiscal year end.	within 2 months after the interim Consumption tax period (3 months from the beginning of the taxable period) e.g., The end of May, August and November in case of December fiscal year end.	1st month in the tax period: within 2 months after the 2 months of the beginning of the tax period e.g., the end of Aprill in case of December fiscal year end After 10 months : within 2 months after the interim Consumption tax period. e.g., The end of April to January in case of December fiscal year end. As a result 2 sets of interim Consumption tax return filing and payment are required.
Interim Consumption tax amount (based on prior year's tax method)		6/12 of the national consumption tax amount immediately preceding tax period + local consumption tax calculated based on the interim national consumption tax	3/12 of the national consumption tax amount immediately preceding tax period + local consumption tax calculated based on the interim national consumption tax	1/12 of the national consumption tax amount immediately preceding tax period + local consumption tax calculated based on the interim national consumption tax
Number of Consumption tax filing	Only 1 final Consumption tax return filing	Final Consumption Tax filing + 1 time interim Consumption tax filing	Final Consumption Tax filing + 3 times interim Consumption tax filing	Final Consumption Tax filing + 11 times interim Consumption tax filing

2. Calculation of interim consumption tax

There are two methods of calculating interim consumption tax.

(1) Prior year method

Interim consumption tax is calculated based on the national consumption tax for the prior year, prorated by months:

- In the case of an annual interim return, 6/12 of the national consumption tax of the prior years.
- In the case of quarterly interim returns, 3/12 of the national consumption tax of the prior year.
- In the case of monthly interim returns, 1/12 of the national consumption tax of the prior year.

(2) Provisional calculation method

Interim consumption tax is calculated by treating the interim period as a taxable period. Even if the interim consumption tax is negative, no refund is given.

Taxable enterprises can freely choose their preferred calculation method.

Q65 Simplified Consumption Tax Returns

We are a small corporation. Is there any way to reduce the administrative burden of consumption tax compliance?

A:

You may consider filing a simplified consumption tax return.

Discussion

The simplified consumption tax return was introduced to reduce the administrative burden of consumption tax compliance for SME enterprises. A simplified tax return calculates input consumption tax based on output consumption tax.

A simplified tax return can only be filed by an enterprise whose taxable sales in the 'Base Period' are JPY 50 million or less (the 'Base Period' is the fiscal year two years prior to the current fiscal year). In order to file a simplified return, an enterprise must submit a 'Notification of Election of Simplified Taxation System'.

In a simplified return, input consumption tax is calculated by multiplying output consumption tax by a deemed 'purchase ratio', determined according to the type of business, as follows:

Type of business		*Deemed purchase ratio*
Type 1	Wholesale business	90%
Type 2	Retail trade, agriculture, forestry and fishing (limited to businesses related to the transfer of food and beverage products)	80%
Type 3	Agriculture, forestry, fishing (except for business related to the transfer of food and beverages), mining, construction, manufacturing, electricity, gas, heat supply and water supply	70%
Type 4	Businesses other than Type 1, Type 2, Type 3, Type 5 and Type 6	60%
Type 5	Transport and communications, financial services and insurance, and services (excluding those falling within the restaurant industry)	50%
Type 6	Real estate	40%

Q66 Timing of Input Consumption Tax Credit

We are a Japanese branch of a foreign corporation. Invoices for most of our expenses are sent directly to and paid by us. However, some invoices are sent to and paid by our head office.

We understand that input consumption tax on all expenses should be included in our consumption tax return.

However, we sometimes receive the invoices for certain expenses a long time after the transaction has occurred, and therefore we do not know the exact amount of the invoice when preparing our consumption tax returns.

How should we treat such expenses for consumption tax purposes?

A:

An input consumption tax credit is available for the fiscal year that includes the date of the consumption taxable transaction. Therefore, an input consumption tax credit cannot be taken in the taxable period of the date of issue of the invoice if that differs from the date of the transaction.

A one-month extension of the due date for filing consumption tax returns may be granted, which may provide some extra time to collect invoices for all transactions during the fiscal year.

Discussion

A taxable enterprise is entitled to an input consumption tax credit in the taxable period as follows (JCTA Article 30(1)):

1. Taxable purchases

The date on which a taxable purchase is made.

2. 'Specific Purchases' are made

The date on which the 'Specific Purchases' are made.

3. Goods removed from a bonded area

The date of removal of the goods.

The date on which taxable purchases are made refers to the date on which assets are transferred or borrowed, or services are provided (Consumption Tax Basic Circular Article 11-3-1).

The following examples are provided.

1. Transfer of inventories and/or transfer of fixed assets (Consumption Tax Basic Circular Article 9-1-1, Article 9-1-13)

> The timing of the transfer of inventories or transfer of fixed assets is in principle the date of delivery.

2. Lease of assets under a lease contract (Consumption Tax Basic Circular Article 9-1-20)

The date on which payment is to be received either under the contract or by custom (excluding advance payments).

3. Provision of services (Consumption Tax Basic Circular Article 9-1-5 to Article 9-1-12)

(1) Contracts for work requiring deliverables, delivery date of the deliverables after completion of all agreed work.
(2) Contracts for work not requiring deliverables, the date of completion of all agreed work.
(3) Provision of personal services, excluding contracts for work, the date of completion of the personal services.

As stated above, an input consumption tax credit is only available for the fiscal year in which the transaction occurs.

Since Japanese consumption tax is based on accounting records, there are differences from value added tax (VAT) or goods and services tax (GST) in other countries. Since an invoice system is generally adopted for VAT or GST, the input VAT/GST credit is available based on the date of the invoice. However, for consumption tax purposes, an input consumption tax credit is available based on the date of the taxable transaction. Such difference is sometimes confusing for those who are familiar with VAT or GST.

Japan is planning to introduce a 'qualified invoice system' (which is often referred to as a 'Japanese version of an invoice system') from 1 October 2023 (refer to Q86). However, no amendment to the timing at which an input consumption tax credit can be taken is expected.

Q67 Revenue Recognition and Consumption Tax

We recently signed a contract to provide IT system consulting services to a Japanese customer:

1. The service is tailored for the customer's specific IT system.
2. One of our employees will work at the customer's premises for one year to provide support services.
3. We will not provide any specific deliverables to the customer, although we will submit monthly work reports.
4. Our consulting fee is a fixed monthly fee, but the total fee is invoiced at the time of conclusion of the contract, and thus will be received in advance.
5. In the event of early cancellation, the prepaid fee is not refunded.

For accounting and corporation tax purposes, we will recognise the fees on a monthly basis.

What is the consumption tax treatment?

A:

Consumption tax should be recognised upon completion of a service. In this case, the completion of the service may be considered as the end of the contract.

However, if the fee is fixed on a monthly basis, and if the services are considered to be completed each month, consumption tax should also be recognised on a monthly basis.

Discussion

Revenue recognition for corporation tax purposes follows the accounting standard (*see* Q28).

However, the revenue recognition for consumption tax purposes does not follow the accounting standard, so consumption tax should be recognised at the time of the 'Transfer of Assets'.

The time of 'Transfer of Assets' where the transfer is the provision of personal services is the date of completion of the personal services (Consumption Tax Basic Circular Article 9-1-5). This applies even where payment is made in advance (Consumption Tax Basic Circular Article 9-1-27).

In this case, although the contract period is one year, the fee is fixed and the services are rendered on a monthly basis. Thus, the 'Transfer of Assets' is each month, when the services are completed.

On the other hand, if the fee was fixed on an annual basis, and the services were to be completed on an annual basis, then the date of the 'Transfer of Assets' would be the end of the contract.

Q68 Taxable and Exempt Enterprises for Consumption Tax Purposes

We are a subsidiary of a multinational group, and were incorporated in the current year with a registered capital of JPY 1 million. We import goods from overseas and sell them to customers in Japan. Our annual sales are expected to exceed JPY 10 million. No other group company has any business in Japan. When do we need to submit a consumption tax return?

A:

You will be exempt from filing a consumption tax for your first year of business.

In your second year, if taxable sales and salaries each exceed JPY 10 million in the 'Specified Period', you will become a taxable enterprise.

For the third year and later, as your taxable sales will exceed JPY 10 million in the 'Base Period', you will be a taxable enterprise.

Discussion

1. Taxable and exempt enterprises

Most enterprises are required to collect consumption tax from customers and to pay that tax to the competent national tax office. Enterprises that are obliged to pay consumption tax are referred as 'taxable enterprises'.

However, small enterprises with taxable sales of JPY 10 million or less in the 'Base Period' are, in principle, not obliged to pay the consumption tax they collect from customers to the tax office (JCTA Article 9(1)). Enterprises such as this that are exempt from paying the consumption tax they receive to the tax office are generally referred to as 'exempt enterprises'. Exempt enterprises are not only exempt from paying the consumption tax they receive to the tax office but also have no right to claim an input consumption tax credit.

2. Base Period Exemption

A corporation with taxable transactions for consumption tax purposes of JPY 10 million or less during the 'Base Period' for a fiscal year is in general treated as an exempt enterprise ('Base Period Exemption'). The Base Period is the fiscal year two years prior to the current year (JCTA Article 2(1)(xiv)).

3. Specified Period

Even if taxable sales in the Base Period are JPY 10 million or less, if taxable sales in the 'Specified Period' exceed JPY 10 million, an enterprise becomes a taxable enterprise (JCTA Article 9-2(1)). Salaries, wages and severance payments paid to Japanese residents can also be used for the 'Specified Period', whichever gives the best result for the enterprise (JCTA Article 9-2(3)). As a result, even if taxable sales in the 'Specified Period' exceed JPY 10 million, if salaries, wages and severance payments in the 'Specified Period' do not exceed JPY 10 million, the enterprise is not an exempt enterprise. The Specified Period for corporation is the six-month period from the beginning of the previous fiscal year (JCTA Article 9-2(4)(ii)).

4. Exception for newly established corporations

Newly established corporations will technically not have a Base Period and thus should be exempt from filing consumption tax returns for at least the first fiscal year under the Base Period Exemption. However, the Base Period Exemption is not available and a newly established corporation is automatically treated as a taxable enterprise for its initial two fiscal periods if the following conditions are met (JCTA Article 12-2):

(1) it has a registered capital of JPY 10 million or more; or
(2) it is controlled by another corporation which owns 50% or more of its shares, and the taxable sales for consumption tax purposes of that controlling corporation exceed JPY 500 million.

5. Election to become a taxable enterprise

Even if an enterprise is an exempt enterprise, it is possible to become a taxable enterprise by submitting a 'notification for election to become a taxable enterprise' to the competent national tax office (JCTA Article 9(4)). This notification must be submitted by the day before the first day of the fiscal year to which it is to be applied. Such election is in practice used when an enterprise expects to be in a consumption tax refundable position.

Once an enterprise chooses to become a taxable enterprise, it cannot become an exempt enterprise for at least two years (JCTA Article 9(6)). In addition, if the taxable enterprise purchases certain fixed assets during the following fiscal year, the taxable enterprise cannot become an exempt enterprise for three years from the fiscal year in which the fixed assets are purchased (JCTA Article 9(7)).

6. The current case

As you are a newly established corporation, there is no Base Period. In addition, your registered capital is only JPY 1 million, so it is less than the JPY 10 million threshold referred to above. Furthermore, there are no taxable sales of any related enterprise.

As a result, you are an exempt enterprise for your first fiscal year.

Since you sell goods to Japanese customers and thus will recognise taxable sales, there should be no advantage in filing a notification to become a taxable enterprise.

In your second fiscal year, if your taxable sales and salaries, wages and severance payments in the Specified Period exceed JPY 10 million, you will become a taxable enterprise. Otherwise, you will also be an exempt enterprise for your second fiscal year.

From your third fiscal year on, if taxable sales in the Base Period exceed JPY 10 million, or if taxable sales and salaries, wages and severance payments in any Specified Period exceed JPY 10 million, you will become a taxable enterprise:

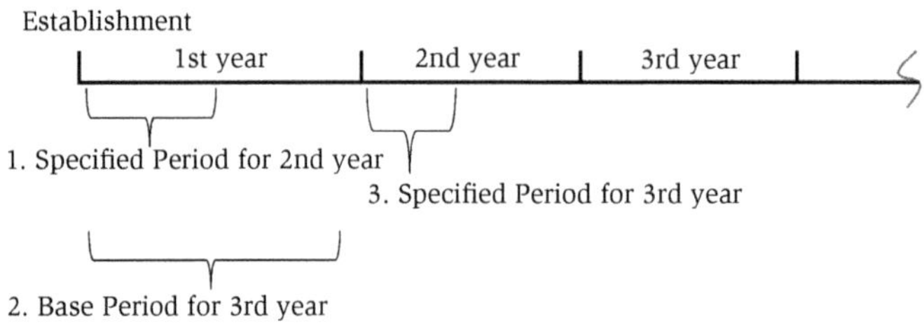

1st year	exempt enterprise, as the registered capital is JPY 10 million or less taxable enterprise
2nd year	-if the taxable sales in the Specified Period (i.e., first half of 1st year) are JPY 10 million or more; and - the salaries and wages in the Specified Period (i.e., first half of 1st year) are JPY 10 million or more otherwise, exempt enterprise
3rd year	taxable enterprise, - if the taxable sales in the Base Period (i.e., 1st year) are JPY 10 million or more; or - if the taxable sales in the Specified Period (i.e., first half of 2nd year) are JPY 10 million or more; and - the salaries and wages in the Specified Period (i.e., first half of 2nd year) are JPY 10 million or more

Q69 Base Period for Foreign Corporations

We are a foreign corporation without any offices, employees or related corporations in Japan. We were established two years ago with registered capital equivalent to JPY 10 million. We started distribution of games through the internet to Japanese customers this year, and sales in the first half of the year exceeded JPY 10 million. Do we need to pay consumption tax in Japan?

A:

For your first fiscal year, you have no taxable sales in the Base Period or the Specified Period, so you are an exempt enterprise.

For your second fiscal year, taxable sales in the Specified Period are expected to exceed JPY 10 million; however, as there are no offices in Japan and therefore no salaries, wages or severance payments made to Japanese residents, you should be an exempt enterprise.

As a result, you should become a taxable enterprise and need to pay consumption tax from your third fiscal year.

Discussion

The distribution of games on the internet is treated as the provision of electronic services to consumers, and accordingly, that part of the transaction where Japanese consumers are beneficiaries is subject to consumption tax (JCTA Article 4(3)(iii)).

Enterprises with taxable sales of JPY 10 million or less in the Base Period are not obliged to pay consumption tax (JCTA Article 9(1)). Therefore, your taxable sales in the Base Period are important to consider whether you are a taxable enterprise or an exempt enterprise. The Base Period is the fiscal year two years prior to the current year (JCTA Article 2(1)(xiv)).

However, even if taxable sales in the Base Period are JPY 10 million or less, if taxable sales in the Specified Period exceed JPY 10 million, the enterprise becomes a taxable enterprise (JCTA Article 9-2(1)). Salaries and wages can also be used instead of taxable sales in the Specified Period (JCTA Article 9-2(3)), whichever gives the best result for the enterprise. The Specified Period is six months from the beginning of the enterprise's previous fiscal year (JCTA Article 9-2(4)).

1. Tax liability for the current fiscal year

Although you have been distributing online games to customers in Japan since this year, you were established two years ago. Therefore, that year is your Base Period. However, your taxable sales in the Base Period should be zero, as you did not sell any games to customers in Japan at that time.

The Specified Period for the current fiscal year is the first six months of last year. Taxable sales in the Specified Period should also be zero, as you did not sell any games to customers in Japan at that time.

As a result, you should be an exempt enterprise for the current fiscal year, and thus you do not have an obligation to pay the consumption tax you receive from Japanese consumers to the Japanese tax authorities:

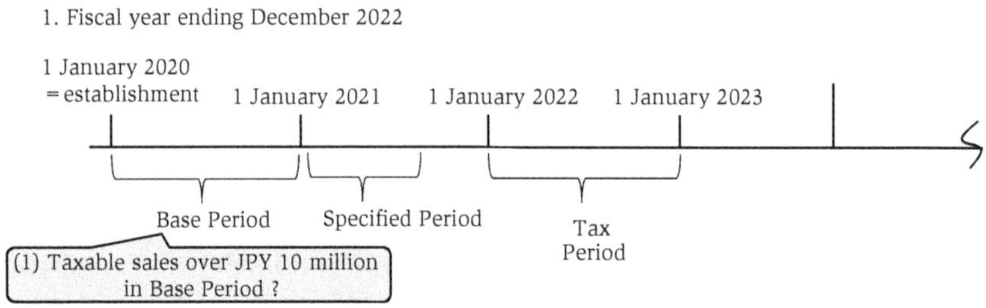

2. Tax liability for next fiscal year

The Base Period for next fiscal year is the last fiscal year. The Specified Period for next fiscal year is the first six months of the current year.

As you did not sell any games to customers in Japan in the Base Period, your taxable sales in the Base Period should be zero.

However, your taxable sales in the Specified Period exceed JPY 10 million. Consequently, you could become a taxable enterprise from the next fiscal year.

However, salaries and wages can be used to assess taxable status, instead of taxable sales, in the Specified Period. Salaries and wages are those paid to Japanese residents in Japan.

As you do not have any employees in Japan, you should have no salaries and wages in the Specified Period. Accordingly, you will be an exempt enterprise and are not liable to pay consumption tax next fiscal year:

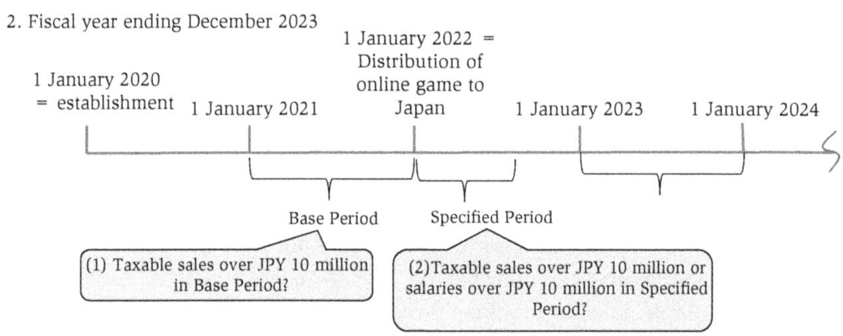

3. Tax liability for fiscal year after next

The Base Period for the fiscal year after next is the current fiscal year.

Since your taxable sales in the Base Period are expected to exceed JPY 10 million, you will be a taxable enterprise in the fiscal year after next, and therefore you will be liable to pay consumption tax at that time.

Q70 Consumption Tax Refunds for Foreign Corporations

We are a foreign corporation that made taxable purchases in Japan. Since we have no sales in Japan or to any Japanese consumers, we are not required to file a consumption tax return. Can we claim a consumption tax refund on our purchases?

A

You may be able to claim a consumption tax refund after making an election to become a consumption taxable enterprise.

In order to obtain a refund, you will need to elect the itemised method for calculating your input consumption tax credit.

Once you have elected to become a taxable enterprise, you are required to keep that status for at least two years.

Discussion

Japanese consumption tax is imposed on the sale of assets in Japan. Therefore, even if you are a non-resident or a foreign corporation, if you purchase assets and the transaction occurs in Japan, you can still be subject to consumption tax.

However, if you have no taxable sales in the Base or Specified Periods, you are an exempt enterprise, and, therefore, an input consumption tax credit cannot be applied.

On the other hand, exempt enterprises can elect to become taxable by submitting a 'notification of election to become a taxable enterprise' to the competent national tax office.

Taxable enterprises have the right to claim a consumption tax refund if their input consumption tax exceeds their output consumption tax.

There are two methods to calculate input consumption tax: the itemised method and the proportional method (*see* Q81). In order for a foreign corporation with no sales in Japan or to Japanese consumers to claim a consumption tax refund, the itemised method must be used to calculate the input consumption tax credit.

Under the itemised method, input consumption tax can be credited where taxable purchases: (1) are related to taxable sales, and (2) are related to both taxable sales and non-taxable sales (i.e., using the taxable sales ratio).

The taxable sales ratio is calculated based on the following formula:

taxable sales / (taxable sales + non-taxable sales)

If there are no taxable or non-taxable sales, the NTA has issued an opinion that the taxable sales ratio is zero. Therefore, only input consumption tax for (1) can be credited.

Under the itemised method, however, input consumption tax related to sales made outside Japan is treated as input consumption tax related to taxable sales under (1) above (Consumption Tax Basic Circular Article 11-2-13). Therefore, if your taxable purchases in Japan are related to sales made outside Japan, input consumption tax on those sales will fall within the scope of (1) above.

If you elect to become a taxable enterprise and apply the itemised method, you may claim a refund of input consumption tax. However, once you elect to become a taxable enterprise, you cannot change back to an exempt enterprise for two years.

Q71 Shortening of the Consumption Taxable Period

We provide marketing support services in Japan for our foreign parent corporation, which is our sole customer. As a result, all of our sales are exempt for consumption tax purposes, so we obtain a refund when we file our consumption tax return each year.

Is there any way to obtain this refund earlier?

A:

Taxable enterprises can apply to shorten the consumption taxable period by submitting a 'notification of election or change of special taxable period for consumption tax' to the competent national tax office. The taxable period can be shortened to one month, three months or six months.

However, as it is necessary to submit a consumption tax return for each taxable period, it is important to consider the costs of compliance against the benefits of an earlier refund, before deciding whether to make the election to shorten the taxable period.

Discussion

Taxable enterprises are obliged to file a consumption tax return for each taxable period to the competent national tax office within two months from the day following the end of that taxable period (JCTA Article 45(1)).

Refunds are generally paid after filing the final consumption tax return and after confirmation of the refund calculation by the tax authorities.

The taxable period of a corporation is, in principle, the fiscal year (JCTA Article 19(1)(ii)). Therefore, in principle, the final consumption tax return should be submitted within two months from the end of the fiscal year.

However, if an election is made, the taxable period can be shortened to one month, three months or six months (JCTA Article 19(1)(iii-ii),(iv), (iv-ii)). The election is made by submitting a 'notification of election or change of special taxable period for consumption tax' to the competent national tax office prior to the start of the first shortened taxable period.

When the 'notification of election or change of special tax period for Consumption tax' is submitted, the enterprise must also file a consumption tax return from the beginning of the fiscal year to the date before the beginning of the shortened tax period. For example, if your fiscal year ends on 31 December and your first shortened tax period of three months begins on 1 October, you must first submit a consumption tax return for the period 1 January to 30 September. From 1 October onwards, you must submit a consumption tax return every three months.

Unless the business is discontinued, for at least two years from the date of application of the shortened taxable period, the following will not be allowed (JCTA Article 19(5)):

1. not applying the shortened taxable period; or

2. changing from a taxable period of every three months to a taxable period of every one month or vice versa.

Consumption tax returns must be filed for each taxable period, so if the taxable period is shortened to three months, four consumption tax returns must be filed; if the taxable period is reduced to one month, twelve returns must be filed.

Therefore, before deciding whether to shorten the taxable period, it is important to compare the costs of this additional administrative work with the benefits of accelerated cash flow.

Q72 Consumption Tax-Exempt Sales (Election to Become a Taxable Enterprise)

We are a newly established company with registered capital of JPY 1 million, and provide market research services to our foreign parent corporation. We understand these services are exempt sales for consumption tax purposes.

Can we obtain a consumption tax refund from our first year of business?

A:

Since your registered capital is less than JPY 10 million, you are, in principle, an exempt enterprise for your first two years of business.

Given the services you provide are exempt sales for consumption tax purposes, you should be in a refund position. However, since you are an exempt enterprise for two years, you do not have the right to claim a consumption tax refund unless you elect to become a taxable enterprise.

Discussion

1. Consumption tax on the provision of services to non-residents

Consumption tax is imposed on the transfer of assets in Japan. For the provision of services, the transfer is considered to occur in Japan when the services are provided in Japan (JCTA Article 4(3)).

Where the provision of services is conducted both in Japan and outside of Japan, and where the place of provision of the services is not clear, the services are deemed to be provided at the location of the office of the enterprise providing the service (JCTAEO Article 6(2)(vi)). This also includes services provided consecutively in Japan and outside Japan, and where services are provided in Japan and outside Japan to the same person, the remuneration for such services is not reasonably distinguishable as between the services provided in Japan and outside Japan (Consumption Tax Basic Circular 5-7-15).

Your type of service is generally considered to be a combined service which is provided in Japan (i.e., market research service) and provided outside Japan (i.e., reporting to foreign customers). As a result, such services are generally treated as the provision of the services where the place of provision of the services is not clear, and thus where the amount of remuneration for each service is not reasonably distinguishable.

As your services are provided in an office located in Japan, the provision of services is deemed to be provided in Japan.

On the other hand, the provision of services to non-residents (other than those services where the benefit is directly received in Japan) is treated as exempt sales, similar to an export sale of goods (JCTA Article 7(1)(v), JCTAEO Article 17(2)(vii), Consumption Tax Basic Circular Article 7-2-1(11)).

Non-residents for consumption tax purposes are defined as non-residents pursuant to the Foreign Exchange and Foreign Trade Act (JCTAEO Article 1(2) (ii)).

Non-residents are natural persons and juridical persons other than Japanese residents. Japanese residents are natural persons having their domicile or residence in Japan and juridical persons having their principal office in Japan (Foreign Exchange and Foreign Trade Act Article 6(1)(vi)). Therefore, a foreign corporation with its principal office outside Japan is considered a non-resident for consumption tax purposes.

In order to prove that the services being provided are similar to export sales (i.e., exempt sales), an agreement, invoices or other documents which show the following information should be preserved (JCTAER Article 5(1)(iv)):

- Name and address of the enterprise performing the services.
- Date of provision of the services.
- Details/contents of the services.
- Remuneration for the services.
- Name and address of the counterparty.

As far as documents containing the above information are in place, your services will be treated as exempt sales.

If your services are exempt sales, while your purchases of goods and services in Japan are taxable transactions, you would generally be in a consumption tax refund position.

2. Election to become a taxable enterprise

Since you are a newly established corporation with registered capital of JPY 1 million, you should be an exempt enterprise (*see* Q68). An exempt enterprise is not obliged to pay consumption tax received to the national tax authorities, but is also not entitled to receive a consumption tax refund.

However, if you elect to become a taxable enterprise, you will be able to claim a refund. An election is made by submitting a 'notification for election to become a taxable enterprise' by the end of the taxable period preceding the first taxable period for which you would be a taxable enterprise.

Q73 Consumption Tax-Exempt Sales (Sales to Foreign Embassies)

We sell our products to customers in Japan, including to foreign embassies. Are these sales subject to consumption tax?

A:

In principle, consumption tax applies to the transfer of assets in Japan. However, if this transfer is made to a foreign embassy in Japan, it may be an exempt sale for consumption tax purposes if the following criteria are met:

(1) the seller is a 'designated shop';
(2) the transfer is made for use in diplomatic or consular activities; and
(3) the transfer is made in a prescribed manner.

It is also necessary to maintain certain documents, such as the tax-exempt purchase form from the foreign embassy.

Discussion

1. Exempt sales under laws other than the Consumption Tax Act

Consumption tax is levied on the transfer of assets in Japan, but under the Consumption Tax Law, exports from Japan are exempt (JCTA Article 4(1), Article 7(1)).

In addition, the following transactions are also exempt sales for consumption tax purposes, however, pursuant to laws other than the Consumption Tax Act:

- Transfer of assets to be loaded on ocean-going ships (STMA Article 85).
- Transfer of assets to foreign embassies (STMA Article 86).
- Transfer of assets to US navy exchanges and PX (STMA Article 86-2).
- Transfer of assets to the US Army or an authorised procurement agency of the US Army (Act on Temporary Special Provisions of the Income Tax Act, etc., in Connection with the Implementation of the Agreement on Facilities and Areas under Article 6 of the Treaty of Mutual Cooperation and Security between Japan and the United States of America and on the Status of United States Armed Forces in Japan Act Article 7(1)).

2. Transfer of assets to foreign embassies

The transfer of assets to foreign embassies will be treated as exempt for consumption tax purposes if the following conditions are satisfied (STMA Article 86(1), STMAEO Article 45-4(1), STMAER Article 36-2):

(1) The transfer is to a foreign embassy, legation, consulate or other equivalent organisation in Japan or a foreign ambassador, minister, consul or other equivalent person dispatched to Japan.

(2) The assets are transferred in accordance with a 'specified procedure', and are necessary for the performance of diplomatic, consular or other duties.

The 'specified procedure' is as follows:

(i) The seller is a 'designated shop'.
(ii) The foreign embassies purchase the assets for the performance of diplomatic, consular or other duties.
(iii) The foreign embassies present the seller with an 'exempt card', which is a certificate issued by the Ministry of Foreign Affairs.
(iv) The foreign embassies present the seller with a document describing the details of the assets or services purchased ('tax exempt purchase form for foreign embassies'). The seller must maintain this form for seven years.

Therefore, in order for your sales to foreign embassies to qualify as exempt sales, you will need to be a 'designated shop', by filing an application to the Ministry of Foreign Affairs. You will also need to check the 'exempt card' presented by the foreign embassy, and receive and maintain the 'tax exempt purchase form for foreign embassies' for at least seven years:

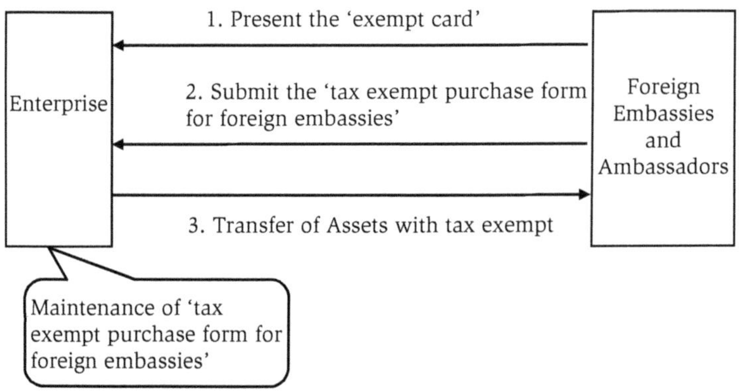

Example of 'exempt card'

免税カード（※注）第 － － 号
年 月 日まで有効
○物品
（公館名） ○サービス
（官職名） 写 真
（氏 名）
年 月 日 外務省発行 省印

Q74 Sales and Purchases of Goods Located in Japan by a Foreign Corporation

We are planning to upgrade our machinery. The new machinery will be purchased from a Japanese vendor. However, the Japanese vendor refuses to sell directly to us.

As a result, our foreign parent corporation will purchase the machinery from the Japanese vendor and will then resell it to us. The machinery will be delivered directly to us from the Japanese vendor's factory in Japan. What are the consumption tax implications of this transaction?

Our parent has never had taxable sales in Japan in the past.

A:

Both transfers from the Japanese vendor to your parent and from your parent to you are treated as taxable transactions.

However, since your parent should be an exempt enterprise, they will not be liable to pay consumption tax on these transactions.

Discussion

1. Consumption tax implications of the transactions

Consumption tax is imposed on the transfer of assets in Japan (JCTA Article 4(1)). A transfer is considered made in Japan when the assets are located in Japan at the time of the transfer (JCTA Article 4(3)(i)).

The sale from the Japanese vendor to your parent ('Transaction 1') is a taxable transaction since the machinery is located in Japan.

The sale from your parent to you ('Transaction 2') is also a taxable transaction for the same reason.

2. Consumption tax liability of foreign parent corporation

Since your parent has never had any taxable sales in Japan, their taxable sales in the Base Period should be less than JPY 10 million. Therefore, your parent is an exempt enterprise.

The Japanese vendor will charge consumption tax on Transaction 1. However, as your parent is an exempt enterprise, they cannot obtain an input consumption tax credit from Transaction 1.

On the other hand, your parent will charge consumption tax to you on Transaction 2. As an exempt enterprise, however, they do not need to pay this output consumption tax to the tax authorities.

If the price of the machinery exceeds JPY 10 million, your parent will become a taxable enterprise after two years, which will be relevant if they have taxable sales at that time.

2. Your input consumption tax credit

You are required to pay consumption tax to your parent on Transaction 2, and are entitled to claim an input consumption tax credit when filing your next consumption tax return. This is because input consumption tax credits can be obtained regardless of whether the seller of the asset is a taxable or exempt enterprise.

However, due to the introduction of the proposed qualified invoicing system from 1 October 2023, the above analysis will change for transactions made on or after that date:

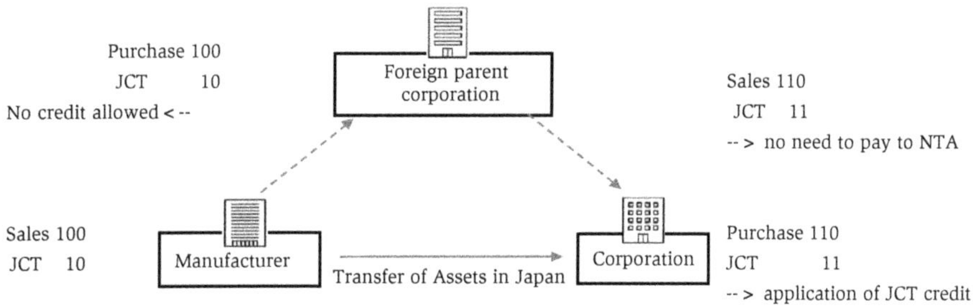

※ Dot line: commercial, Solid line: logistics

Q75 Provision of Services to Non-residents (Storage of Goods in Japan)

We have temporarily stored some goods in our warehouse that our foreign parent corporation purchased in Japan. We are planning to charge a storage fee to our parent. Is the storage fee subject to consumption tax?

A:

Although the provision of services in Japan is subject to consumption tax, most services provided to non-residents are exempt sales. However, if the benefit of the services is in Japan, the services will be treated as taxable transactions. The benefit of storing goods in Japan is clearly in Japan, and thus your storage fee is subject to consumption tax.

Discussion

Consumption tax is imposed on the transfer of assets in Japan. For the provision of services, consumption tax is imposed when the services are provided in Japan (JCTA Article 4(3)).

Despite the above, the provision of services to non-residents is exempt sales (*see* Q72) other than the following (JCTA Article 7(1)(v), JCTAEO Article 17(2)(vii), Consumption Tax Basic Circular Article 7-2-1(11)):

1. Transportation or storage of assets located in Japan.
2. Eating, drinking or accommodation in Japan.
3. Services equivalent to (1) and (2), where the benefits are enjoyed directly in Japan.

The provision of services to non-residents that are not exempt from consumption tax includes the following (Consumption Tax Basic Circular 7-2-16):

1. Transportation or storage of assets located in Japan.
2. Management and repair of real estate located in Japan.
3. Construction of buildings.
4. Transportation of passengers.
5. Eating, drinking or accommodation in Japan.
6. Hairdressing or beauty services.
7. Medical treatment or recuperation.
8. Provision of services such as theatrical performances.
9. Domestic telephone and postal services.
10. Provision of Japanese language education services.

Your provision of storage services is treated as a taxable transaction even though the services are provided to a non-resident since the benefit of the services is in Japan.

Accordingly, the fees charged to your parent will be subject to consumption tax. On the other hand, your parent may claim a refund of this tax by electing to become a taxable enterprise (*see* Q70).

Q76 Reimbursement of Expenses

We asked a Japanese law firm for a legal opinion. In order to prepare this opinion, lawyers of the firm had to travel outside Japan. The law firm paid the travel expenses, and these expenses were recharged to us at the same time as the fee for the legal opinion. Do we have to pay consumption tax on the travel expenses?

A:

Consumption tax will be levied on the travel expenses.

The provision of services in Japan is a taxable transaction, and consumption tax will be charged on the total remuneration paid for those services.

Since the travel expenses are considered a part of the remuneration for the legal opinion, they will also be subject to consumption tax, irrespective of whether the travel expenses are incurred in Japan or outside Japan.

Discussion

Consumption tax is imposed on the total consideration paid for a transfer of assets. The total consideration includes all money or non-monetary items, rights or other economic benefits received or to be received. It does not include the consumption tax itself that is imposed on the transfer of taxable assets (JCTA Article 28).

The consideration paid for legal services is generally understood to include any money paid to the law firm in connection with the provision of the law firm's services. This means that reimbursement of expenses is generally treated as part of the consideration for legal service (NTA Q&A, Consumption Tax, Reimbursement of Expenses).

However, consumption tax is not imposed on the following expenses:

(i) Registration tax, vehicle weight tax, vehicle acquisition tax and similar fees to be borne by an enterprise, but which are paid on the enterprise's behalf and recharged (Consumption Tax Basic Circular Article 10-1-4). Such taxes and fees must be accounted for separately.

(ii) Accommodation and transport costs paid directly by the enterprise. In addition, even where such expenses are not paid directly by the enterprise, if the invoice/receipt from the service provider is clearly addressed to the enterprise, it is deemed to have been paid directly by the enterprise.

Since the travel expenses charged to you by the law firm are not included in the list above, such expenses should be a consumption taxable transaction.

The following is a numerical example of the above:

- Legal fee: JPY 1,000,000.
- Domestic transportation fee (including consumption tax): JPY 20,000.
- Overseas transportation and accommodation: JPY 50,000.

The law firm's invoice would show:

	JPY
Legal fee	1,000,000
Domestic transportation expenses	18,182
Overseas transportation expenses	50,000
Subtotal	1,068,182
Consumption tax	106,818
Invoice amount	1,175,000

In practice, there is often confusion over the consumption tax treatment of reimbursement of expenses or payments made on behalf of an enterprise. As illustrated above, there is a difference in the consumption tax treatment between reimbursement of expenses and certain payments made on behalf of an enterprise.

Q77 Tax Treatment of Transfers of Assets Outside Japan

We import goods from our foreign parent corporation and sell them to Japanese customers. We were recently asked by our parent to sell goods to a Chinese corporation.

In this transaction, the goods will not be imported into Japan, but will be delivered directly from our parent to the Chinese customer. Will this transaction be subject to consumption tax?

A:

Consumption tax will not be imposed on this transaction since it is not a transfer of assets in Japan.

Discussion

Consumption tax is imposed on the transfer of assets in Japan (JCTA Article 4(1)). Transfers are made in Japan if the assets are located in Japan at the time of the transfer (JCTA Article 4(iii)).

The goods you purchased from your parent and sold to the Chinese customer are outside Japan throughout the entire transaction. As a result, the transaction is out of scope for consumption tax purposes.

In addition, Consumption Tax Basic Circular Article 5-7-1 clarifies that this type of triangular transaction should be treated as a foreign transaction, which is out of scope for consumption tax purposes, regardless of the accounting treatment.

Q78 Tax Treatment of the Cross-Border Supply of Electronic Services (B2B Transactions)

We receive cloud services from a third party in the US. The cloud services are used for our business in Japan. What is the consumption tax treatment of this transaction?

A:

The provision of cloud services is treated as the 'provision of electronic services'. Under the Consumption Tax Act, the 'provision of electronic services' is deemed to be conducted in Japan, and therefore subject to consumption tax, if the recipients of the electronic services are located in Japan.

'B2B electronic services' is the provision of electronic services where, due to the nature of the services or the terms and conditions on which they are provided, the recipients are usually limited to businesses.

For B2B electronic services, the reverse charge method is applied. Under this method, the output consumption tax liability is transferred from the service provider to the recipient of the service. At the same time, however, the recipient can claim an input consumption tax credit. In addition, under current transitional measures, if your consumption taxable sales ratio is 95% or more, to simplify administrative processes, the provision of B2B electronic services is deemed not to have taken place.

Discussion

1. Provision of electronic services to businesses

Consumption tax is levied on the transfers of assets (excluding transfers of 'Specific Assets') and specific purchases (i.e., the transfers of 'Specific Assets' received) made by an enterprise in Japan (JCTA Article 4 (1)). As a result, an enterprise that has received assets or made specific purchases is liable for consumption tax.

Transfers of 'Specific Assets' are defined as the provision of B2B electronic services and the provision of 'Specific Services' (JCTAO Article 2(1)(viii-ii)).

'Provision of electronic services' means the provision of services via telecommunications lines. It includes the provision and licensing of 'Copyrighted Works' (as defined in the Copyright Act Article 2(1)(i)) via telecommunications lines. It excludes the use of telecommunications networks themselves, and services notifying the results of transfers of assets via telecommunications networks when the notification is ancillary to the transfer of other assets (JCTA Article 2(1)(viii-iii)).

Where electronic services provided by foreign enterprises are limited to businesses, due to the nature of the services, or the terms and conditions on which they are provided, such services are classified as the provision of 'B2B electronic services' (JCTA Article 2(1)(viii-iv)). The provision of any other electronic services is generally referred to as the provision of electronic services for consumers ('B2C electronic services').

Services that allow customers to use software and databases in the cloud are considered the provision of electronic services, as these services are provided via telecommunications networks.

Although it may depend on the terms and conditions of the contract, it is likely that the cloud services you receive from the US third party will be treated as B2B electronic services since they are used for your business purposes (Consumption Tax Basic Circular Article 5-8-4).

2. Taxation of the provision of B2B electronic services

Under the Consumption Tax Act, a taxable enterprise making a transfer of taxable assets is generally required to submit a consumption tax return and make payment of the consumption tax on the transfer. However, an enterprise receiving B2B electronic services is liable to submit a consumption tax return and remit the output consumption tax to the tax authorities since the 'provision of B2B electronic services' conducted by a foreign service provider is deemed a sale of 'Specific Assets' and accordingly, the 'reverse charge' method is applied. At the same time, however, the enterprise receiving the services can recognise an input consumption tax credit for the purchase of the 'Specific Assets' (JCTA Article 30). As a result, the actual tax payable by the service recipient theoretically becomes zero under the reverse charge method after offsetting the output tax liability of the foreign service provider against the service recipient's own input tax credit.

Under current transitional measures, if an enterprise receiving B2B electronic services has a taxable sales ratio of 95% or more, or if it applies the simplified consumption taxation method, no 'B2B electronic services' are considered provided (Amendment Act Supplementary Provision to Partially Amendment the Income Tax 2015 Article 42, 44). It is not clear how long the transitional measures will continue. However, at some time in the future, an enterprise receiving B2B electronic services with a taxable sales ratio of 95% or more, or if it applies the simplified consumption taxation method, will need to apply the reverse charge.

In such cases, it is not necessary to report the output tax liability of the foreign service provider or the service recipient's own input tax credit for the B2B electronic services in the service recipient's consumption tax return.

On the other hand, if an enterprise's taxable sales ratio is less than 95%, and that enterprise receives B2B electronic services, the reverse charge method is applied. In this case, the foreign service provider's output tax liability must be recognised in the enterprise's consumption tax, together with its own input tax credit on the purchase. Due to the taxable sales ratio being below 95%, there will be some tax to be paid to the tax authorities; i.e., the impact will not be zero.

The taxable sales ratio is as follows:

Taxable sales ratio = taxable sales amount/ (taxable sales amount + non-taxable sales amount)

As the taxable sales ratio may not be known until the end of the taxable period, purchases of 'Specific Assets' should be appropriately accounted for in case it is necessary to apply the reverse charge method at the end of the year.

When a foreign service provider provides 'B2B electronic services', it must notify the service recipient in advance that the transaction is a 'provision of B2B electronic services' (JCTA Article 62, Consumption Tax Basic Circular 5-8-2). However, even if the foreign service provider fails to notify in advance, the reverse charge method should still be applied. Accordingly, the failure to notify has no impact on the tax liability:

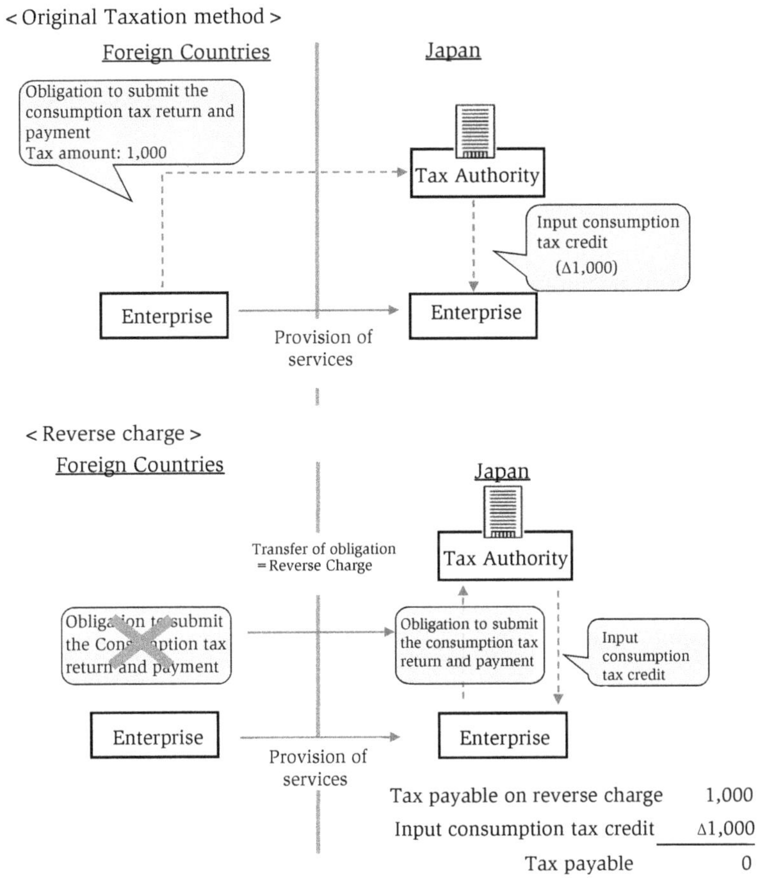

Q79 Tax Treatment of the Cross-Border Supply of Electronic Services (B2C Transaction)

We currently subscribe to a print newspaper in Japan that is published by the Japanese subsidiary of a US newspaper corporation. We plan to replace this print subscription with an online subscription of the same newspaper provided directly by the US newspaper corporation. What are the consumption tax implications of this online subscription?

A:

The provision of e-books, online newspapers, music, videos, and software (including applications such as games) via the internet is treated as the 'provision of electronic services'. Under the Consumption Tax Act, the 'provision of electronic services' is treated as being conducted in Japan, and therefore subject to consumption tax if the recipients of the services are located in Japan.
'B2B electronic services' is the provision of the electronic services, where, due to the nature of the services or the terms and conditions on which they are provided, the recipients are usually limited to businesses. The provision of electronic services other than B2B is the 'provision of B2C electronic services'.

It is difficult to limit the provision of newspaper subscriptions to businesses. Therefore, your online subscription will likely be treated as the provision of B2C electronic services.

Foreign service providers are required to submit consumption tax returns and pay output consumption tax themselves for B2C electronic services.

However, other than under the exception noted below, recipients of B2C electronic services such as yourself cannot currently claim an input consumption tax credit on B2C electronic services. An exception is available if the foreign service provider is registered as such, and if you preserve the invoices (which satisfy the necessary documentary requirements, such as the registration number of the registered foreign service provider). In this case, it is possible to obtain an input consumption tax credit on the subscription payment to the US newspaper corporation.

Discussion

1. Provision of B2C electronic services

The provision of e-books, digital newspapers, music, videos, and software (including applications such as games) via the internet is treated as the 'provision of electronic services'. Under the Consumption Tax Act, the 'provision of electronic services' is treated as conducted in Japan, and therefore subject to consumption tax if the recipients of the electronic services are located in Japan.

'B2B electronic services' is the provision of electronic services, where, due to the nature of the services or the terms and conditions on which they are provided, the recipients are usually limited to businesses (JCTA Article 2(1)(viii-iv)). The provision of all other electronic services is generally referred to as the 'provision of B2C electronic services'.

Your online US newspaper subscription should be classified as the 'provision of B2C electronic services' under the following conditions:

(1) The digital version of the newspaper is available to both businesses and consumers and that, given the nature of the service, it cannot be said that those receiving the service are limited to businesses.
(2) The subscription is based on general terms and conditions, and it cannot be said from those terms and conditions that those receiving the services are normally limited to businesses.

2. Taxation of the provision of B2C electronic services

The 'provision of B2C electronic services' is subject to the foreign business tax return method, which means that the foreign service provider is responsible for submission of a consumption tax return, and for paying the output consumption tax received to the tax authorities.

Enterprise recipients of B2C electronic services are currently not able to claim an input consumption tax credit (Amendment Act Supplementary Provision to Partial Amendment the Income Tax 2015 Article 38(1), Consumption Tax Basic Circular Article 11-1-3 Note 2).

However, if the foreign service provider is registered as such, the taxable enterprise receiving B2C electronic services from that foreign service provider can claim an input consumption tax credit if the enterprise has preserved the relevant invoices and those invoices satisfy the necessary documentary requirements, as listed below (JCTA Article 30(7), Amendment Act Supplementary Provision to Partial Amendment the Income Tax 2015 Article 38(1), (2), Consumption Tax Basic Circular Article 11-1-3 Note 2):

(i) the name and registration number of the document issuer,
(ii) the date of provision of the services,
(iii) the content of the services,
(iv) the payment amount,
(v) the name of the customer receiving the invoice, and
(vi) indication that the registered foreign service provider is liable for consumption tax

Accordingly, if the US newspaper corporation is a registered foreign service provider, and you preserve the invoices issued by them (which satisfy the above requirements), you can claim an input consumption tax credit for the input consumption tax paid on the subscription fees.

The list of registered foreign service providers is available on the NTA's website. You can check if the US newspaper corporation is registered and whether the subscription start date is on or after the date of their registration. Input consumption tax credits are only available for transactions occurring after the date of registration of the foreign service provider on the NTA's list:

登録国外事業者名簿
(Registered Foreign Businesses List)

令和3年12月23日現在
(As of December 23, 2021)
国税庁
(National Tax Agency)

所得税法等の一部を改正する法律(平成27年法律第9号)附則第39条第4項の規定に基づき、登録国外事業者の登録番号等を以下のとおり公表します。
(National Tax Agency hereby publishes the Registered Foreign Businesses' Registration Number etc. under Paragraph 4 of Article 39 of the Act for Partial Revision of the Income Tax Acts and other Acts(Act No.9 of 2015).)

登録番号 Registration Number	登録状況 Registration Status	氏名又は名称(日本語) Name(In Japanese)	氏名又は名称(英語) Name(In English)	国外にある住所又は居所/本店又は主たる事務所の所在地 Address or Domicile /Location of the head office or principal office outside Japan	国内において行う「事業者向け電気通信利用役務の提供」以外の電気通信利用役務の提供に係る事務所等を国内に有する場合の所在地 Location of the office providing other than B2B electronic service in Japan	登録年月日 Registration Date (MM/DD/YY)	法人番号 Japan Corporate Number	備考欄 Notes
00001	有効 (Valid)	ザ・フィナンシャル・タイムズ・ジャパン・リミテッド	The Financial Times Japan Ltd	Number One Southwark Bridge, London SE1 9HL, UNITED KINGDOM	東京都千代田区内幸町一丁目1番7号 NBF日比谷ビル21階	平成27年10月1日 10/01/2015	7700150000788	
00002	有効 (Valid)	アドビシステムズ ソフトウェア アイルランド リミテッド	Adobe Systems Software Ireland Limited	4−6 Riverwalk Citywest Business Campus Dublin 24 Ireland	該当なし(N/A)	平成27年10月1日 10/01/2015	3700150007275	
00003	有効 (Valid)	アマゾン サービス インターナショナル エルエルシー	Amazon Services International LLC	410 Terry Avenue North, Seattle, WA 98109−5210 U. S. A.	該当なし(N/A)	平成27年10月1日 10/01/2015	2700150006138	令和3年7月1日 Amazon Services International, Inc. から名称変更 (7/1/2021 Name changed)
00004	有効 (Valid)	アマゾン ウェブ サービス インク	Amazon Web Services, Inc.	410 Terry Avenue North, Seattle, WA 98109−5210 U. S. A.	該当なし(N/A)	平成27年10月1日 10/01/2015	-	
00005	有効 (Valid)	アマゾン サービス ヨーロッパ エス・エー・アール・エル	Amazon Services Europe S. à. r. l.	5 Rue Plaitis, L−2338, Luxembourg	該当なし(N/A)	平成27年10月1日 10/01/2015	1700150006139	
[illegible]	有効	[illegible]	[illegible]	1 Washington Park, 16th Floor,	[illegible]	平成27年10月1日	[illegible]	

Q80 Requirement to Become a Registered Foreign Service Provider

We are a foreign corporation which distributes online games worldwide, including customers in Japan. As our services are considered B2C electronic services, we have been filing consumption tax returns and remitting the output consumption tax collected from our customers.

Is it worthwhile for us to become a registered foreign service provider?

A:

Under the current consumption tax system, foreign taxable enterprises do not have to become registered foreign service providers (*see* Q68 for details of taxable enterprises). Since the advantage of registering is so that business customers can apply for input consumption tax credits, if your customers are primarily consumers as in your case, there is no advantage to registering.

Discussion

1. Provision of B2C electronic services

'B2B electronic services' is the 'provision of electronic services', where, due to the nature of the services or the terms and conditions on which they are provided, the recipients are limited to businesses (JCTA Article 2(1)(viii-iv)). The provision of all other electronic services is referred to as the 'provision of B2C electronic services'.

The provision of online games by foreign corporations is treated as the 'provision of B2C electronic services' since recipients of online games are not limited to businesses.

2. Taxation of the provision of B2C electronic services

Foreign taxable enterprises providing B2C electronic services are responsible for submission of a consumption tax return and the payment of output consumption tax collected to the tax authorities.

Whether or not a foreign enterprise is a consumption taxable enterprise is determined by the enterprise's taxable sales in the Base Period and taxable sales in the Specified Period (*see* Q68 for details of taxable enterprises).

3. Registered foreign service providers

Other than the exception noted below, recipients of B2C electronic services are currently not able to claim input consumption tax credits (Amendment Act Supplementary Provision to Partial Amendment the Income Tax 2015 Article 38(1), Consumption Tax Basic Circular Article 11-1-3 Note 2).

However, if the foreign service provider is registered, and if the recipients have preserved invoices that satisfy the necessary documentary requirements (*see* Q79), the recipients can claim input consumption tax credits (Amendment Act Supplementary Provision to Partial Amendment the Income Tax 2015 Article 38(1), Consumption Tax Basic Circular Article 11-1-3 Note 2). [The reason for this exception is that taxable enterprises receiving similar services from Japanese electronic service providers would be able to claim input consumption tax credits on payments for those services. As a result, foreign enterprises providing B2C electronic services whose customers are primarily taxable enterprises may be at a disadvantage compared to domestic businesses in terms of price competitiveness. Once a foreign service provider is registered, taxable enterprises receiving their B2C electronic services can claim an input consumption tax credit, so there should be no disadvantage to the foreign service provider.]

Registration is not mandatory, but is at the option of the foreign service provider.

In order to register, the following requirements must be met, and an application form and attached documents must be submitted to the competent national tax office (Amendment Act Supplementary Provision to Partial Amendment to the Income Tax 2015 Article 39(2)):

(1) The service provider is consumption taxable enterprise.
(2) The service provider provides or will provide B2C electronic services.
(3) The service provider has an office in Japan to provide B2C electronic services.
(4) If the service provider does not have an office as stated in (3), it must appoint a tax agent (i.e., qualified tax advisor) for consumption tax purposes.
(5) If enterprise does not have an office in Japan, it must appoint a tax representative (i.e., anyone domiciled in Japan or a Japanese corporation which handles the tax issues on behalf of the service provider).
(6) The service provider has no outstanding national tax liabilities.

As discussed above, the advantage of registering is that customers who are taxable enterprises can apply for input consumption tax credits. Thus, if the customers are only consumers, there is no advantage to registering. It is therefore important for B2C electronic services operators to ensure that they are also providing services to business customers when considering registration.

As most customers for online games are consumers and therefore not eligible for an input consumption tax credit anyway, there will be no difference in price competitiveness if a foreign service provider is not registered.

Accordingly, in this case, there is no benefit to registering.

The registered foreign service provider system will be abolished upon introduction of the qualified invoice system from October 2023.

Q81 Itemised Method and Proportional Method

We are a taxable enterprise.

We have been informed that there are different methods to calculate input consumption tax credits. How do they differ?

A:

For taxable enterprises whose taxable sales are less than JPY 500 million and with a taxable sales ratio of 95% or more, the entire amount of input consumption tax can be credited.

Taxable enterprises whose taxable sales exceed JPY 500 million can choose to apply either the itemised method or the proportional method.

The itemised method is only applicable when the input consumption tax amount can be classified as: (i) input consumption tax on taxable purchases related to taxable sales, (ii) input consumption tax on taxable purchases related to non-taxable sales, and (iii) input consumption tax on taxable purchases related to both taxable sales and non-taxable sales. When applying the itemised method, in practice, it is advisable to classify input consumption tax as described above on the date of the transaction.

Discussion

Consumption tax payable in Japan is calculated by deducting from consumption tax related to taxable sales ('output consumption tax') consumption tax related to taxable purchases ('input consumption tax').

The input consumption tax credit (i.e., the deduction) is only available if the taxable enterprise preserves appropriate books of account and relevant documents (e.g., invoices, receipts) for the taxable period for which input consumption tax is claimed (JCTA Article 30(7)).

The calculation of the input consumption tax credit depends on whether the consumption taxable sales for the taxable period are JPY 500 million or less and whether the taxable sales ratio is 95% or more.

The taxable sales ratio is calculated as follows:

Taxable sales ratio = taxable sales amount / (taxable sales amount + non-taxable sales amount)

1. If consumption taxable sales for the taxable period are JPY 500 million or less and the taxable sales ratio is 95% or more

The entire input consumption tax amount during the taxable period can be credited from the output consumption tax during the taxable period.

2. If consumption taxable sales during the taxable period are more than JPY 500 million or the taxable sales ratio is less than 95%

The input consumption tax credit is only available for purchases related to taxable sales. The amount of creditable input consumption tax must be calculated in accordance with either: (i) the itemised method or (ii) the proportional method.

(1) Itemised method (JCTA Article 30(2)(i))

Under the itemised method, all input consumption tax should be classified into the following three categories:

(i) Input consumption tax related to taxable sales,
(ii) Input consumption tax related to non-taxable sales,
(iii) Input consumption tax related to both taxable sales and non-taxable sales.

After the above classification, the input consumption tax credit for the taxable period can be calculated as follows:

Input consumption tax credit = (i) + ((iii) * taxable sales ratio)

The itemised method can be used only if the enterprise can classify its input consumption tax into the above three categories. In addition, this classification should be made when the taxable purchases are made, although it is permitted to make it before the end of the taxable period (Consumption Tax Basic Circular Article 11-2-20). However, practically, it is difficult to make the classification later; therefore, it is recommended to make the classification when accounting for the purchase.

Some accounting systems, particularly foreign systems, do not permit such classification. In such cases, the itemised method cannot generally be applied.

(2) Proportional method (JCTA Article 30(2)(ii))

Under the proportional method, the input consumption tax credit for the taxable period can be calculated as follows:

input consumption tax credit = input consumption tax *taxable sales ratio

If an enterprise has chosen the proportional method, it cannot change to the itemised method for two years (JCTA Article 30(5)).

Q82 Input Consumption Tax Credits for Purchases Related to Sales Outside Japan

We import products from Germany and sell them to customers in Japan.

At the request of a Japanese customer, we will sell products to the customer's German subsidiary. The products are to be shipped directly from a German warehouse to the German customer. As the transfer of the products will take place in Germany, we understand that no consumption tax will be levied on these sales.

Since this is a new transaction for us, we discussed it with our Japanese lawyers. The invoice they rendered to us includes consumption tax. Can we claim an input consumption tax credit for this amount?

We apply the itemised method to calculate our input consumption tax credit.

A:

Input consumption tax credits are available for taxable purchases related to the transfer of assets made outside Japan.

Input consumption tax related to sales outside Japan is categorised as input consumption tax related to taxable sales under the itemised method (*see* Q81). As a result, you can claim the entire amount of input consumption tax paid on the legal fees.

Discussion

Consumption tax payable in Japan is calculated by deducting from the consumption tax related to taxable sales the consumption tax related to taxable purchases.

If taxable sales are JPY 500 million or less and the taxable sales ratio is 95% or more, the entire input consumption tax credit can be obtained. On the other hand, if taxable sales are more than JPY 500 million, either the itemised method or the proportional method must be applied.

Where the itemised method is applied, input consumption tax must be classified into: (i) input consumption tax related to taxable sales, (ii) input consumption tax related to non-taxable sales, and (iii) input consumption tax related to both taxable sales and non-taxable sales (JCTA Article 30(2)(i)).

The transfer of assets outside Japan is not subject to consumption tax. On the other hand, input consumption tax related to the transfer of assets outside Japan can be included in the input consumption tax credit (Consumption Tax Basic Circular Article 11-2-13). In addition, for the purpose of itemised method (*see* Q81), the input consumption tax corresponding to transfer of assets outside Japan shall be deemed to be classified as input consumption tax related to taxable sales.

This is because input consumption tax related to taxable sales is defined among others, as 'total input consumption tax from taxable purchases required for the transfer of taxable assets' (JCTA Article 30(2)(i)(a)). For this purpose, 'the transfer of taxable assets' is the transfer of assets other than those that are non-taxable (JCTA Article 2(1)(ix)). As 'non-taxable transfer of assets' is a defined list of transfers conducted in

Japan, any transfer of assets conducted outside Japan falls under the category 'transfer of Taxable assets'.

Given the above, an input consumption tax credit is available for taxable purchases, such as the legal fee paid in this case, where it is classified as input consumption tax related to taxable sales.

This transaction may also be subject to value added tax (VAT) in Germany, so it is important to discuss German VAT issues with a German tax specialist.

Q83 Tax Treatment of Transfers of Small Value Assets: Invoices

Our accounting officer, who is newly seconded from our parent corporation, has raised a question about the small amounts of transportation expenses used by our employees for business purposes, which are reimbursed without receipts/invoices. In many countries, if there are no receipts/invoices, input VAT credits cannot be obtained, even for small amounts.

We understand that receipts/invoices are often not issued for small amounts, especially for short-distance transportation expenses. What is the consumption tax treatment in this case?

A:

In order to obtain input consumption tax credits, taxable enterprises need to preserve appropriate accounting records and invoices. However, for small taxable purchases with a value of less than JPY 30,000 per transaction, the preservation of the invoices is not required, but only preservation of the accounting records.

Discussion

Consumption tax payable in Japan is calculated by deducting from the consumption tax related to taxable sales the consumption tax related to taxable purchases.

If an enterprise fails to preserve appropriate accounting records and relevant documents relating to input consumption tax credits, the input consumption tax credit may be denied (JCTA Article 30 (7)).

The accounting books and relevant documents that must be preserved are as follows:

1. Books of account (JCTA Article 30(8)):

(1) For the Transfer of Assets, the following information needs to be stated;
  (i) Name of the supplier to whom the taxable purchase is made
  (ii) Date when taxable purchases are made
  (iii) Description of the assets or services in the taxable purchase
  (iv) Amount of consideration paid for taxable purchases

(2) For the Specific Purchase, the following information needs to be stated;
  (i) Name of the supplier of Specific Purchase
  (ii) Date of Specific Purchase
  (iii) Description of Specific Purchase
  (iv) Amount of consideration paid for Specific Purchase
  (v) The fact that the transaction is Specific Purchase

(3) For importation of the goods, the following information needs to be stated;
  (i) The date of receipt of the taxable goods from the bonded area (where a special declaration has been submitted for Customs duty purpose, the date of receipt from the bonded area and the date of submission of the special declaration or the date of receipt of notification of the decision on the special declaration)

(ii) Description of taxable goods
(iii) The amount of national consumption tax and local consumption tax, or the total amount thereof, in respect of the receipt of taxable goods.

2. Vouchers (JCTA Article 30 (9)):

(1) Invoices, delivery notes and other similar documents issued by other Enterprises who Transfer of Taxable Assets which contain the following items (in the case where the Transfer of the Taxable Assets is in the retail business, the item listed in (i) to (v))
   (i) Name of the Enterprise who prepared the document
   (ii) Date of Transfer of Taxable Assets
   (iii) Description of assets or services for the Transfer of Taxable Assets
   (iv) Amount of consideration for Transfer of Taxable Assets
   (v) Name of the Enterprise to whom the documents are issued
(2) A statement of purchase, a calculation of purchase, or any other similar document prepared by an Enterprise with respect to taxable purchases, which contains the following items and which has been confirmed by the other enterprise
   (i) Name or title of the Enterprise who prepared the document
   (ii) Name of the Enterprise to whom the taxable purchase is made
   (iii) Date when taxable purchases were made
   (iv) Details of the assets or services involved in the taxable purchase
   (v) Amount of consideration for taxable purchases
(3) Documents certifying that permission for importation of the taxable goods, issued by the director-general of customs offices, which contain the following items
   (i) Name of director-general of the relevant customs office
   (ii) The date on which the taxable goods became available for pick-up from the bonded area (where a special declaration has been submitted for Customs duty purpose, the date on which the goods became available for pick-up from the bonded area and the date on which the special declaration was submitted or the date on which the decision on the special declaration was notified)
   (iii) Description of taxable goods
   (iv) The amount of Consumption tax levied on the taxable goods, and the amount of national consumption tax and local consumption tax payable on the receipt of the goods
   (v) Name of the Enterprise to whom the documents are issued.

3. Special provisions for the preservation of small value invoices

The preservation of invoices is not required for consumption tax purposes in the following cases (JCTA Article 30(7), JCTAEO Article 49(1)):

(i) Where the total amount of consideration paid for taxable purchases is less than JPY 30,000.
(ii) Where the total amount of the consideration paid for the taxable purchase is JPY 30,000 or more, and there are unavoidable circumstances for not having received the invoice.
(iii) Where the purchase relates to a Specific Purchase.

The JPY 30,000 referred to in 3(i) above is determined based on the consumption tax inclusive amount in each transaction, not per product (Consumption Tax Basic Circular Article 11-6-2).

Based on the above, when calculating the input consumption tax credit for small transportation expenses, it is only necessary to preserve the accounting records where the amount is less than JPY 30,000.

However, this provision will be abolished effective 1 October 2023. From that time, it will be necessary to preserve invoices even for small value transactions. The only exceptions will be the following:

- Public transportation of less than JPY 30,000.
- Vending machine purchases of less than JPY 30,000.
- Postal services for which postage stamps are used.
- Admission tickets which are collected upon admission.
- Second-hand goods and pawned goods purchased by second-hand dealers and pawnbrokers.
- Lump sum travel allowances paid to employees.

Q84 Foreign Exchange for Foreign Currency Transactions

We purchase goods from our foreign-related corporations. All purchase prices for these goods are denominated in foreign currencies.

What exchange rates should be applied to such foreign currency transactions?

A:

The foreign exchange rate applicable to foreign currency transactions is generally the telegraphic transfer mid rate on the transaction date ('TTM'), which is the same rate as for corporation tax purposes.

Discussion

Consumption tax must be paid in Japanese yen. For this reason, transactions denominated in foreign currencies should be converted into Japanese yen and recorded in the accounts as such.

Under Consumption Tax Basic Circular Article 10-1-7, the exchange rate for foreign currency transactions for consumption tax purposes is the same as for corporation tax purposes. This means that the foreign exchange rate on foreign currency transactions will generally be the TTM on the transaction date (Corporation Tax Basic Circular Article 13-2-1-2, *see* Q42).

Q85 Consumption Tax Treatment on Bad Debt Losses

One of our customers, with whom we have a long-term relationship, has fallen into financial difficulties and payment for our accounts has been delayed, although the customer has not been subject to bankruptcy, corporate reorganisation act or any other legal proceedings.

Under our group accounting policy, we must establish a bad debt reserve for accounting purposes of 50% of the doubtful debt if collection is delayed more than three months. In the event of a delay in payment of more than six months, the full amount of the receivable is recorded as a bad debt loss.

Since the payment from the customer has been delayed for more than six months, we have recorded the full amount as a bad debt loss.

What is the consumption tax treatment in this case?

A:

Where accounts receivable or other receivables cannot be collected, the consumption tax corresponding to the uncollectable amount shall be creditable from the consumption tax on sales for the taxable period in which the receivable becomes uncollectable.

However, bad debts are only recognised in certain circumstances for consumption tax purposes. So it is likely no consumption tax credit will be available in the current situation.

Discussion

Where accounts receivable or other receivables cannot be collected, the consumption tax corresponding to the amount of the bad debt is creditable from the output consumption tax for the taxable period in which the receivable becomes a bad debt.

However, for consumption tax purposes, bad debts are only recognised in the following cases (JCTA Article 39, JCTAEO Article 59, JCTAER Article 18):

1. Bad debt losses where a receivable has been waived under the law (legal bad debts)

(1) Amounts waived in accordance with the provisions of the Corporate Reorganization Act, Act on Special Measures for the Reorganization Proceedings of Financial Institutions, the Companies Act, and the Civil Rehabilitation Act.

(2) Amounts waived on a reasonable basis at a voluntary meeting of creditors not governed by law, or at a discussion mediated by a government or financial institution.

(3) The amount is waived in writing to the debtor when the debtor has been insolvent for a considerable period and is unable to meet its debts.

2. Bad debt losses where a receivable is effectively uncollectible (factual bad debts)

If it becomes apparent that the debtor is unable to collect the full amount of the debt due to the debtor's lack of assets or inability to pay, the receivable is considered uncollectible in the fiscal year in which it becomes apparent. However, if there is collateral, the receivable will not be deemed to be uncollectable until the collateral has been disposed of.

Where a guarantee has been given, the receivable will not be considered uncollectible until after the guarantee has been fulfilled.

3. Bad debt losses where a receivable is formally uncollectible (formal bad debts)

Where any of the following events occurs, the account receivable, less the residual value (generally JPY 1), can be treated as a bad debt loss. Formal bad debt losses are limited to accounts receivable and therefore do not include other receivables such as loans:

(1) where a debtor with whom the corporation has had a continuous business relationship ceases to do business due to deterioration in the debtor's assets or ability to pay, at least one year must have elapsed since the latest of the time of the cessation of business and the time of the last payment (except in the case where the receivables are secured by collateral). Note that this treatment does not apply to accounts receivable from debtors who do not have a continuous business relationship with the corporation, such as in a real estate transaction.

(2) where the total amount of accounts receivable from debtors in the same area is less than the collection costs and no payment has been made after reminding the debtor to pay.

The above is the same treatment as for bad debt losses under the corporation tax law (*see* Q37).

As your customer has not taken any legal procedure, the receivable does not qualify as a legal bad debt. In addition, unless your customer provides evidence that they are unable to pay the full amount of the debt due to the lack of assets or inability to pay (e.g., insolvency), it does not qualify as a factual bad debt. Further, since the delay of the payment is only six months, it does not qualify as a formal bad debt.

Accordingly, it cannot be treated as a bad debt loss for consumption tax purposes.

However, if you cannot collect the bad debt for more than one year from the date of cessation of your business with the customer, the bad debt amount less the residual value may be treated as a bad debt for consumption tax purposes.

In that case, the consumption tax corresponding to the amount of the bad debt would be credited from output consumption tax in the taxable period in which more than one year has elapsed since the last payment by the customer.

In order to be able to credit consumption tax on bad debts, documents evidencing the fact that the receivable is uncollectible and other documents explaining the fact of the bad debt must be maintained.

Q86 Japanese Invoice System

We are a Japanese subsidiary of a German corporation. We have just been established, and we are issuing invoices for the first time in Japan. Our parent corporation has asked us about the requirements for invoices. It seems that in Germany there are detailed requirements for invoices; are there any similar regulations in Japan?

A:

Under the current consumption tax law, there are no stipulated requirements for issuing invoices.

However, enterprises that apply for input consumption tax credits are obliged to keep invoices that contain certain information (*see* below).

In addition, a qualified invoice system (i.e., a Japanese version of the European invoice system) will be effective from 1 October 2023. Under this qualified invoice system, enterprises that are qualified invoice issuers will be obliged to issue qualified invoices, with specific requirements.

Discussion

Under the current consumption tax act, there are no provisions stipulating the requirements for invoices. However, taxable enterprises applying for input consumption tax credits are required, in principle, to preserve invoices containing the following information (JCTA Article 30 (9)):

(i) Name of the Enterprise who prepared the document
(ii) Date of Transfer of Taxable Assets
(iii) Description of assets or services for the Transfer of Taxable Assets
(iv) Amount of consideration for Transfer of Taxable Assets
(v) Name of the Enterprise to whom the documents are issued.

From 1 October 2023, the qualified invoice system (i.e., the Japanese version of the invoice system) will come into force. Under the qualified invoice system, an enterprise that is a qualified invoice issuer must issue and deliver qualified invoices, with specific invoice requirements, and retain a copy of those qualified invoices, except in certain circumstances where it is difficult to issue a qualified invoice.

The information which should be contained in qualified invoices is as follows:

(i) Name and registration number of the qualified invoice issuing Enterprise
(ii) Date of transaction
(iii) Description of the transaction (including that the item is subject to a reduced tax rate)
(iv) The total amount of consideration (excluding or including tax) by each tax rate and the applicable tax rate
(v) Consumption tax amount (fraction must be made per the total amount of invoice by the tax rate)
(vi) Name of the Enterprise to whom the documents are issued.

Although the content of invoices will not change significantly after the qualified invoice systems come into effect, qualified invoice issuers will be required to issue qualified invoices from that time on.

In order to be a qualified invoice issuer, an enterprise must be a taxable enterprise and registration as 'qualified invoice issuer'.

Q87 Consumption Tax Account Summary

We have been subject to a consumption tax audit and are required to submit a 'consumption tax account summary'. What is this?

A:

A consumption tax account summary is a list of accounts which are summarised by type of consumption tax (i.e., standard rate, reduced rate, tax-exempt, non-taxable, or out-of-scope).

The consumption tax account summary is used to check overall whether there are any material errors in the recording of consumption tax in the accounts. A consumption tax account summary is generally required to be submitted in a Japanese tax audit.

Discussion

The input consumption tax credit is designed to prevent the accumulation of consumption tax liabilities, but it must be supported by evidence of taxable purchases. In Japan, this is done by using accounting and invoice. This is the preservation of 'books of account and vouchers' relating to taxable purchases (*see* Q83).

A consumption tax account summary is a list of accounts summarised by type of consumption tax (i.e., standard rate, reduced rate, tax-exempt, non-taxable, or out-of-scope).

A consumption tax account summary can be used to check overall whether there are any material errors in the recording of consumption tax in the accounts. It is generally automatically prepared by accounting systems from Japanese IT vendors. However, it would not generally be prepared in accounting systems provided by non-Japanese IT vendors (although in some cases, it may be provided as an add-on).

If a consumption tax account summary cannot be prepared automatically in your accounting system, you will need to prepare it manually.

The following is an example of a consumption tax account summary:

Output Consumption Tax

	TB	Taxable		Exempted sales	Non-taxable sales	Out-of-scope	Total
		Standard rate	Reduced rate				
Sales	100,000,000	80,000,000	0	20,000,000	0	0	100,000,000
Other income	5,000,000	1,500,000	0	250,000		3,250,000	5,000,000
Total		81,500,000					
		10%	8%				
		8,150,000	0				
	TB	8,150,000					
	Diff	0					

Input Consumption Tax (proportional method)

	TB	Taxable		Non-taxable/ Exempted/ Out-of-scope	Total
		Standard rate	Reduced rate		
Purchase of inventories	70,000,000	70,000,000			70,000,000
Salary	12,000,000			12,000,000	12,000,000
Legal welfare	1,500,000			1,500,000	1,500,000
Office supply	650,000	650,000			650,000
IT expenses	150,000	150,000			150,000
Rent	1,200,000	1,200,000			1,200,000
Travel	500,000	150,000		350,000	500,000
Insurance	300,000			300,000	300,000
Communication	250,000	200,000		50,000	250,000
Other taxes	100,000			100,000	100,000
Depreciation	1,500,000			1,500,000	1,500,000
Utilities	500,000	400,000	100,000		500,000
Entertainment	150,000	100,000	50,000		150,000
Professional fee	1,200,000	1,200,000			1,200,000
Bank charge	300,000	200,000		100,000	300,000
Purchase of fixed assets	800,000	800,000			800,000
Total		75,050,000	150,000	15,900,000	
		10%	8%		
		7,505,000	12,000		
	TB	7,505,000	12,000		
	Diff	0	0		

www.ingramcontent.com/pod-product-compliance
Ingram Content Group UK Ltd.
Pitfield, Milton Keynes, MK11 3LW, UK
UKHW020805290926
15470UKWH00003B/969

9 789403 543109